Transforming Civil War Prisons

During the Civil War, 410,000 people were held as prisoners of war on both sides. With resources strained by the unprecedented number of prisoners, conditions in overcrowded prison camps were dismal, and the death toll across Confederate and Union prisons reached 56,000 by the end of the war. In an attempt to improve prison conditions, President Lincoln issued General Orders 100, which would become the basis for future attempts to define the rights of prisoners, including the Geneva Conventions. Meanwhile, stories of horrific prison experiences fueled political agendas on both sides, and would define the memory of the war, as each region worked aggressively to defend its prison record and to honor its own POWs.

Springer and Robins examine the experience, culture, and politics of captivity, including war crimes, disease, and the use of former prison sites as locations of historical memory. *Transforming Civil War Prisons* introduces students to an underappreciated yet crucial aspect of waging war and shows how the legacy of Civil War prisons remains with us today.

Paul J. Springer is Associate Professor of Comparative Military Studies at Air Command and Staff College. He is the author of *America's Captives: The History of US Prisoner of War Policy*.

Glenn Robins is Professor of History at Georgia Southwestern State University. He is the editor of *They Have Left Us Here to Die: The Civil War POW Diary of Sgt. Lyle G. Adair, 111th US Colored Infantry*.

Critical Moments in American History

Edited by William Thomas Allison, Georgia Southern University

Transforming Civil War Prisons

Lincoln, Lieber,
and the Politics
of Captivity

*Paul J. Springer and
Glenn Robins*

Routledge
Taylor & Francis Group

NEW YORK AND LONDON

First published 2015
by Routledge
711 Third Avenue, New York, NY 10017

and by Routledge
2 Park Square, Milton Park, Abingdon, Oxon OX14 4RN

Routledge is an imprint of the Taylor & Francis Group, an informa business

© 2015 Taylor & Francis

The right of Paul J. Springer and Glenn Robins to be identified as author of this work has been asserted by them in accordance with sections 77 and 78 of the Copyright, Designs and Patents Act 1988.

Library of Congress Cataloging in Publication Data
Springer, Paul J.
   Transforming Civil War prisons: Lincoln, Lieber, and the politics of captivity/Paul J. Springer, Glenn Robins.—First edition.
   pages cm.—(Critical moments in American history)
   1. United States—History—Civil War, 1861–1865—Prisoners and prisons. 2. Military prisons—United States—History—19th century. 3. Military prisons—Confederate States of America—History. 4. Prisoners of war—United States—History—19th century. 5. Prisoners of war—Confederate States of America—History. 6. Lincoln, Abraham, 1809–1865. 7. Lieber, Francis, 1800–1872. 8. War—Moral and ethical aspects. 9. Military ethics. I. Robins, Glenn. II. Title.
   E615.S67 2014
   973.7'7—dc23
   2014008037

ISBN: 978-0-415-83336-3 (hbk)
ISBN: 978-0-415-83337-0 (pbk)
ISBN: 978-0-203-49458-5 (ebk)

Typeset in Bembo and Helvetica Neue
by Florence Production Ltd, Stoodleigh, Devon, UK

Printed and bound in the United States of America by Publishers Graphics, LLC on sustainably sourced paper.

Dedicated to our parents, Perry and Milly Springer and Marvin and Phyllis Robins, who always provided the love and support we needed to reach for our dreams.

Contents

Series Introduction

Welcome to the Routledge *Critical Moments in American History* series. The purpose of this new series is to give students a window into the historian's craft through concise, readable books by leading scholars, who bring together the best scholarship and engaging primary sources to explore a critical moment in the American past. In discovering the principal points of the story in these books, gaining a sense of historiography, following a fresh trail of primary documents, and exploring suggested readings, students can then set out on their own journey, to debate the ideas presented, interpret primary sources, and reach their own conclusions—just like the historian.

A critical moment in history can be a range of things—a pivotal year, the pinnacle of a movement or trend, or an important event such as the passage of a piece of legislation, an election, a court decision, a battle. It can be social, cultural, political, or economic. It can be heroic or tragic. Whatever they are, such moments are by definition "game changers," momentous changes in the pattern of the American fabric, paradigm shifts in the American experience. Many of the critical moments explored in this series are familiar; some less so.

There is no ultimate list of critical moments in American history—any group of students, historians, or other scholars may come up with a different catalog of topics. These differences of view, however, are what make history itself and the study of history so important and so fascinating. Therein can be found the utility of historical inquiry—to explore, to challenge, to understand, and to realize the legacy of the past through its influence of the present. It is the hope of this series to help students realize this intrinsic value of our past and of studying our past.

William Thomas Allison
Georgia Southern University

Figures

Acknowledgments

The authors would like to thank Bill Allison, Kimberly Guinta, and Genevieve Aoki at Routledge Press, as well as all of their dedicated colleagues, for the unstinting assistance provided in the preparation of this work. In addition, both authors owe a debt of research gratitude to the staff at the Andersonville National Historic Site and the National Archives of the United States in Washington, D.C. Special thanks goes to former superintendents Fred Boyles and Brad Bennett, Chief of Interpretation Eric Leonard, and Cultural Resources Specialist Alan Marsh.

Paul J. Springer would like to thank the entire staff at the Muir S. Fairchild Research and Information Center on the campus of Air University. Thanks also go to Air Command and Staff College colleagues Tom Deale, Mack Easter, Mary Hampton, Kenneth Johnson, Mike Pavelec, Jim Selkirk, Bob Smith, John Terino, and Ryan Wadle. Paul was lucky to have wonderful parents, K. Perry and Mildred Springer, who he dedicates this book to, and is grateful to the rest of his family, including Lorraine Springer; Jeff, Michelle, and Sean Gibbs; Ed, Sharon, and David Hansen; and Val, Alex, and Kendall McKinney. Of course, he would be nothing without the love and support of his wife Victoria, who deserves all of the credit for any of his success.

Glenn Robins would like to thank the entire staff at the James Earl Carter Library on the campus of Georgia Southwestern State University, particularly access services supervisor John Wilson. Thanks also go to GSW colleagues, Richard Hall, John Stovall, DeDe Reyes, Ellen Cotter, Brian Parkinson, Gary Kline, Dean of Arts & Sciences Kelly McCoy, and Vice President for Academic Affairs Brian Adler. Glenn is blessed to have supportive and caring parents, Marvin and Phyllis Robins, who he dedicates this book to, and is grateful for a wonderful set of in-laws, Buddy and Virginia Douglas. Glenn's deepest gratitude, love, and affection go to his wife Kim for her patience and unconditional love.

Timeline

July 5, 1861	The first Confederate prisoners arrive at Camp Chase
July 21, 1861	The First Battle of Bull Run results in the capture of 1,050 Union prisoners
August 28, 1861	The War Department releases all Federal paroled prisoners from service
October 21, 1861	Colonel William Hoffman is appointed Commissary General of prisons and prisoners by War Department Special Order 284
February 16, 1862	Fort Donelson, Tennessee, surrenders to Ulysses S. Grant, including 15,000 prisoners
February 21, 1862	The first Confederate prisoners arrive at Camp Douglas
February 22, 1862	The first Confederate prisoners arrive at Camp Morton
February 24, 1862	Camp Douglas has over 7,000 prisoners and only one surgeon
February 27, 1862	John H. Winder is appointed provost marshal of Richmond, putting him in charge of nearly all Confederate prisoner of war camps
March 26, 1862	The first Union prisoners arrive at Libby
April 6–7, 1862	The Battle of Shiloh includes the capture of more than 3,000 prisoners
April 16, 1862	The Confederate Congress authorizes conscription
April 25, 1862	The city of New Orleans surrenders to Union forces
June 16, 1862	Hoffman orders all Confederate officer prisoners sent to Johnson's Island
July 11, 1862	Confederate prisons in Richmond hold more than 8,000 Federal prisoners
July 22, 1862	Dix-Hill Cartel is signed, establishing guidelines for prisoner exchange
August 3, 1862	The first exchange of prisoners under the Dix-Hill Cartel occurs at Aiken's Landing on the James River, freeing a total of more than 6,000 prisoners
August 26, 1862	Captain Henry Wirz assumes command of the POW camps in Richmond
November 10, 1862	Hoffman orders camp commanders to withhold rations for the purpose of creating prison funds for prisoners' welfare
December 23, 1862	Confederate President Jefferson Davis announces that captured African-American troops will be punished for servile insurrection
January 1, 1863	The Emancipation Proclamation goes into effect, authorizing the enlistment of African-American troops
February 28, 1863	Camp Douglas returns show 387 of 3,884 prisoners died in the month of February, most due to a smallpox outbreak
May 2–4, 1863	The Battle of Chancellorsville results in the capture of 6,000 Federal and 2,000 Confederate prisoners

July 1–3, 1863	During the Battle of Gettysburg, each side captures more than 5,000 prisoners
July 4, 1863	Vicksburg surrenders, including 29,500 Confederate prisoners
December 3, 1863	The first Confederate prisoners arrive at Rock Island
February 9, 1864	109 Union prisoners escape from Libby Prison, 59 reach Union lines
February 25, 1864	The first Union prisoners arrive at Andersonville
March 14, 1864	Union prisoner John Ransom arrives at Andersonville
March 27, 1864	Captain Henry Wirz is assigned to command at Andersonville
April 12, 1864	Confederate troops under General Nathan Bedford Forrest massacre hundreds of African-American troops attempting to surrender at Fort Pillow, Tennessee
April 17, 1864	General Ulysses S. Grant unilaterally halts prisoner exchanges until the Confederacy releases enough prisoners to equal earlier Federal releases and treats all POWs equally, regardless of skin color
May 8, 1864	Of the 12,954 POWs received at Andersonville, 728 have died thus far
May 10, 1864	Hoffman authorizes a pay rate of $.10 for ten hours work by Confederate POWs
June 1, 1864	Confederate POW rations are reduced in Federal camps
July 6, 1864	The first Confederate prisoners arrive at Elmira
July 11, 1864	The Union prisoner gang known as the Raiders are hanged by their fellow inmates at Andersonville
August 9, 1864	Andersonville returns show 33,006 prisoners, the highest total at the prison
August 31, 1864	Wirz reports that 2,993 prisoners died in August at Andersonville
September 13, 1864	The first Union prisoners arrive at Camp Lawton
November 21, 1864	John H. Winder becomes Commissary General of Confederate prisons
January 21, 1865	Bowing to political pressure, Grant reinstitutes limited exchanges
February 7, 1865	John H. Winder dies of a heart attack
April 9, 1865	General Robert E. Lee surrenders the Army of Northern Virginia, with less than 8,000 effectives on-hand
April 14, 1865	President Abraham Lincoln is shot by John Wilkes Boothe, and dies the next day
April 27, 1865	The *Sultana* sinks in the Mississippi River resulting in the death of more than 1,500 Union prisoners of war
May 5, 1865	Colonel George Gibbs abandons his post as commander of Andersonville
August 14, 1865	Clara Barton participates in the dedication of the Andersonville National Cemetery
August 25, 1865	The war crimes trial of Henry Wirz begins
July 11, 1865	The last Confederate prisoners leave Elmira
November 10, 1865	Captain Henry Wirz is hanged for war crimes
September 20, 1889	The Libby Prison Museum opens in Chicago, Illinois
February 3, 1899	The New Jersey Monument is dedicated in the Andersonville National Cemetery
June 7, 1902	A monument to Confederate prisoners is dedicated at Camp Chase
November 26, 1908	The Indiana Monument is dedicated in the Andersonville National Cemetery
May 12, 1909	The Henry Wirz Monument is dedicated in the town of Andersonville, Georgia
April 29, 1914	The New York Monument is dedicated in the Andersonville National Cemetery
November 8, 1985	President Ronald Reagan signs legislation creating the Prisoner of War Medal
April 9, 1998	The National Prisoner of War Museum is dedicated at the Andersonville National Historic Site

CHAPTER 1

Prisoner of War Policy and Practice

April 24, 1863 dawned unseasonably cold and rainy in Washington, D.C. After two years of bloody civil war, the armies of the United States and the Confederate States stood poised to launch their spring campaigns. If the trends of the previous two years provided any clear indication of the coming struggle, 1863 would be a terrible year for the soldiers of both sides. With commanders of both armies beginning to grasp the fundamental nature of warfare in the industrial age, the spring and summer battles would undoubtedly bring about the battlefield deaths of tens of thousands of young men, with many times that number brought down by disease and malnutrition. It seemed that the conflict was doomed to bring out the very worst behaviors in its participants, and might very well destroy the nations involved.

President Abraham Lincoln faced a dire political situation in the spring of 1863. His Republican Party lost nearly two dozen seats in Congress in the 1862 elections, retaining control of the House only through a tepid alliance with pro-war Democrats who broke from their prewar affiliation to form the Unionist Party. His Emancipation Proclamation, which went into effect with the new year, had formally banned slavery in the portions of the Confederacy not under Union occupation. Thus, it freed no slaves in practice, but it did infuriate many Northern citizens who had not supported the war as an abolitionist crusade. Lincoln's diplomats worked tirelessly to ensure that no foreign power would intervene in the conflict, although many European observers considered diplomatic recognition of the Confederacy to be almost inevitable. The Federal government resorted to conscription to fill the ranks on March 3, 1863 with the passage of the Enrollment Act. This law demonstrated that the Union Army's constant need for manpower could no longer be supplied solely through volunteers, even with increasing enlistment bounties.

The Union's military situation was not much better than the political position held by the Lincoln administration. Although Union armies had launched a series of massive offensives in both the Eastern and Western Theaters, most of the Confederacy remained free of occupation. The Union blockade had stifled the South's ability to export most of its cotton crop, but could do little to hinder the internal movements of resources on the rivers. The Confederates also had the significant advantage of fighting on the defensive, making the shift of troops and supplies along internal lines of communication much easier. With three of the five deadliest battles of the war occurring during 1863, the year had the potential to be the decisive campaign season. It also might involve a devolution into abject brutality on one or both sides, with disastrous consequences.

Although the warring governments had signed a prisoner of war (POW) exchange cartel the preceding spring, accusations of perfidy from both sides threatened to end the exchanges and subject the unfortunate troops who fell into enemy hands to unspeakably bad treatment within the ad hoc prison systems established by each government. Although Lincoln and his secretary of war, Edwin M. Stanton, had long considered ways to mitigate the worst aspects of military engagements and occupation, they had no means of forcing reciprocity upon the enemy, and had little control over the behavior of their own troops in the field. In consultation with the chief of staff of the army, Major General Henry W. Halleck, Lincoln issued a transformational general order that codified the laws of war for the United States and set the expectations for the behavior of armies in the field. Although formally titled General Orders No. 100, it is more well-known by the name of its chief author, Professor Francis Lieber of Columbia College. The Lieber Code clarified an enormous number of vexing issues regarding the treatment of enemies on the battlefield, captured prisoners of war, and civilians in the pathway of armies. Although it was primarily intended to ameliorate the worst aspects of the current war, it soon became clear that the Lieber Code would have a far greater effect than its author expected or intended. Foreign observers seized upon the code as a good starting point for attempts to codify the international laws of warfare.

Although not all of the provisions of the Code were strictly applied to every Union POW camp, its regulations almost certainly prevented the POW crisis of the last years of the war from becoming substantially worse. By setting at least a minimum standard of acceptable treatment, the Code represented an effort to mitigate the worst elements of military prison camps. It also made the key distinction that all POWs should be considered captives of the national government, and not the units that took them as prisoners. Thus, all decisions regarding the disposition of prisoners could be handled by a central authority, rather than recreating the haphazard systems of captivity and exchange that had been practiced in earlier American wars. While the resulting system had significant flaws, it was markedly better than the treatment of POWs in the Confederacy.

General Orders No. 100 continued to guide the treatment of POWs by American forces for the next seven decades, before finally being superseded by Amery regulations for POW treatment. The document quickly spread throughout the world, and had a major influence upon the development of international laws governing armed conflict. Much of the exact wording of the Code can be found in later multilateral treaties, such as the Hague Conventions of 1899 and 1907 and the Geneva Conventions of 1929 and 1949. Its definitions of lawful combatants, unlawful combatants, and civilians, and how each classification should be treated by the enemy, remain the underpinning of international military laws today.

For this transformation to be accepted, it was probably necessary for the war that produced it to be characterized by horrific POW conditions. Just as the Civil War was the bloodiest conflict in American history for the troops that fought in it, the war was also the deadliest in American history for the POWs held captive during the conflict. The public memory of the Civil War is a very complicated one, and includes key elements of regionalism, ethnicity, and American subcultures. For some, the war is remembered as a period of heroic deeds by great men, while others view it as the most tragic period of the nation's history. If the outcome included the welcome end of chattel slavery, it came at a terrible price: the loss of 600,000 citizens and a sitting president. Virtually all historians agree that Civil War prisoners faced horrific conditions in the prison camps created by both sides. These stories told by prisoners who survived clearly demonstrated the need to improve the lot of the unfortunate troops who fell into enemy hands.

This book is designed to show the terrible situation in the prison camps, and thus illustrate the absolute necessity of better guidance for future conflicts. The first chapter begins with an examination of previous American POW programs, from the Revolutionary War until 1860, and then moves into a discussion of the official government policies of the war regarding POWs. Chapter 2 demonstrates the gradual breakdown of the inadequate and improvised systems of captivity created by each government. Chapter 3 analyzes the captivity experience of prisoners held in both the Union and the Confederacy from the perspectives of the prisoners. Chapter 4 discusses the politics associated with the prison systems, particularly in the aftermath of the Civil War. Chapter 5 examines the ways in which the victims of the captivity experience have been honored in the decades since the end of the war. The final chapter analyzes the gradual changes in how the Civil War prison systems have been understood and portrayed since the end of the conflict. The documents provided after the narrative chapters were chosen to illustrate the differences between the planned approach to Civil War prisons and the actual practices within the camps.

Students are encouraged not only to focus upon the awful situations faced by captive soldiers, but also the means by which they confronted their individual situations in the quest for survival. Although General Orders No. 100 could not immediately solve all of the captivity problems of the Civil War, and did not address every possible issue that might arise in future conflicts, it deserves credit for the generally better treatment meted out to millions of POWs held in later conflicts. It provided the baseline for negotiations between the most powerful nations on Earth regarding acceptable behavior in wartime, and illustrated that, even in the most difficult of circumstances, it is possible to fight an enemy without losing one's humanity. Readers should examine the behavioral prescriptions put forth in the Lieber Code, and evaluate the net effects of this transformative document upon the practice of warfare.

REVOLUTIONARY WAR PRECEDENTS

Prior to the Civil War, the United States had fought a pair of wars with Great Britain, invaded Mexico, and had faced continual internal conflicts with Native American tribes. Each of these wars served to shape the U.S. perspective on how the enemy should be treated, and had an influence on the final form of General Orders No. 100. In the American Revolution, much of the U.S. policy was derived from existing British policies, and in fact, General George Washington vowed to his British counterpart, General Thomas Gage, "I shall regulate my Conduct towards those Gentlemen, who are or may be in our Possession, exactly by the Rule you shall observe towards those of ours, now in your custody."[1] Washington was not simply conceding all POW decisions to his enemy, rather, he was reminding Gage that the American forces had captured hundreds of British troops to date, and were likely to capture thousands more. Because the British commander had suggested the possibility of considering all American rebels taken in arms as treasonous subjects, who might be executed for their actions, Washington was subtly letting Gage know that retaliatory actions would follow. In this manner, he was able to influence Gage's decision of how to handle captured American patriots, without offering a direct threat to the safety of British POWs.

The British tended to hold their POWs in prison hulks near New York City and other harbors under their direct control. These old ships, stripped of sails and rigging, offered a relatively easy way to securely house prisoners, with few opportunities for escape. Unfortunately, overcrowding and poor rations allowed a substantial amount of disease to spread through the POW ranks, and thousands died during the course of war. Such treatment was considered normal, and evoked little protest from many of the American commissioners named to check on the welfare of the prisoners.[2] At George Washington's suggestion, the Patriots usually placed their British and German captives into encampments in the countryside, as far from the front lines as possible.[3] They often encouraged POWs to desert and enlist in the Continental Army, or to hire out as wage laborers for local farmers and businesses. Many of the Germans refused to return to Europe at the end of the war, preferring to remain in their imprisonment communities as citizens of the new republic.[4]

On October 17, 1777, General John Burgoyne signed a capitulation agreement at Saratoga, surrendering his forces on the condition that they be marched directly to Boston and allowed to take ship for England. They would remain ineligible for service in North America until exchanged, although they might be sent elsewhere in the British Empire to free up troops for service against the rebels. When the Continental Congress learned the terms of the deal, its members were livid. They reneged on the agreement, citing technicalities in the surrender that had not been followed to the letter by the British, and ordered Burgoyne's troops into captivity in Virginia. Naturally, the British commanders of the war effort, Sir William Howe and Sir Henry Clinton, protested the abrogation of the capitulation, but they refused to compound the injustice by offering American captives in exchange for Burgoyne's men, and as a result, the entire POW exchange system threatened to collapse. Burgoyne's forces were some of the last to leave captivity; by the time they were released in 1783, nearly half of his force had deserted or escaped.[5]

The Treaty of Paris required the return of all captives from the war, and recognized American independence. It also established the western border of the new nation at the Mississippi River, virtually guaranteeing that whites migrating westward would come into conflict with Native Americans already living in the region. When wars erupted with Native Americans, the U.S. government saw no reason to apply the customs of "civilized warfare" and thus the wars tended to be fought under the assumption that no quarter would be offered. Even noncombatants could not expect to peacefully surrender to any of the belligerents involved. This mindset carried over into the War of 1812, as British troops employed Native American auxiliaries, especially near the Canadian border.

WAR OF 1812 PRECEDENTS

When the United States and Great Britain went to war in 1812, it was a relatively minor distraction for the British, who were locked in a titanic struggle with Napoleon Bonaparte on the European continent. For the United States, the war had much greater ramifications, and hence a stronger sense of urgency. It was fought along the Canadian frontier, on the Great Lakes, along the Atlantic seaboard, and in the southeastern states against British regulars, the Royal Navy, Canadian militia, and Native Americans allied with the British. In short, it was an exceedingly complex conflict, which produced POWs from a wide variety of locales and from many different sources. For the British, the captives were simply added to the existing POW facilities, which already housed thousands of French troops and could accommodate thousands more Americans. For the United States, the Revolutionary War system sufficed for a time, with British prisoners held in encampments far from any potential rescue attempt, where they might be induced to labor or desert their service.

One of the primary causes of the conflict was the British habit of impressing American citizens into the Royal Navy. The British contended that any individual born on British soil could be compelled to serve. The United States allowed individuals to become American citizens through naturalization, which included renouncing previous citizenship and its accompanying allegiance.[6] Most British judgments of origin revolved around a person's accent, thus captives with an Irish brogue were assumed to be British subjects. In 1812, American captives taken along the Canadian frontier were interviewed, and 23 were accused of treason due to their Irish heritage. British authorities pulled them from the captive population and announced plans to try them in an Admiralty court. In retaliation, Secretary of War John Armstrong ordered 23 British officers held in close confinement, hostages against the fate of the Irish-Americans singled out. The British, in turn, retaliated by placing 46 American officers in a similar situation. The escalations threatened to continue until all captives on both sides were closely confined and in mortal danger of retaliatory execution. Thankfully, some quick diplomacy convinced both sides to release most of their hostages, and eventually the British chose not to try the original 23 for treason. The incident, which became a cause célèbre in England and the United States, demonstrated one of the great problems of holding POW populations—the temptation to retaliate upon them, and the possibility of a misunderstanding ballooning into a tragic outcome, made the development of an exchange cartel a high priority.[7]

On May 12, 1813, American and British negotiators agreed to an exchange system, with a much more rational composition system than the one created for the previous conflict.[8]

This allowed specially designated cartel ships to sail on a regular basis, taking POWs home on credit, secure in the knowledge that both sides would uphold the system. When the United States realized it had fewer POWs to exchange, it created a bounty system, inducing privateers to retain captured merchant ships'

A New Composition Scheme

In the exchange cartel of May 12, 1813, each military rank was assigned a value in "privates."

Rank	War of 1812 Value	Revolutionary War Value
Non-commissioned officers	2 privates	2 privates
Lieutenants	4 privates	6 privates
Captains	6 privates	16 privates
Majors	8 privates	28 privates
Lieutenant Colonels	10 privates	72 privates
Colonels	15 privates	100 privates
Brigadier Generals	20 privates	200 privates
Major Generals	30 privates	372 privates
Lieutenant Generals	40 privates	1,044 privates
Commanding Generals	60 privates	5,000 privates

crews rather than dropping them in neutral ports.[9] The system was not flawless, and tempers occasionally flared over who should pay the upkeep costs while prisoners awaited release.

Another complicating factor was the question of captured slaves. Britain abolished the slave trade in 1807, although it did not formally abolish slavery within the empire until 1833. The 1807 law made the transfer of slaves illegal, hence any slaves captured in the United States could not be retained in bondage. Having adopted the moral high ground against the United States (and previously against French attempts to put down a Haitian slave revolt), the British refused to send any freed slaves back into captivity. They also refused to provide any compensation to former slaveholders for taking their "property." Long after the war had ended, the tsar of Russia agreed to arbitrate the captured slave claims. On September 11, 1822, he ruled that the British should either return the captured slaves as confiscated property, or pay compensation of $1.2 million. The British government paid the sum in 1827, under protest, rather than effectively supporting slavery by sending captives back after more than a decade of freedom.[10] Native Americans also represented a thorny issue, as they tended not to take POWs, and on several occasions massacred U.S. troops who had surrendered to the British. In return, most U.S. troops did not offer quarter when facing Native American troops. The pattern of killing rather than capturing remained the dominant norm for eight more decades of war between whites and Indians in the United States.[11]

On April 6, 1815, with the war ended and the Treaty of Ghent in effect, hundreds of American privateers captured by the Royal Navy remained in captivity in England, awaiting transportation home. At Dartmoor Prison, a riot broke out among the captive population over the conditions in the prison and the delays in their release. Prison guards opened fire upon the American prisoners, killing seven immediately and wounding dozens more. These final casualties of the War of 1812 remain a stark testament to the conditions of POWs in the nineteenth century.[12]

MEXICAN WAR PRECEDENTS

The War with Mexico included the first substantial American military victories on foreign soil, and with the battlefield successes came thousands of captives. American field commanders had neither the resources nor the desire to guard such large bodies of enemy POWs, nor did they wish to transport them back to the United States. As a result, both Major General Zachary Taylor and Major General Winfield Scott chose repeatedly to parole large bodies of Mexican troops on the promise that they would not return to the fighting unless exchanged. Many of the parolees were forced back into the ranks by Mexican authorities, putting Taylor and Scott in a difficult position when they were recaptured, as happened on a number of occasions. To execute them would probably provoke some form of protest and possibly partisan activity by the civilian population, but to release them again would demonstrate that the parole agreement had no meaning. Both commanders enlisted the assistance of the Catholic Church, asking parish priests to administer the parole oath. This created a much more effective and binding parole, and few paroled troops returned to the fight under the new system.[13]

Interestingly, Irish-American POWs became the subject of intense scrutiny in Mexico, just as they had three decades earlier in the War of 1812. Mexican authorities attempted to induce the desertion of immigrant soldiers serving the United States, particularly those from a Catholic background. In particular, they targeted Irish-American soldiers, largely on the basis of Catholic solidarity. Hundreds of recently-arrived immigrants abandoned the U.S. flag and joined a special Mexican artillery unit, the San Patricio Battalion. They were promised land grants by the Mexican government in exchange for their service, to be distributed at the end of the war. Their leader, Sergeant John Riley, and a number of others, deserted before the declaration of war. When captured, they were tried and sentenced to banishment, as well as having a "D" branded into their cheek. Those who deserted during wartime and were subsequently captured received a death sentence. For 30 men, it was carried out en masse on September 13, 1847, with the prisoners held on a scaffold watching the Battle of Chapultepec Castle in the distance. When the castle's Mexican flag was replaced by an American flag, the signal was given and the men were hanged.[14]

PRISONERS IN THE CIVIL WAR

The experience in Mexico shaped many of the Civil War commanders' views about conflict in general, and POWs in particular. Many proved skeptical about the value of paroles, especially from enlisted personnel, and advised that prisoners be held until their actual exchanges could be arranged. Administratively, the Civil War had much more in common with the War of 1812. POWs were given acceptable rations and reasonable accommodations in the first years of the war, and once an exchange system had been established it followed the same system of composition that was created in the May 12 Cartel. Because Native Americans did not serve in most of the Civil War engagements, their earlier treatment had little effect upon Civil War POW policy and practice. Captured slaves, on the other hand, became an increasingly contentious issue as the war dragged on. Encroaching Union units served as magnets to nearby slaves, who expected to earn their freedom by crossing Union lines. By the end of 1863, the Union Army was enlisting African-American troops, including entire regiments of former slaves. In turn, Confederate officials vowed to enslave any captured black troops and execute any white officers leading them, a threat that all but guaranteed the end of any program of exchanges. Union political and military leaders looked to previous conflicts and the treatment of POWs to determine the best course of action for the current conflict, although they did not always learn the lessons of the past.

A number of issues presented thorny problems at the outset of the Civil War. Like the British in the Revolutionary War, the Union faced an enemy that sought to break away into a separate republic. Thus, by some definitions, anyone who took up arms in support of the Confederate cause could be considered guilty of treason, and executed for joining the rebellion. Of course, the rebels were not out to overthrow the government so much as to simply stop being under its authority, and some legal scholars argued that they were thus not treasonous. In any event, the practical result of mass executions would almost certainly have been a massive amount of reprisals, particularly after Confederate troops won a few early engagements and held the balance of prisoners taken in 1861. Even if the Lincoln administration had chosen to pursue execution of rebel troops, getting soldiers to carry out such executions against individuals they perceived as fellow citizens would have been difficult at best. It would also have been likely to trigger a massive amount of partisan activity and blurred the lines between troops and noncombatants. Thankfully, the course of executing the rebels did not have much backing outside of the most radical opponents of the South, and their efforts to demonize the enemy hinged more upon the institution of slavery than upon legal definitions of treason.

If the administration did not want to execute rebels, neither did it want to release them. The parole violation experience of the Mexican War had soured many on the concept. Exchange seemed to be an obvious course of action, especially as the number of U.S. volunteers held in the South started to grow, but it presented its own legal issue. To enter into exchange negotiations on anything but a local basis might be construed as a de facto recognition of the Confederate government, whose President, Jefferson Davis, also understood the potential ramifications of diplomatic negotiations. Just as Lincoln refused to call the naval blockade of the Confederate coastline a blockade, which would indicate a state of war between the governments, he hesitated to recognize Confederate negotiators. When the total number of captives reached into the thousands, Lincoln finally had to admit the inevitable and name a negotiating party, although they remained under strict instructions to confine their discussions to the mechanics of an exchange protocol.

The Union Army was unsure of how to handle their own returning paroled troops. They could not be exchanged until rebels had been captured in the field, and the War Department leadership had no interest in trying to force its troops to violate paroles. Some of the parolees agreed to serve on frontier duty in the West; for that reason, most of the regulars remained on the frontier for the entire war. At the very least, their service could free up Western militia units to be nationalized and brought into service against the revolt. Some of the higher-ranking officers had little chance of parole for months or even years, and were unfit or unnecessary for frontier service. Many wound up in administrative functions needed by the burgeoning military, including the Union commissary general of prisons and prisoners, Colonel William Hoffman.[15] For enlisted personnel sent north on parole, the first proposed solution was simply to release them from any service obligation and send them home. Because the war was not expected to last more than a season or two, the government assumed it would be cheaper to recruit new volunteers than to pay the upkeep of a paroled soldier awaiting exchange. The Congressional limit on the size of forces recruited for the suppression of the rebellion may have also contributed to the decision, as paroled prisoners awaiting exchange still counted towards a state's recruitment quota, even if they contributed nothing to the war effort.

Of course, the release from service obligations gave an incentive to some soldiers to surrender at the first opportunity, give their parole, and head home early, keeping

Figure 1.1 Colonel William Hoffman and his staff. Photo courtesy of Library of Congress.

any enlistment bonus. In early 1862, the system changed, and freed POWs were no longer released from service. This created its own headaches, as the government now needed to keep some degree of control over its own parolees. They had a decided tendency to desert, feeling that they had fulfilled any obligation to the government. As a result, the War Department established Camp Parole, Maryland, where prisoners were held under guard by their own comrades-in-arms as a means to maintain control. Prisoners from the Western Theater were sent to Benton Barracks in St. Louis and Camp Chase in Indianapolis. The three camps suffered from overcrowding, poor sanitation, and a pervasive boredom for their occupants. At their height, the parole camps held over 30,000 Union POWs. As camp overseers interviewed the parolees, they found the practice of surrendering to obtain discharges had become widespread. The paroled men, finding that they would not be released from service, refused to perform any military duties, and soon resembled a sullen mob more than a collection of Federal soldiers. In one noteworthy instance, Brigadier General Daniel Tyler led 8,000 parolees to Camp Douglas, where they soon rioted and virtually destroyed the camp.[16]

With all of the problems of handling paroled prisoners, it is unsurprising that the Union did not have a coherent plan for how to hold Confederate POWs.[17] In the first year of the war, they tended to be stashed in existing jails and prisons, or else held in open stockades under armed guards. In particular, the Old Capitol Prison in Washington, D.C., held thousands of prisoners in a facility designed for no more than 500. While this could be endured for a short period of time, it would not serve if the system of paroles and exchanges could not be quickly settled. In the West, where far fewer and smaller permanent installations existed, many prisoners were simply shoved into warehouses or barracks, copying one typical British approach from the Revolutionary War. Hoffman submitted a plan to Quartermaster General Montgomery Meigs for how to confine and supply enemy prisoners only two weeks after being named the Commissary of Prisoners, but his plan was far too small for the numbers that the Union soon faced.[18] Unfortunately, when confronted with the actual volume of prisoners held by the Union, Hoffman simply did not have the capacity for his job. According to historian Benton McAdams, "In Hoffman's case, power did not corrupt. It overwhelmed."[19] It did not just overwhelm the man, it overwhelmed the entire system that he designed and administered.

The leadership of the Confederacy believed that keeping prisoners under guard but near the border would facilitate exchanges. Most Union POWs who were not immediately released on parole were gathered in Richmond, mainly in converted tobacco warehouses or other improvised structures. This concentration meant that the city's provost marshal, General John H. Winder, effectively became Hoffman's equivalent for the South, although he did not formally receive responsibility for all of the POW system until 1864. Because the Confederacy's logistical capability was weaker, these men tended to receive very poor rations and other supplies. Only the temperate climate and adequate shelter prevented them from worse suffering. Their proximity to the front lines made successful escapes more likely, as prisoners who made it outside of their compound were often only a day's journey from reaching friendly forces. The propensity of Union captives to escape contributed to the decision to build camps in the Confederate interior in 1864 and 1865. In the short term, it led to the establishment of a camp at Belle Isle, in the middle of the James River, under the assumption that most prisoners would not attempt to swim to the shore in an escape.

Although the Lincoln administration feared that POW negotiations might offer de facto recognition to the Confederate government, the desire to alleviate suffering and regain lost troops pushed the Federal government toward exchange talks. On February 11, 1862, Secretary of War Edwin M. Stanton instructed John E. Wool, commanding Fort Monroe, to begin negotiations for a POW exchange cartel. Wool contacted Benjamin C. Huger, who commanded at Norfolk, Virginia. In turn, Huger sent Howell Cobb as the Confederate representative to meet with Wool. The men met on February 23, and had little difficulty agreeing to use the May 12, 1813 Cartel as a guide for the immediate exchange of all prisoners, either rank-for-rank or by composition, as needed.[20] Any remaining prisoners could give their parole and return to their lines to await a later exchange. Although Wool and Cobb needed only a day to negotiate, their quick agreement began to fall apart almost immediately. On February 16, General Ulysses S. Grant had accepted the unconditional surrender of Fort Donelson and its 15,000 defenders.

When added to existing prisoner counts, these captives heavily tipped the balance of prisoners in favor of the Union. Stanton feared that the Confederate troops would either violate their paroles or be used to free up other troops for service against the impending Union spring campaign. As such, he cancelled the paroles, although he did allow exchanges to proceed. Cobb sputtered and fumed, but could not force Stanton to change his mind. Regrettably, the seeds of mistrust had been sown, and would permeate all future POW negotiations.

THE DIX–HILL CARTEL

In June, Stanton consented to another round of talks, and dispatched Major General John A. Dix to resolve the question of exchange. He met Major General Daniel Harvey Hill for several weeks of discussions to hammer out an acceptable approach to regular exchanges. On July 22, they signed the Dix–Hill Cartel, a relatively simple document with only six articles. Under its terms, all captives would be exchanged in the most expeditious fashion possible. Soldiers and sailors could be traded interchangeably, with the provision that exchanges should proceed according to dates of capture. Regardless of which side held a surplus of prisoners, all captives were ordered forward to exchange points along the front lines for parole within ten days of capture. Thus, most POW upkeep expenses would be borne by the government to which each soldier belonged, which would alleviate any charges of deliberate mistreatment or other forms of improper conduct. Commissioners of exchange for each side were ordered to maintain lists of all prisoners released on parole, and would reconcile exchanges on a regular basis. It would then fall to the receiving government to notify its own troops that they had been exchanged and were eligible for a return to service.[21]

The Dix–Hill Cartel was balanced, eloquently short-winded, and efficient. It created a workable system that reduced the costs of POW upkeep, alleviated the

Grant at Forts Henry and Donelson

In early 1862, Brigadier General Ulysses S. Grant moved his forces to threaten Fort Henry on the Tennessee River and Fort Donelson on the Cumberland River 10 miles away. He worked well with his navy counterpart, Flag Officer Andrew Foote, to quickly reduce Fort Henry, which had been poorly sited and flooded easily in the winter rainy season. Most of its defenders had already fled to Donelson, a much better built fortification on a high bluff overlooking the river. Foote's river gunboats could do little against the well-placed Confederate artillery batteries, and soon had to withdraw downriver. Grant's land forces surrounded the fort, and after being bloodily repulsed in their attempt to storm the position, settled in to besiege it. Commanding the fort was Brigadier General John B. Floyd, who had served as the secretary of war under President James Buchanan. Floyd feared he would be tried for treason if captured, and thus he relinquished command to Brigadier General Gideon Pillow and escaped. Pillow also feared his fate if taken with the fort, and handed his command to Brigadier General Simon Bolivar Buckner before taking flight.

Buckner and Grant had known each other while cadets at the U.S. Military Academy at West Point. Grant graduated in 1843, just one year before Buckner, in a period when the academy graduated less than 50 cadets per year. Buckner expected their personal relationship would play some part in negotiating the surrender of the fort, and he sent a messenger under flag of truce on the morning of February 16 to ask what terms Grant might offer in exchange for possession of the fort. At the least, Buckner expected his men to be paroled and sent home until exchanged, and he held out hope that they might retain their sidearms and personal baggage. Grant's response to the request absolutely stunned Buckner, who did not expect such a blunt reply from his old friend and comrade. Grant wrote "No terms except an unconditional and immediate surrender can be accepted. I propose to move immediately upon your works." Buckner had only a few minutes to decide the fate of his army, and he elected to capitulate to Grant's demand rather than prolong the inevitable surrender with additional bloodshed. He never forgave Grant for the humiliating terms, although Grant proved relatively magnanimous as the victor.

Grant's message earned him the wartime sobriquet "Unconditional Surrender" Grant. It demonstrated his single-minded focus upon the capture of a position and the annihilation of enemy forces. One thing Grant seemed to grasp much better than his contemporaries was the incredible difficulty of eliminating an enemy army. Even in the bloodiest of Civil War battles, the battlefield casualties represented only a fraction of the forces engaged. When an army could be induced to surrender, on the other hand, it simply and completely ceased to exist until exchanged. Grant managed to achieve the capture of three separate Confederate armies during the war. No other general on either side accomplished the feat more than once.

overcrowding of facilities, and made governments responsible for their own troops, rather than those of the enemy. When it went into effect in July of 1862, both sides began to forward all of the prisoners under their control. Over the next 10 months, the cartel essentially emptied the POW camps of all but a handful of prisoners held back under special circumstances, such as allegations of war crimes against noncombatants. By May of 1863, over 20,000 Confederate and 12,000 Union POWs had been sent home, and most had received notice of their formal exchange. The system worked so well that a cynic would be tempted to call it too good to last, and unfortunately would be correct. The cartel was destined for a catastrophic breakdown and complete collapse, with dire results for the prisoners caught in the bureaucratic fight that followed.

EARLY PROBLEMS WITH EXCHANGE AND THE COLLAPSE OF THE CARTEL

Although the exchange system itself functioned, it also exposed a fundamental inequality in the treatment of prisoners. Union troops returning from captivity in the South often suffered from severe medical problems, most related to inadequate nutrition. The perception that the Confederates were mistreating their captives was enhanced by the Southern habit of sending the sickest and weakest prisoners North for exchange, for humane reasons.[22] Scurvy, although not a virulent killer of POWs, affected most returning Federal POWs to some degree, making them unfit for future service without a substantial period of recuperation. Chronic dysentery, although not technically caused by diet, was often exacerbated by the coarsely-ground cornmeal that usually comprised the bulk of the POWs' rations in the South. In comparison, Confederate captives under Union control were far more likely to suffer from infectious diseases, in part because they usually did not receive inoculations, in part because the colder winters forced the men to remain inside cramped quarters for warmth, making the spread of germs much easier. Most Confederate POWs who died in captivity succumbed to smallpox, pneumonia, and dysentery and diarrhea, which left few lasting effects if the victim survived. Those who were exchanged could normally return to service fairly quickly. Many field commanders, especially Ulysses S. Grant, objected to exchanges on the grounds that returning Confederates would simply return to the lines and have to be overwhelmed once more. Fighting on the tactical offensive tended to produce more casualties, thus every Confederate exchanged might cost multiple Union troops in the future, while providing the return of only a disabled soldier at the time of exchange. While the principle of seeking the return of one's own troops still held sway, Grant and others believed more Union troops would be saved overall if exchanges were halted and the war simply prosecuted in the most vigorous manner possible.

On July 17, 1862, Congress passed two acts formally allowing African-Americans to enlist in Union regiments for service in putting down the rebellion, although the official activation of federal black units under the designation "U.S. Colored Volunteers" did not commence until early 1863. Some state and volunteer units had already seen a limited amount of service. These units had white officers in command,

and received less pay than their white counterparts. In theory, they could be used for the same duties as white units, although in practice, most were designated for garrison, occupation, and fatigue duties far more often than comparable white units. The formal acceptance of black troops into the Union Army followed more than a year of escaped slaves serving the Union, mostly as temporary auxiliaries in the occupied portions of the South. Lincoln saw it as a necessary political move, in that it shored up his support among abolitionists eager to prove that African-Americans could serve just as ably as other soldiers. It also tapped a previously unutilized pool of recruits, who eventually comprised nearly 10 percent of the Union Army's total wartime strength. The move, coupled with the Emancipation Proclamation that went into effect on January 1, 1863, did not garner universal support in the North, but it did not provoke much resentment, either.

In the Confederacy, the idea of arming freed slaves and unleashing them upon the Southern population was met with sheer horror and a determination to prevent or end the practice by any means available. Confederate leaders did not just fear the addition of thousands of fresh troops to the Union Army, they also suspected the move was designed to incite a widespread slave revolt across the South. Because most able-bodied men had joined the army and been sent to the frontiers, they would not be able to protect their families from such an uprising. Even the much resented exemption of slave overseers from conscription did not leave enough forces on the home front to quell a slave rebellion. The only way to prevent the widespread killing of noncombatants and destruction of the Southern economy, in the minds of some, was to make the consequences of enlisting black troops far worse than any gain they might offer to Union commanders.

To stop the enlistment plans in their tracks, the Confederate Congress and President Jefferson Davis both vowed that black troops would be treated as rebellious slaves, even if they had been born free or manumitted at any point. White officers would be charged with inciting a slave revolt, a crime punishable by execution. Any black troops who managed to surrender to Confederates without being shot out of hand would be eligible for a return to slavery, either under a claim by their previous owner or through public auction. Some Confederate field commanders suggested that they would offer no quarter if their armies met African-American units in the field. On a number of occasions, Confederate troops engaged in full scale massacres against black Union troops. The most notorious incident, the Fort Pillow Massacre on April 12, 1864, was by no means an isolated incident.[23] That said, neither General Nathan Bedford Forrest nor any other Confederate commander sought to slaughter every African-American soldier that his troops encountered.[24]

Lincoln could not ignore the idea that Union troops might be killed on the basis of race. He wavered between ordering black troops to be held back from front-line service and threatening retaliation against Confederate POWs for any confirmed abuses. Grant strongly urged him to halt exchanges unless the Confederates promised to treat all POWs equally, in accordance with the Dix–Hill Cartel, and Stanton seconded the idea. Grant had already realized that most exchanged Confederate troops went immediately back into the lines, while a substantial portion of Union troops never returned to service after exchange. From 1861 until 1863, this was largely due to the end of their enlistment periods—by the time they had been duly exchanged and sent back to their units, they had fulfilled their service obligations. However, by 1864, those Union troops who returned did so in poor physical health, with little prospect of a rapid recovery that might make them fit for service again. He recognized how harsh his actions might be perceived, informing Benjamin Butler:

> It is hard on our men held in Southern prisons not to exchange them, but it is humanity to those left in the ranks to fight our battles. Every man we hold, when released on parole or otherwise, becomes an active soldier against us at once either directly or indirectly. If we commence a system of exchange which liberates all prisoners taken, we will have to fight on until the whole South is exterminated. If we hold those caught they amount to no more than dead men.[25]

Thus, when Grant urged a halt to the exchange system, he did so for reasons of military efficiency, but in the larger picture, it also included a certain degree of humanitarian concerns.

If anyone understood the importance of holding prisoners of war from a campaign standpoint, it was Grant. He had captured an army at Fort Donelson in 1862, and he repeated the feat at Vicksburg on July 4, 1863. Although Grant had a reputation of demanding unconditional surrender, he tended to be quite generous once the capitulation occurred. The Vicksburg captives, who included 30,000 troops but accounted for 42,000 privates when reduced by the composition system, were allowed to return home on parole. Grant believed their appearance in hometowns across the South would demoralize the citizens with their personal stories of defeat on the Mississippi River. If they were allowed to return to service, though, he would have to overwhelm them again, at some other fortified point of their choosing. If threats against African-American troops provided a handy excuse to end the exchange system, Grant was in favor of such a plan. It might be disguised as a temporary halt, but he knew that once the exchanges stopped, it was quite likely that they would not start again in time for the 1864 campaign season.

To halt exchanges without a breach of honor, Northern leaders at least needed a plausible excuse. They found one in the question of how to treat captured black troops. President Lincoln expressed his expectation that all Union troops would receive the same treatment as POWs, while the Confederate leadership announced that all captured black troops would be enslaved.[26] Until the Confederacy promised to provide the same level of care to all Union POWs, the Union unilaterally halted all exchanges. This promised to deprive the Confederate Army of returning troops for the summer campaign season of 1864. The Confederate exchange commissioners protested vehemently that they had already forwarded a surplus of prisoners on parole, in the expectation that the Union would maintain good faith and uphold the exchange convention. The Southern commissioners had a good legal point, as the cartel made no mention of equal treatment to all POWs, given that it was negotiated before the enlistment of African-Americans into the Union Army. On the other hand, there was little practical way to force the return of prisoners held by the Union. Confederate exchange commissioner Robert Ould announced that the Confederacy would deem all paroled POWs duly exchanged, regardless of Union objections, and this freed up thousands of men for service. It also guaranteed that the Union would stop sending captives back to the South on parole, and effectively abrogated the exchange cartel.

The exchange system broke down just as the number of captives began to sharply rise. The surety of exchange and a return home had eliminated a major barrier to surrender, and some of the largest campaigns of the war began in 1863. General Robert E. Lee's invasion of Pennsylvania, which culminated at Gettysburg; Grant's siege of Vicksburg; and the running fights throughout southeastern Tennessee all swelled the prison camps.[27] If paroles and exchanges completely stopped, both sides would have to scramble to construct or convert new locations to serve as prisons. Many Union training and recruitment depots quickly became POW compounds. In the Confederacy, the military and political leadership, determined to ease the strain on Richmond and other city facilities, decided to construct a series of massive compounds as far from the front lines as possible. The stage had been set for the terrible camp systems by which the Civil War POWs are most often remembered today.

Just as hardly anyone had expected a protracted war prior to the commencement of the conflict in 1861, when exchanges broke down, hardly anyone expected a permanent failure. Both sides made the mistake of assuming that the enemy would cave on the pivotal issues preventing exchanges, and then the system would resume operations. This unfounded optimism slowed efforts to construct permanent holding facilities to house the tens of thousands of prisoners who would be retained for much longer periods of time. In turn, the officials charged with overseeing the POW operations on both sides found themselves scrambling to improvise a means of housing and feeding the captives, while constrained by a lack of resources and little interest from political and military leaders. Although a number of existing locations were converted into holding facilities, they were ill-suited to the purpose.[28] On the other hand, prison compounds specifically designed to house POWs did little better, as they became magnets to which field commanders sent their captives, with little or no consideration for the problems that a flood of new arrivals might create. For their part, the senders were simply happy to dispose of their prisoners and dump their care upon someone else; they cared nothing about the eventual outcome of the problem.

THE LIEBER CODE

While the POW situation began to worsen, the law governing the treatment of POWs substantially improved. When the War Department issued General Orders No. 100, it was immediately distributed to every Union command, and compliance with its provisions became the norm. Naturally, there were incidents of violating the orders, but the vast majority of Union leaders complied to the best of their abilities. The orders triggered a great deal of correspondence from field commanders requesting clarifications of certain articles, but the explanations that followed mollified the interrogators, and helped regulate the implementation of the orders. Unfortunately, while the Lieber Code supplied the broad outlines governing how POWs should be treated, it did nothing to supply the necessary resources. Prison camps and their inhabitants remained a low priority throughout the war, thus even a generous commandant had no way to obtain extra rations, medical supplies, or any luxuries for his charges. The War Department, and its chief bureaucrat for POW policy, Hoffman, determined how much to issue to prisoners. Because the Lieber Code allowed for retaliatory measures against enemy POWs, the reports of mistreatment that emerged from Southern prisons triggered a series of retaliatory measures in the North. Specifically, Hoffman ordered reductions in both the quantity and quality of rations issued to prisoners.

Francis Lieber's reputation as a legal scholar brought him into contact with General Henry W. Halleck, who also had a strong academic reputation. On August 1, 1862, Lieber had sent Halleck some thoughts on the topic of guerrilla warfare. In particular, Lieber's opinion upon the legality of guerrilla attacks, and how captured guerrillas should be treated, caught Halleck's eye. Halleck was unsure of whether irregular troops should be extended the traditional protections of belligerents, or if they should be treated as lawless brigands who could not claim the protections of laws and customs that they violated through their normal activities. Lieber fell firmly on the side of the argument that guerrillas should be considered illegal combatants. Halleck ordered Lieber's pamphlet, a succinct 16-page guide, printed and distributed throughout the Union officer corps. When Halleck then decided to form a committee to codify the laws of war, he invited Lieber to join its chair, Major General Ethan A. Hitchcock, who was also serving as the commissioner of exchange of prisoners for the Union.

On April 24, 1863, the War Department issued General Orders No. 100, under the heading "Instructions for the Government of Armies of the United States in the Field." This document contained 157 articles, of which 38 covered the capture, treatment, and release of POWs. The orders, which came to be known as the Lieber Code, served as the foundation for every subsequent international agreement regarding POWs. Although it was initially intended to guide and inform American officers, the well-considered statements had an immediate appeal to individuals wishing to mitigate the worst aspects of warfare. The Code defined who should be considered a lawful combatant and strictly forbade the use of violence by individuals outside the definition. By clarifying who had a right to participate in war, it sought to protect everyone else in society, as much as possible, from the worst aspects of conflict. However, if an unlawful combatant chose to take up arms, they forfeited all of their protections and could be very harshly treated by the authorities. Lincoln, who had practiced law before entering politics, quickly grasped the importance of the Code. He not only ordered it to be printed and sent to every Union command, he also had copies provided to the fielded forces of the Confederacy, on the assumption that it might eliminate some of the worst and most unnecessary excesses committed by both sides of the conflict.[29]

Section III of the Code dealt with, among other things, prisoners of war. It began with a definition of POWs, something that had previously been largely left to individual commanders in the field. POWs included almost anyone directly attached to an enemy army, to include individuals who arose en masse against an invader, civilians accompanying the army, diplomats, and chief officials of the enemy government. Criminals and people who attacked an occupying force after it came into control of a region were not considered POWs. Medical personnel were exempted from capture unless needed to care for other POWs, in which case they could be held at the commander's discretion. In a major departure from earlier wars, the Code declared hostages rare in modern warfare, although it did allow for their usage in extreme circumstances. In practice, this made retaliations extremely uncommon, a major break with previous American POW habits.[30]

Francis Lieber

Francis Lieber was born in Berlin in 1800, and as a teenager joined the Prussian Army just in time to be wounded at the Battle of Waterloo in 1815. He attended the University of Jena to study mathematics, but soon volunteered for the Greek War of Independence in 1822. He emigrated to Boston in 1827, with the intention of running a gymnasium and swimming program for the city. At the same time, he edited the *Encyclopaedia Americana*, which was published in 13 volumes between 1829 and 1833. After a short stint at Philadelphia's new Girard College, Lieber accepted a professoriate of history and political economics at South Carolina College in Columbia, South Carolina, where he wrote a number of treatises upon legal and ethical subjects. In 1856, he transferred to Columbia College in New York City, where he became the first professor of political science in the United States.

Despite his two decades in South Carolina, Lieber strongly identified with the Union cause during the Civil War. He had agitated in the South for an end to secession movements, and maintained that states had no legal right to leave the Union. During the war, Lieber founded and ran the Legal Publication Society of New York, a group that amassed pro-Union newspaper articles and distributed them to Union troops. He wrote 10 pamphlets discussing legal issues for the society, an activity that brought him to the notice of the general-in-chief of the Union Army, Major General Henry W. Halleck. In 1862, Lieber wrote "Guerrilla Parties Considered with Reference to the Laws and Usages of War." This short piece discussed whether or not guerrilla troops should be entitled to the privileges and protections of the laws of war, a topic of special interest in the hotly-contested border states of Kentucky and Missouri. It's clear style and lucid analysis induced Halleck to invite Lieber to join a newly-formed committee tasked with codifying the laws of war. This process resulted in the creation of General Orders No. 100, issued on April 24, 1863. Lieber's influence in the creation of the final document led many to simply refer to it as the "Lieber Code."

After the war, Lieber accepted the task of compiling and organizing the records of the Confederate States government. He also served as an arbitrator to resolve several diplomatic disputes between the United States and Mexico, a position he held at the time of his death in 1872. Lieber had three sons, two of whom served in the Union Army and survived the war. His eldest son, Oscar Montgomery Lieber, joined the Confederate Army and died from wounds received during the Union's invasion of the Jamestown Peninsula near Richmond in 1862.

Once captured, POWs could not be intentionally harmed through malnutrition, attacks, close confinement, or humiliation. On a related note, belligerents could not refuse POW status to enemies on the grounds of class or color, a deliberate clarification of the disputed status of African-American captives. Also, if an enemy enslaved any U.S. troops, it was considered grounds for severe retaliation, including by execution of an equal number of prisoners. While armies could not issue blanket no-quarter orders, individual units could, under dire circumstances, refuse to take prisoners, although this did not allow killing already-wounded troops incapable of further resistance. Dressing in enemy uniforms or using enemy flags for deception caused the actors to forfeit all claims to protection under the laws of war, and American troops were expressly forbidden from any such activities.[31]

The Lieber Code had an interesting provision that noted that the object of modern wars was not to kill the enemy, but rather to achieve a political object. As such, unnecessary killing was specifically prohibited, such as attacks upon sentinels or pickets that were not followed by attacks by a large body of troops. Poisoning the enemy in war was also forbidden, despite the fact that no nation had yet put substantial effort into researching chemical or biological weapons. In this regard, the Code attempted to establish that certain behaviors and technologies were simply beyond the pale of acceptable behavior, even in wartime, and should be shunned by all civilized, law-abiding nations. When POWs surrendered, they had to hand over any weapons or large sums of money beyond what was needed for their own upkeep. Everything else on their person was considered private property and exempted from seizure. While many of the provisions of the Code were fairly well followed, this particular requirement failed in almost every Civil War camp, where prisoners from either side tended to be stripped not just of valuables, but of any item that might serve as a souvenir of the war.[32]

The Lieber Code made the important distinction that prisoners belong to the government, not the capturing unit or individuals. No POW could be ransomed or otherwise released except by the government's designated representative. The government was expected to house, clothe, and feed them, but could compel their labor in exchange for those considerations, with no restrictions upon the type of labor to be performed. They could also expect medical care, to the same standards as the captor's troops, and to be free of interrogation. POWs were permitted to attempt escapes, although they could legally be shot in the attempt. If successful, the escape could not be held against them if recaptured, although they might be placed in closer confinement to prevent further escapes.[33]

The Lieber Code did not cover every possible eventuality that might be faced by POWs, and their captors, but it did an excellent job of setting limits and expectations upon the behavior of both. It directly affected the later international conventions created at The Hague (1899, 1907) and Geneva (1929, 1949) regarding prisoners of war, including a number of examples where the wording remained identical in each document. The Code did not get everything perfect, of course, but it did a remarkable job of consolidating the laws of war from only a collection of previous customs to a single, coherent set of provisions. In that regard, it was a remarkable achievement whose importance, both to the eventual outcome of the Civil War and in subsequent conflicts, cannot be overstated.

RETALIATION AND NEGLECT

In the North, the official policy in 1861 was that POWs should receive the same ration as Union troops in the field. Because the prisoners were concentrated in a few locations, the strain upon the logistical system was relatively light, and thus POWs typically received at least the equal of soldiers on campaign. However, the Confederate POWs contributed little, if anything, to their own upkeep, and performed almost no labor.[34] Thus, some began to actually put on weight, a sight that prompted complaints from guard personnel and civilians visiting the camps. Returning Union POWs did not show such improvements in their health from their time in captivity, and thus it was probably only a matter of time before calls for reduced rations became common. There was no compelling reason to change Union policy, save the idea of retaliation, although certain administrators, including Hoffman, showed a tendency to obsess over saving the smallest amounts of money in the upkeep of prisoners. If Confederate authorities did not provide sufficient victuals for Union POWs, Hoffman would not authorize anything but equal treatment. On April 20, 1864, the first order for a reduction in rations cut the Confederate POW's food allowance by one third.[35] While they probably still received enough food to maintain their weight, it probably was not enough to support immune systems that had to fight the chronic diseases periodically sweeping through the camps. Also, the variety and nutritional content of the rations declined, opening the door for dietary diseases like scurvy. While almost no Confederate POWs died from scurvy, a substantial portion showed its effects, and it became a significant contributing factor to their overall declining health.

While the Union's leadership deliberately reduced rations, causing a rise in the POW mortality rate, it is harder to directly assign blame in the Confederacy for one specific policy that hurt the POWs. Instead, the Union POWs suffered due to a series of poorly-considered decisions by Confederate authorities. To reduce the overcrowding in Richmond prisons, and to handle the possible influx from the 1864 campaign season, the Confederate War Department authorized the construction of several new compounds. Unfortunately, the primary consideration in the location of these camps was that they be deep in the interior, safe from marauding Union cavalry that might seek to release the POWs en masse. This put the camps in areas with poor access to the limited rail resources of the Confederacy, meaning the camps would rely upon their immediate local area for sustenance. Few locations in the Confederate interior produced enough agricultural surplus to support a large, idle population, even though a number of areas had converted from cash crops to food harvests to support the war effort. There might have been ample space, and even resources to build the camps, but sustaining the men inside them proved almost impossible, especially when security-conscious camp commandants refused to allow large amounts of prisoner labor outside the walls.

The breakdown in exchanges created the conditions for disaster among the POWs, and the subsequent decisions of authorities on both sides virtually guaranteed it would happen. As the camp populations began to skyrocket in the spring of 1864, the foolish decisions became evident, but there was little impetus to alleviate the situation. Union leaders believed Grant's spring offensive might soon conclude the war, and thus resolved to accept a certain amount of suffering among the captives as the price of victory. The Southern leadership had to scramble to survive the Union onslaught on five fronts, and thus spared little thought for the suffering unfortunates in captivity. If word of the terrible conditions leaked northward, as it almost inevitably would, that might simply create more pressure to resume exchanges, providing fresh troops to fill the earthworks guarding every key Southern position. Also, with the Confederate logistical system strained to the breaking point just to keep a minimum flow of supplies to the field armies, there was little thought given to diverting precious resources to enemy prisoners.[36]

Did these decisions constitute a deliberate policy of mistreating captives? That question has been a subject of debate for historians since the end of the war. Neither government expressly ordered a blanket policy of mistreatment, but both took actions that created a predictably awful situation. There is no doubt that both sides could have done a great deal more to alleviate the suffering, without hindering military operations in the slightest. As in previous American conflicts, POWs were often perceived as instruments of retaliation. When the Confederate Congress announced a policy of sending captured African-American troops into slavery, and executing any white officers who led them, the U.S. War Department immediately announced a retaliatory plan. Of course, because the Union had no intention of enslaving any captives, regardless of race, only the question of retaliatory executions could be easily presented. For any Union soldier placed into slavery, regardless of his former status as a slave, Lincoln vowed to place one Confederate POW in close confinement. For the most part, the quick Union response probably worked, at least from the standpoint that few reports of enslaved POWs emerged from the South. However, it also probably backfired to a certain extent, in that Confederate troops on at least a few occasions simply refused to accept the surrender of black Union troops, obviating the question of close confinement of Confederate prisoners but creating an entirely different problem at the same time.

One retaliatory action of note came when Major General Benjamin Butler learned that African-American Union POWs had been compelled to work upon Confederate earthworks at Mobile, a violation of the traditional norms of warfare. In addition, slaveowners in the area had been notified of their presence, and were encouraged to come and claim any of their former slaves.[37] Other black prisoners were used in a similar capacity at Fort Gilmer. In retaliation, Butler ordered 110 Confederate POWs to perform hard labor on behalf of Union troops at Dutch Canal.[38] One of the more notorious incidents of POW retaliation came in 1864 at Charleston, involving the captured batteries of Fort Sumter. As Union forces sought to capture the "Cradle of the Confederacy," they found the defenses too tough to be easily overwhelmed. From Morris Island, Union mortars began to lob enormous shells into the city, in the hopes of compelling its surrender. If that did not work, the attacks might disable the Confederate shell factory and the docks used by blockade-runners, rendering the city irrelevant to the war effort. Confederate authorities decried the bombardment on the grounds that its almost random nature effectively targeted civilians, who had not received sufficient notice to evacuate the city. When their protests did nothing to halt the shelling, Major General Sam Jones requested the transfer of Union officer POWs to share the risks of the civilians.[39] This move enraged Secretary of War Stanton, who ordered the shipment of 600 Confederate prisoners to Morris Island in retaliation. Major General William T. Sherman's army, which had approached fairly close to Andersonville, triggered an effort to shift some of its captives elsewhere before they could be freed by a raid. Nearly 1,000 wound up in the Charleston city jail, which stood directly in the path of the shells fired into the city. Amazingly, despite the enormous potential for disaster, none of the POWs being used as human shields were killed by shellfire, either from their own side or from enemy shells falling short. The harsh conditions of captivity, including poor rations, exposure to extreme temperatures, and waves of yellow fever and other diseases killed dozens of POWs on each side, but would have likely been encountered in any of the war's compounds.

Grant and General Henry W. Halleck, who had generated substantial friction with one another while commanding together in the Western Theater, were in total agreement regarding the need to halt prisoner exchanges. When Grant learned that Union and Confederate commanders in the vicinity of Charleston had entered into negotiations for a local exchange, which might free all of the human shield prisoners, he immediately notified General John G. Foster that no such POW swap should occur.[40] In Grant's view, sending Confederates back to swell the ranks in the height of the campaign season would prove a great folly.[41] Halleck agreed, although he expressed remorse that the policy of ending exchanges would abandon Union POWs to be slowly tortured to death at the hands of their Confederate captors. By this time, it was clear that Grant's army would not capture Richmond, or its primary rail supply line at Petersburg, without a protracted siege. To send more forces into Lee's entrenchments would only create more Union casualties in the assaults that would be needed to capture the city and potentially end the war.

Grant and his enemy counterpart, Lee, exchanged repeated correspondence upon the topic of POWs and the possibility of resuming exchanges during the nine months of siege operations around Petersburg. Each repeated the accusations thrown out by the exchange commissioners, naturally placing blame for the breakdown upon the enemy. Grant refused to consider any exchanges until the Confederacy promised to treat all Union troops the same, regardless of race; a demand he did not think they would ever entertain. Lee argued that the terms of the Dix–Hill Cartel allowed the Confederacy to declare unilateral exchanges of its own paroled prisoners if the Union refused to swap lists for exchange. He also entreated Grant to consider escaped slaves as stolen property, which under the laws of warfare should be returned to its owner if recaptured, although he was willing to exchange captured African-American troops who had never been enslaved.[42] In short, neither commander was willing to give an inch to the other's position, but the end of exchanges served Grant and the Union far better. Lee expressed his frustration, but could do nothing to budge his stubborn opponent; appeals to both honor and humanity fell upon deaf ears. The two men could not come close to reconciling their diametrically-opposed positions, thus it is little surprise that their governments could not do so, either.

By the fall of 1864, it had become clear that the enormous prison compounds created that year had become a disastrous and embarrassing spectacle. In the South, Confederate authorities finally moved to alleviate the terrible conditions at Andersonville, by transferring as many of the prisoners as could be safely moved to other prisons.[43] Unfortunately, many of the new destinations quickly became

Ulysses S. Grant and Henry W. Halleck

Ulysses S. Grant was by far the most successful Union commander when it came to capturing enemy troops. Ironically, his successes in the field brought him into substantial conflict with his superior in the Western Theater from 1861–1862, Major General Henry W. Halleck. Halleck had a strong academic reputation, earning him the moniker "Old Brains." Despite his very strong intellect, Halleck was not particularly skilled at field command. However, he was a very jealous individual who perceived most of his colleagues as rivals. As Grant's star began to rise, and even eclipse his own importance, Halleck sought to undermine him on a number of occasions. He strongly hinted to Secretary of War Edwin M. Stanton and President Abraham Lincoln that Grant had a serious drinking problem that hindered his command performance. On July 23, 1862, Halleck was called to Washington to serve as the general-in-chief of the Union Army. Upon his departure, he left Grant as the senior officer in the West, and moved to assume control over the entire war effort. Grant's capture of Vicksburg and victory at Chattanooga, both in 1863, prompted Lincoln to push for his promotion to lieutenant general and for him to succeed Halleck as general-in-chief, leaving his former boss to hold the administrative position of chief of staff of the army. With this, Grant finally outranked his former nemesis, but rather than removing him from influence, he harnessed Halleck's talents and kept him in a vital post. Each remained in his respective position for the remainder of the war, and both played major roles in the eventual defeat of the Confederacy. Grant is remembered as the paramount Union hero, while Halleck's legacy is far more mundane, in part because of their respective behaviors in this one-sided rivalry.

overcrowded and incapable of supporting their swelling POW populations, meaning that the worst problems had simply been shifted from one location to another, with little or no alleviation. The move reduced the official Andersonville death toll, as thousands of recent inhabitants died en route to their next camp, or shortly after arriving in the new hellhole.[44] In the North, efforts to shift the main camps to the West, where they would be closer to agricultural supplies and less likely to interfere with military supply operations, swelled the size of camps in Illinois, Indiana, and Ohio, but at least those locations had the local resources necessary to house and feed their captives. While disease remained a constant problem, largely due to Union refusals to inoculate POWs, outbreaks tended to be fairly well contained through rapid quarantine measures.

When the spring campaign season commenced in 1865, it quickly became evident that Richmond could not be held for long against renewed Union pressure. Its POW population had already been evacuated to the newer interior camps, most of which were in danger of being overrun by Union forces rampaging throughout the Southern countryside. The entire Confederate military structure teetered on the brink of collapse, and desertion among POW camp guards was rampant. When the final collapse of military resistance came in April and May, many of the camp guards simply disappeared, making no effort to inform the prisoners that the war had ended and they could go home. In some cases, Union cavalry units captured the vicinity of the compounds and announced the situation to the grateful captives, but in other cases the camps were so remote that the prisoners did not hear of the Confederate collapse until weeks later. When possible, Union leaders made arrangements to transport the prisoners back to consolidation points in the North, where they could receive medical care, if necessary, and be furloughed or dismissed from the service, as necessary. Little thought was given in 1865 to providing the long-term care that many POWs required due to chronic conditions that they developed while imprisoned.

If the precedents of previous wars strongly influenced the POW policies of both the Union and Confederate governments, so too did the Civil War policies, particularly of the victorious North, heavily influence the behavior of belligerents in later conflicts. In particular, the Lieber Code played a vital role in the national and international laws governing acceptable behavior in armed conflicts. Unfortunately, by the time General Orders No. 100 had been issued by the U.S. War Department, the practices of captors in both the North and the South had begun to crystallize into a continual habit of neglect and occasional abject cruelty. Neither side had expected to house and feed thousands of enemy prisoners, and upon having the problem arise, both sides did a poor job handling the necessary tasks. Rather than devote the precious and limited resources needed to provide an adequate standard of care to the enemy captives, political leaders from both governments preferred to make wild accusations about the enemy's nefarious practices, laying all blame for the deplorable state of affairs at the feet of the opponent. If the intended policies for the treatment of POWs had reached new heights of civilization, the practice of the new ideals lagged considerably behind, setting the stage for a catastrophic performance of POW operations in the later years of the war.

NOTES

1   George Washington to Thomas Gage, August 11, 1775, *The Writings of George Washington from the Original Manuscript Sources, 1745–1799*, Ed. John C. Fitzpatrick, 39 vols. (Washington, D.C.: Government Printing Office, 1931–1944), 3: 416–417.

2   David L. Sterling, "American Prisoners of War in New York: A Report by Elias Boudinot," *William and Mary Quarterly* 13 (July 1956): 376–393.

3   Washington to the President of Congress, November 17, 1775, Washington, *Writings*, 4: 73.

4   Paul J. Springer, *America's Captives: Treatment of POWs from the Revolutionary War to the War on Terror* (Lawrence: University Press of Kansas, 2010), 18–19.

5   Richard Sampson, *Escape in America: The British Convention Prisoners, 1777–1783* (Chippenham, UK: Picton Publishing, 1995), 82–88.

6   For a full examination of the argument between Great Britain and the United States over the question of citizenship and service obligations, see Rising Lake Morrow, "The Early American Attitude toward Naturalized Americans Abroad," *American Journal of International Law* 30 (October 1936): 647–663 and Ralph Robinson, "Retaliation for the Treatment of

Prisoners in the War of 1812," *American Historical Review* 49 (October 1943): 65–70. A full case study of U.S. Navy ships in New York in 1808 found that more than half of the enlisted crewmen were not born in the United States. See Christopher McKee, "Foreign Seamen in the United States Navy: A Census of 1808," *William and Mary Quarterly* 42 (July 1985): 383–393.

7   Springer, *America's Captives*, 48–49; Robert C. Doyle, *The Enemy in Our Hands: America's Treatment of Enemy Prisoners of War, from the Revolution to the War on Terror* (Lexington: University Press of Kentucky, 2010), 63–65.

8   "Cartel for the Exchange of Prisoners of War between Great Britain and the United States of America," May 12, 1813. Document 190, Box 10, Entry 127, Record Group 94, National Archives, Washington, D.C.

9   See Winslow Lewis to John Mason, November 23, 1814, and J. Pleasonton to John Mason, December 3, 1814, both in Box 611, Entry 464A, Record Group 45, National Archives, Washington, D.C.

10   Arnett G. Lindsay, "Diplomatic Relations between the United States and Great Britain Bearing on the Return of Negro Slaves, 1783–1828," *Journal of Negro History* 5 (October 1920): 391–419, contains a full account of the treatment and fate of captured slaves during the Revolutionary War and the War of 1812.

11   One of the worst massacres came in the aftermath of the surrender of Fort Dearborn. For a full examination, see Milo M. Quaife, "The Fort Dearborn Massacre," *Missouri Valley Historical Review* 1 (March 1915): 531–573, and Robert S. Quimby, *The U.S. Army in the War of 1812: An Operational and Command Study*, 2 vols. (East Lansing: Michigan State University Press, 1997), 1: 137–138.

12   Several contemporary authors described the Dartmoor Massacre in great detail. See Charles Andrews, *The Prisoners' Memoirs or Dartmoor Prison* (New York: Self-Published, 1815); and *Horrid Massacre at Dartmoor Prison* (Boston: Nathaniel Conerly, 1815). Historical studies of note include Reginald Horseman, "The Paradox of Dartmoor Prison," *American Heritage* 26 (February 1975): 13–17, and Vivian Bird, *The Dartmoor Massacre: A British Atrocity against American POWs at Princetown Jail during the War of 1812* (Washington, D.C.: Barnes Review, 2002).

13   Robert Ryal Miller, *Shamrock and Sword: The Saint Patrick's Battalion in the U.S.-Mexican War* (Norman: University of Oklahoma Press, 1989), 122; K. Jack Bauer, *The Mexican War, 1846–1848* (New York: Macmillan, 1974), 336–337.

14   Peter F. Stevens, *The Rogue's March: John Riley and the St. Patrick's Battalion* (Washington, D.C.: Brassey's, 1999), 2–3. Approximately 20 percent of Irish-American soldiers deserted during the war. See also Miller, *Shamrock and Sword*.

15   Montgomery Meigs to William Hoffman, October 7, 1861, U.S. War Department, *The War of the Rebellion: A Compilation of the Official Records of the Union and Confederate Armies*, 127 vols. (Washington, D.C.: Government Printing Office, 1880–1901), Series II:3:49. Hereafter cited as *OR*.

16   George Levy, *To Die in Chicago: Confederate Prisoners at Camp Douglas, 1862–1865* (Evanston, IL: Evanston Publishers, 1999), 109–114.

17   Montgomery Meigs to Simon Cameron, July 12, 1861, Henry W. Halleck to Lorenzo Thomas, December 25, 1861, *OR*, II:3:8, II:3:169.

18   Hoffman to Meigs, October 22, 1861, *OR*, II:3:54–57.

19   Benton McAdams, *Rebels at Rock Island: The Story of a Civil War Prison* (DeKalb: Northern Illinois University Press, 2000), 204.

20   Wool and Cobb's proposals can both be found in the *OR*, II:3:302–309.

21   The full cartel is located in the *OR*, II:4:266–267.

22   Arch Fredric Blakey, *General John H. Winder, C.S.A.* (Gainesville: University of Florida Press, 1990), 171.

23   Edwin Stanton to Abraham Lincoln, May 5, 1864, *OR*, II:7:113–114. Stanton recommended a strict policy of retaliation for the atrocities at Fort Pillow, and a new policy of treating Confederate prisoners in the exact way that Union troops were treated in Southern prisons, but Lincoln resisted any action that promised to make the conduct of the Civil War even more unpleasant.

24   William Marvel, *Andersonville: The Last Depot* (Chapel Hill: University of North Carolina Press, 1994), 154–155. Marvel suggests, incorrectly, that the black POWs at Andersonville had a much lower mortality rate, due to their opportunities to work on labor details outside the prison, and hence receive a larger ration. A study of the Andersonville graves shows that their mortality rate was equal to the camp as a whole.

25   Ulysses S. Grant to Benjamin Butler, August 18, 1864, *OR*, II:7:606–607.

26   "Proclamation of the President of the Confederate States," December 23, 1863, *OR*, II:5:905–908; "Joint resolutions adopted by the Confederate Congress on the subject of retaliation, April 30–May 1, 1863," *OR*, II:5:940–941.

27   McAdams, 57–58.

28   William O. Bryant, *Cahaba Prison and the Sultana Disaster* (Tuscaloosa: University of Alabama Press, 1990), 2; Michael P. Gray, *The Business of Captivity in the Chemung Valley: Elmira and Its Civil War Prison* (Kent, OH: Kent State University Press, 2001), 28; James R. Hall, *Den of Misery: Indiana's Civil War Prison* (Gretna, LA: Pelican Publishing, 2006), 35.

29   The full text can be found in the *OR*, II:5:671–682.

30   Articles 49–53, General Orders No. 100, April 24, 1863, *OR*, II:5:674.

31   Articles 56–65, General Orders No. 100, April 24, 1863, *OR*, II:5:674–675.

32   Articles 68–73, General Orders No. 100, April 24, 1863, *OR*, II:5:675–676.

33   Articles 74–80, General Orders No. 100, April 24, 1863, *OR*, II:5:676.

34   William Hoffman, "Circular," July 7, 1862, *OR*, II:4:152.

35   William Hoffman, "Circular," April 20, 1864, *OR*, II:7:73; William Hoffman to Edwin M. Stanton, May 19, 1864, *OR*, II:7:150–151; William Hoffman, "Circular," June 1, 1864, *OR*, II:7:183–184.

36   John H. Winder to Samuel Cooper, June 24, 1864, *OR*, II:7:410–411.

37   Mobile Advertiser and Register, October 16, 1864; Richmond Examiner, October 11, 1864.

38   Benjamin Butler to Robert Ould, October 12, 1864, in Box 2, Entry 149, RG 249, National Archives.

39   Charles W. Sanders, Jr., *While in the Hands of the Enemy* (Baton Rouge: Louisiana State University Press, 2005), 227.

40   Ulysses S. Grant to Edwin M. Stanton, August 21, 1864, *OR*, II:7:662; Henry W. Halleck to John G. Foster, September 30, 1864, *OR*, II:7:895.

41   Ulysses S. Grant to Benjamin Butler, August 18, 1864, *OR*, II:7:606–607; Ulysses S. Grant to William H. Seward, August 19, 1864, *OR*, II:7:614–615.

42   Robert E. Lee to Ulysses S. Grant, October 19, 1864, *OR*, II:7:1009–1012.

43   John K. Derden, *The World's Largest Prison: The Story of Camp Lawton* (Macon, GA: Mercer University Press, 2012), 56, 70–71.

44   Ibid., 219–220.

CHAPTER 2

The Captivity Experience

Civil War prisoner of war policy might have been improvised and idealistic, but at least both the Union and Confederate governments made an attempt to standardize their approach to handling their captive enemies. Unfortunately, there tended to be major gaps between the official POW policy and the actual practice of maintaining prisoners, in both the North and the South. While each government might decree certain standards for upkeep, such a decree tended to carry very little force, even when prisoners were held in the national capitals. Leaders on both sides envisioned orderly camps where captives would be held for a short period, well-fed, clothed, and sheltered until they could be paroled or exchanged and sent home. None of the political and military high command imagined a catastrophic breakdown in the exchange system any more than they had expected a protracted war involving millions of troops, where thousands of soldiers might die in a single day's battle, without bringing the conflict any closer to completion. By the time those same officials truly realized the awful situation in the prison camps, they could do little to solve the problem. Other wartime crises always took priority, and if they could not solve the problem, they preferred to avoid investigating its depths.

The problems of POW practice began at the very highest levels. Neither president understood how his political and military decisions of 1861 would play out. Lincoln bent over backwards to avoid antagonizing the states that remained in the Union, particularly the border states where slavery remained legal. He could ill-afford the defection of any more states, and thus he sought early in the war to protect the wavering states from many of the worst aspects of the war. He did, of course, insist that every state loyal to the Union furnish volunteers for the war effort, but he did so using his powerful talents for persuasion far more than his equally imposing capacity for coercion. Much of his attention early in the conflict was devoted to holding Missouri, Kentucky, Maryland, and Delaware in their fragile allegiance. While he concentrated upon this vital political question, he largely delegated the military mission to others, beginning with his first secretary of war, Simon Cameron. The regular army at the beginning of 1861 stood at less than 20,000 officers and men, some of whom chose to serve the Confederacy. Most of those who remained were posted along the Western frontier, serving in pacification duties that did not end when the Confederate revolt began. Thus, any attempt to invade the South would require an entirely new force's creation, a massive logistical undertaking that overwhelmed the meager resources of the War Department. Although commissary generals of prisoners had been appointed for the Revolutionary War and the War of 1812, those conflicts had involved the capture of enemy soldiers from a foreign nation, not misguided Americans. Thus, there was no immediate impetus for creating such a post, much less funding a staff to support the office. Most assumed that any prisoners would only be held for a few days before the violence ended, as had been the case in previous rebellions. The quartermaster general's office could surely handle the task of holding a few militia troops for a short period, until the entire mess was sorted out and they could be turned over to law enforcement or simply released.

COMMANDERS IN CHIEF

Lincoln's counterpart gave the matter even less thought, if that was possible. Jefferson Davis had to oversee the creation of an entirely new government, under a modified version of the U.S. Constitution, while attempting to woo more states to join the secession movement. At the same time, he expected there would be at least one battle before the Union would recognize the new Confederate States of America, and thus he had to build an entire military out of thin air. Davis had served as secretary of war under President Franklin Pierce, and felt eminently qualified to personally handle many of the military decisions, rather than leaving them to his secretary of war, Leroy Pope Walker. In the four years of warfare, Davis managed to name five different men to the office, while reserving most of the military decisions for himself. This command situation led many of the practical decisions upon which an army is built to go unconsidered for too long. Because Davis expected the Confederacy to remain on the strategic defensive, tenaciously protecting its territory but not launching attacks across the borders, the question of prisoners seemed moot—at the very least, it could be put off until the South actually had some captives to maintain. At that point, they could be gathered in Richmond and held at a secure location until their exchange—or better yet, an end to the conflict—could be achieved.

President Lincoln had performed a small amount of military field service, but in his conflict, POWs played no major role. Lincoln served as a volunteer captain in the Black Hawk War, a short struggle in 1832 that mostly consisted of chasing a small band of Native Americans through relatively unsettled areas of Illinois and Wisconsin. When the U.S. forces finally chased down the enemy, a massacre ensued at the Bad Axe River, followed by small attempts to chase down the remaining bands of Black Hawk's followers. There was likely little discussion of how to handle captured enemies, and most officers of the era assumed that the rules of "civilized warfare" did not apply on the frontier in any event. Thus, Lincoln did not instinctively consider the issue of prisoners when he considered the problems of military action.

Davis had a considerably longer service acumen than his rival, beginning with his formal education at the U.S. Military Academy, where he graduated with the class of 1828. Strangely, the West Point curriculum had very little practical military education beyond the practice of infantry drill tactics. The curriculum focused more upon the development of engineers through the study of mathematical and language skills, under the assumption that alumni would learn the art of their military profession once they had been commissioned. Davis resigned in 1835, after seven years of service in the infantry, including the job of escorting Chief Black Hawk to his imprisonment at Fort Monroe, Virginia. In 1846, he raised a regiment of riflemen to serve in Mexico, and held a colonel's commission during the war. When Mexican units surrendered, they often were immediately released upon parole, and no effort was made to confine large numbers of enemy troops, even when thousands of parole-violators were repeatedly captured. Thus, even having served in a major war, Davis had no understanding of the potential problems associated with prisoner operations.

Although nineteenth-century officers in America had little familiarity with the problems of holding POWs, they still believed that enemies had the right to surrender, and that quarter should be given. The linear tactics that filled drill manuals of the era did not dovetail well with the development of new rifled muskets, which could fire with murderous accuracy at 400 yards. In many ways, it is surprising that substantial numbers of enemies could survive the battlefield carnage to attempt a surrender, and yet surrender they did, from the first battle of the war to the last, as individuals and as armies. Once they began to arrive, field commanders had little coherent plan for their detention, and improvised plans to guard them in the open could not continue for long. The obvious facilities, most notably prisons and city jails, soon filled to capacity, and the prospect of much larger numbers loomed as the summer campaigns of 1861 expanded.

SCRAMBLING FOR SPACE

Both the North and South followed simple expedients for early captures, once the jails had filled. They looked for large, relatively secure buildings that could be converted to use as temporary holding facilities. Neither belligerent wished to repeat the mistakes of the past, such as the Revolutionary War practice of holding captives in floating hulks or in abandoned mines. In comparison, the conversion of empty warehouses and other industrial buildings seemed both humane and cost-effective. The governments could rent the necessary space on a short-term basis. In the North, the largest such facility was the Gratiot Street Prison in St. Louis, a converted medical college. In the Confederacy, the most well-known such camps were: the Libby tobacco warehouses in Richmond; the slightly modified slave pens of Atlanta, Charleston, Montgomery, and New Orleans; and an abandoned cotton factory in Salisbury, North Carolina. Most of these buildings had few windows, but those that existed could be partially covered for additional security. Also, guards could be housed on the first floor, with prisoners confined to the higher floors, where escapes would be somewhat more difficult. At first, the solution of using converted buildings worked relatively well—they tended to be in urban locations, making the logistical strain minimal. The prisoners had shelter from the weather, could be easily guarded, and faced more problems from boredom than from any other issue. Of course, as the number of captures rose, so did the crowding inside the facilities, particularly when the Federal government showed no interest in creating a formal exchange cartel. As warehouses became overcrowded, infectious diseases began to spread, and hygiene standards plummeted. Guard personnel continued to cram POWs into the facilities, but gave up enforcing the policing regulations, allowing filth to accumulate.

Bernhard Domschcke spent months inside Libby, and gave a thorough description of the Richmond prison in his memoir:

> The Libby was of three floors. The first consisted of the office together with the so-called supply room (here, a room without supplies) and a place for the sick. The second and third had been storage areas for ships' goods, each about fifty feet wide and sixty deep. Both floors had three such areas . . . Under the first floor something of a cellar served various purposes. There the terrible cells—tiny dark holes infested by rats and other vermin—horrified everybody so maligned as to be locked in them. An olio of things rotted there, polluting the air. Even a short stay in those dungeons amounted, without a doubt, to an aeon of agony. One person, and one alone, took pleasure in them. With hellish delight—the ecstasy that devils are said to feel about the torment of their victims—Dick Turner committed helpless people to bread and water in the black and reeking pits.[1]

The Libby warehouses were never intended for habitation, but they functioned reasonably well as long as they did not become overcrowded. Equally unpleasant were the cotton bays converted to prison duty by the officials in Montgomery, Alabama. In the words of John James Geer,

> The side walls were of brick, twenty inches in thickness and thirteen feet high. The ends were closed by massive iron-clad wooden gates, extending the whole width of the prison. The room was about two hundred feet long, and forty in width. It was used formerly as a cotton depot. There was on either side a narrow shed-roof, sloping inward, extending two-thirds of the entire length of the building. Beneath this shelter were six hundred soldiers, and almost one hundred and fifty political prisoners.[2]

Existing military facilities offered another important location for holding enemy captives. In the first half of the nineteenth century, the United States government had built an enormous number of fortifications, particularly to house coastal defense batteries that defended every major harbor and port along the Atlantic seaboard. These masonry forts were designed to withstand protracted bombardments or sieges by a large invading force, thus they were large, sturdy, secure, and capable of storing enormous supply caches. It took little imagination to seal off portions of the casemates and use them to confine prisoners, particularly near Northern cities that had no likelihood of facing a Confederate invasion, such as New York or Boston. Once those locations became full, the capacity of the camp might be expanded by the construction of temporary barracks on the parade ground, or by the erection of tents on almost any open space. Guard personnel could easily maintain control over the situation from elevated positions along the walls. Not surprisingly, fortifications designed to keep invaders out also did an admirable job of keeping prisoners in, and the number of escapes from these locations was considerably lower than from other types of prisons. Also, because the facilities in question were designed to house and maintain large garrisons in wartime, they tended to be easily supplied by the existing logistical systems. The largest Union forts pressed into service as prisons were Fort Delaware and Fort McHenry, although dozens more such locations were used, particularly in areas far from the front lines, where enemy attack was extremely unlikely and local resources might handle most of the prison's needs. At McHenry, a star-shaped fort completed in 1812, authorities placed a mix of political prisoners and Confederate captives into large brick buildings. When those sturdy locations became overfull, the leftover prisoners were shifted into the fort's stables and the surrounding enclosure. At Fort Lafayette, located on a small island near New York Harbor, the prisoners were placed into the batteries, sleeping beside heavy artillery pieces. Extra captives were placed in damp casemates with only a few small loopholes for light.[3] Confederate authorities considered using coastal forts for prisoners, and did so on a short term basis in several locations, but most such facilities were needed to repel or delay the U.S. Navy's incursions to seize coastal positions. Only the forts in and around Charleston continued to house POWs beyond 1861.

EVOLVING COMMAND STRUCTURES

While captors scrambled for locations to stash their prisoners, the military bureaucracy slowly lurched toward providing the necessary oversight. In the Union Army, Quartermaster General Montgomery Meigs had the massive job of organizing the logistics for an army that grew from 20,000 to over 600,000 by the end of 1861. He had to feed, clothe, pay, and train the men; an enormous task far beyond the capacity of his prewar staff. While states provided vital help, particularly in the early stages of recruiting and training, once the men were in Federal service they were Meigs' problem. He recognized his need for help, and immediately began requesting the detail of professional officers to assist his task. Regulars who had spent decades squeezing everything possible out of the pittance supplied by the government in peacetime had the best chance of success, if they could adapt to the new reality of the war. Of course, their service on battlefields was also absolutely necessary, and given a choice, the vast majority of officers elected to pursue positions in the line, rather than staff billets. Hundreds resigned their commissions to seek state service, and the higher ranks that could be quickly obtained from such moves. Meigs devised a brilliant solution to alleviate some of his problems, seeking the service of officers who had been captured in the initial wave of secessionist uprisings. Many of these men had given their parole not to participate directly in any action against the Confederacy until exchanged, and such exchanges would not occur until the Union captured a large volume of equally-ranked prisoners. Most of the parolees scrupulously followed the terms of their parole, which included refusing to participate in training or drilling of new troops. However, few saw a conflict in holding an administrative staff position, including Colonel William Hoffman. He had been included in the surrender of Federal forces in Texas, and his efforts to secure exchange and command of a regiment had failed. On October 7, 1861, Meigs informed Hoffman that he would serve as the commissary general of prisoners and prisons. Hoffman disliked the idea, but did not refuse the order, although he expected to relinquish the position once exchanged.[4]

William Hoffman was a member of the West Point class of 1829. Other notable classmates included Confederate Generals Robert E. Lee and Joseph E. Johnston, as well as nine graduates who were promoted to flag rank in the Union service.

Hoffman graduated from West Point in 1829, and in over three decades of service saw combat in Florida, the Great Plains, and Mexico.

He was efficient if unimaginative, and pursued the needs of his new position with discipline and energy. Less than two weeks after his appointment, Hoffman sent Meigs his initial plan for housing Confederate prisoners. He spent most of his suggestions upon how to confine Confederate officers, whom he considered to be the higher priority over enlisted personnel. Hoffman wished to construct a new purpose-designed prison for Confederate officers on or near Lake Erie, which would soon be constructed on Johnson's Island near Sandusky, Ohio. For enlisted personnel, Hoffman advocated the conversion of a handful of training depots, which could be quickly converted at a minimal cost.[5] Within a few months, such conversions had occurred at: Camp Butler, Illinois; Camp Chase, Ohio; Camp Douglas, near Chicago; and Camp Morton, Indiana. The states might agree to supply the necessary locations and guard personnel, in exchange for a Federal stipend. Hoffman's plan was sound, in theory, but in application, it was simply far too small. His decades of military service had created a penny-pincher of the highest order, who placed a much greater emphasis upon efficiency than upon effectiveness. Hoffman did not want to spend a dollar more than necessary, insisting that construction be undertaken with the cheapest materials and least skilled labor. Because he assumed that prisoners would not be taken in large numbers, and that those taken would not be held long, he saw no reason to expend resources upon permanent facilities. In addition to Hoffman's desire to save money on shelter, he constantly sought ways to reduce the cost of feeding Confederate prisoners. On a number of occasions, the Union commissary general ordered camp commanders to reduce the rations distributed to prisoners. Sometimes, this was a retaliatory measure, designed to punish the Confederacy for failing to supply Union prisoners in their care. On other occasions, it was purely a cost-saving measure, predicated upon the assumption that idle men did not need as many calories as those in the field, and money saved upon ration issuances could be put to other useful tasks.[6] His miscalculations contributed to the deaths of thousands of Confederates, but it was not due to a callous disregard for the lives of prisoners; it was simply caused by his inability to break out of his prewar mindset. Many field commanders had analogous problems, but circumstances forced them to either adapt or lose their commands. Hoffman had no such pressures, and by the time he realized the true problems, if he ever did, it was too late to solve most of them. In the words of historian Benton McAdams:

Hoffman was not evil: he was narrow. He was unimaginative, humorless, hidebound, and very wise in the way of army politics. He had extremely strict ideas of duty, obligation, and his own career, and he followed those tenets blindly. From that came suffering.[7]

In other words, Hoffman was not a tormentor, so much as he was the consummate bureaucrat, more concerned with the correct processes than the desired outcomes.

While the Union appointed a prisons chief who could not overcome his professional training to confront the realities of the war, the Confederacy chose a man who could not overcome his own family history to do the same job. General John H. Winder came from a military family, and it was only natural that he entered the family profession. His father, William H. Winder, fought in the War of 1812, culminating in his command of American forces at the disastrous Battle of Bladensburg. A later court martial absolved him of any charges stemming from his incompetence, but created a stain upon the family honor that his son spent a career trying to absolve. John Winder graduated from West Point in 1820, and had a modest military career until the Mexican War, where he won two brevets for bravery. In 1861, he resigned his major's commission and offered his services to the Confederate government. In June, Winder received the position of inspector general of the camps of instruction, a job that effectively made him the provost marshal of the Confederate capital, Richmond. In that capacity, Winder had to oversee all of the POW operations, organize the training of a Confederate army, and help to build the military bureaucracy that supported the troops in the field. While he did not formally gain control over the entire Confederate POW system until 1864, an administrative problem that enormously increased the challenge of running the prison system, he was the de facto commissary general of prisons for virtually the entire war. By the end of the summer of 1861, Richmond's holding facilities had already begun to show signs of overcrowding, leading Winder to search for other places to deposit the rising number of captives. As he sought proper facilities, his office received a number of suggestions from concerned citizens about how to properly handle captured enemies. Civilian interference remained a consistent theme for Winder's entire tenure.[8]

Winder's personality, like Hoffman's, was not particularly suited to a position that required enormous work without substantial rewards or recognition. His obsession with redeeming the family name had embroiled him in a series of personal conflicts throughout his career, and if anything, became magnified when he was under stress. By all accounts, Winder's personality was imperious, leading to conflicts with subordinates, peers, and superiors on a regular basis, although his Army service record until his resignation remained honorable and sound. He tended to give broad orders without regard for how they might be interpreted or achieved, and did not hesitate to shift blame for any failures in the POW system to any convenient target. He also shamelessly sought positions behind the lines, especially on his personal staff, for family members and friends, usually with success. Most wartime observers have offered a fairly negative view of Winder, although his most recent biographer, Arch Fredric Blakey, has developed a fairly positive opinion of Winder's service, if not his personality. He argued, "He was not a benevolent man, but neither was he cruel or vindictive."[9] The opinion was not shared by Union prisoners, who unabashedly

William Hoffman and John Winder

The two men who had the greatest effect upon the prisoner of war systems of the Civil War were Major General William H. Hoffman and Brigadier General John H. Winder. Each served as the top administrator of his nation's POW camp system, trying desperately to stretch the inadequate resources assigned to his control for the upkeep of tens of thousands of enemy prisoners. Each was vilified by enemy prisoners and newspapers for deliberately injuring the health of captives, although there is no evidence that either of the men actually bore ill-will against the unfortunate captives held in the prison camps.

Winder was born in 1800 in Maryland, the son of Brigadier General William H. Winder. His father rose to prominence during the War of 1812, and served as a negotiator to establish regular exchanges between the United States and Britain. Hoffman was born in New York in 1807, his father, Lieutenant Colonel William Hoffman, Senior, also served in the War of 1812. Both Winder and Hoffman attended the United States Military Academy in its early years, graduating in 1820 and 1829, respectively. Both graduated near the middle of their classes and accepted commissions in the U.S. Army, Winder in the artillery and Hoffman in the infantry. Winder resigned his commission for four years, and upon his reinstatement in 1827, almost became a contemporary of Hoffman on the seniority lists. They each served in the Indian Wars and the Mexican War, where both earned brevet promotions to lieutenant colonel. After the war, Hoffman's star continued to rise, and he reached the permanent rank of lieutenant colonel in October of 1860. With this promotion, he was transferred to Texas to command an infantry regiment, arriving just in time to surrender his command to secessionist state forces. Winder became a major in 1860, but resigned his commission to join the Southern cause, earning a colonelcy in March, 1861.

Hoffman's surrender meant that he was sent back to the Union on parole, awaiting an exchange before he could honorably play a part in the Union Army's attempt to subdue the Confederacy. For that reason, he refused to command a training camp, although he did agree to serve as the commissary general of prisoners and prisons, reporting to Quartermaster General Montgomery C. Meigs. Although his service freed up a different officer for field service, Hoffman did not consider it a violation of his parole. He was not shirking the battlefield; as soon as his exchange finally came through on August 27, 1862, he began to seek a regimental command, without success. He proved an able administrator for the burgeoning Union POW camp system, especially after he became directly responsible to the secretary of war rather than the quartermaster's office. During the war, he was brevetted to major general, partly as a reward for his efforts and partly to facilitate his ability to obtain cooperation from Union commanders in the field. Hoffman finally got his opportunity to command the 8th Infantry Regiment after the war, and led the unit for three years. He retired from service in 1870, and with his wife opened a school for girls in Rock Island, Illinois, where he died in 1884.

Winder became a brigadier general on June 21, 1861, a rank he held for the remainder of the war. He first served as an inspector of the training camps of

Richmond, a post that somehow included the POW facilities, before being named the provost marshal of Richmond. Eventually, his title was adjusted to commissary general of prisoners, and encompassed the entire POW system. Because the Confederacy initially tried to keep most Union prisoners consolidated at Richmond, Winder was the de facto overseer of the entire Confederate POW bureaucracy for most of the war. When exchanges halted in 1863, he ordered the construction of a series of camps, including the infamous Camp Sumter near Andersonville, Georgia. He had correctly surmised that the Richmond facilities would be unable to hold a rapidly-expanding POW population, but the delays in prison construction meant that the camps would remain primitive in their shelters and ability to supply the POWs with food and fuel. Winder died on February 7, 1865, while inspecting the prison camp near Florence, South Carolina.

cheered when news of Winder's death reached the prisons.[10] Like Hoffman, Winder spent much of his time in his nation's capital, and relied upon others for his ideas about the camps' situation. Unfortunately, reports about the growing problems within camps tended to go unheeded by Winder's office, even when they came from trained medical personnel in the service of the Confederacy.[11]

Neither Hoffman nor Winder had anything approaching the level of resources necessary to adequately perform their jobs. Both made do with minimal staff and

Officer Ranks

Both the Union and Confederate Armies used the same rank structure, although the Confederacy promoted certain individuals to a higher rank, General, than the Union, which used Lieutenant General as its highest rank during the war.

General
Lieutenant General
Major General
Brigadier General
Colonel
Lieutenant Colonel
Major
Captain
Lieutenant

In many sources, including this book, all generals are simply referred to as "General," rather than their full rank. The same convention typically applies to colonels and lieutenant colonels.

limited personal authority. Each held responsibility for tens of thousands of prisoners sprinkled into dozens of holding facilities, along with the uniformed personnel needed to guard and maintain the prisons. Both had relatively junior ranks for their responsibilities—although Winder began his post as a brigadier general, it was in an army that had already named full generals, and he had little authority to order even subordinate officers to perform their duties. It is telling that Winder's choice for the commandant of the South's largest and most important prison, Andersonville, was Henry Wirz, a mere captain with no service record prior to the war. Hoffman received a promotion to colonel while still a POW on parole, a development which probably delayed his formal exchange because such high ranking officers were seldom captured. In an army full of flag officers, though, a colonel's orders regarding POWs went largely unheeded, and Hoffman received little backing from his direct superiors. By the end of the war, he had received the brevet rank of major general, placing him on par with most of the highest-ranking Union officers, but he still found it difficult to compel obedience from field commanders regarding the disposition of captives. Part of Hoffman's problem came from his habit of running the entire POW system from his office in Washington. He remained in the city for most of the war, relying upon others for descriptions of the camp conditions. In particular, Hoffman trusted his subordinate camp commanders, who rarely announced that there were major problems under their command. Occasionally, Hoffman received negative reports from members of the U.S. Sanitary Commission, which attempted to alleviate prisoners' suffering on both sides of the conflict, but rarely did he venture into the field to check conditions for himself. When he finally performed a personal inspection tour in late 1864, he found the conditions in the camps appalling, but then did little to solve the problems that he witnessed.[12]

The lack of emphasis upon the importance of POWs permeated the ranks of men selected to command prison locations. These men tended to be either low-ranking officers or, especially later in the war, men rendered unfit for battlefield leadership positions due to wounds, illnesses, or advanced age. Their temperament varied widely, and had an enormous effect upon the captivity experience. Some had a reputation for cruelty that bordered on the barbaric, with harsh punishments meted out for the slightest infractions of their rules. Others had a seemingly lax attitude, which might make them popular among the prisoners, but also tended to allow breakdowns in camp discipline, hygiene, and security. The War Department tried to help by issuing POW regulations on several occasions during the conflict, which were then augmented by the rules created by individual camp commanders.[13]

Some prisoners considered their jailors to be evil incarnate. Domschcke excoriated the commanders of Libby, finding nothing redeeming in their characters or conduct:

> The commandant, Captain (later Major) Thomas B. Turner. He smacked of noblesse but was a Rebel through and through, an accessory to all offenses to torment prisoners, and a hypocrite who masked with civility the temper that has little or nothing to do with humanitarianism. Though trained at West Point and active and vigilant as a commandant, he had not, so far as we knew, been tested as a soldier in the field.

> The other Turner, Richard, usually called Dick (a captain and the commissary), second in importance. He was about forty years old, thin and wiry, and of moderate height. His hair and beard were black, eyes dark and piercing, features hard and pronounced. The son of perdition itself, vicious, sinister, a born turnkey and a beadle by nature, he should have delighted Jefferson Davis.[14]

Of course, not all prisoners had much to complain about regarding their treatment. Many prisoners offered comparisons of different commandants, as replacements took over their places of confinement. The prisoners studied by James Hall approved of their first commandant at Camp Morton, Indiana, Colonel Richard Owen, who Hall believed did his best to look after prisoners. His replacement, Colonel Ambrose Stevens, a member of the Invalid Corps, seemed determined to obtain revenge for his own wounds by dishing out cruelty to his captives.[15] William Bryant made similar comparisons at Cahaba Prison, where he approved of the approach taken by Captain H.A.M. Henderson, who made the most of a bad situation, but castigated Colonel Sam Jones, the commander of not just the prison but the entire military post, as a man determined to hurt Union troops by any means at his disposal.[16]

Over the course of the war, as conditions for POWs worsened, camp commanders had to adapt to the changing situations. Some succeeded in these endeavors, managing to run their camps according to the dictates from their War Department, while protecting their charges from the worst potential ramifications of the situation they faced. The men who navigated these challenges the best tended to run camps with the lowest mortality rates. They also usually reacted decisively to any threat, real or perceived, such as an outbreak of infectious diseases, and they applied common-sense solutions to the problems they confronted, without waiting for directions from Washington or Richmond. The commanders who ran the deadliest prisons tended to be indecisive and dithering, or ignored the reality they faced in favor of a belief in how things ought to function.

CHOOSING NEW LOCATIONS

In the North, POW camps were dispersed for the entire war. In part, this was due to simple pragmatism—it was easier to maintain smaller camps, especially if they were situated near rail junctions, rivers, or agricultural centers. In part, it was also political—many governors petitioned the War Department to locate prison camps in their states. The camps represented a potential revenue stream for any location that held them, and the larger the prison, the bigger the income. Governors submitted subsistence bids, offering to feed the prisoners a diet in accordance with Federal regulations at a set price per prisoner per day. The states with the largest agricultural bases were already reaping enormous profits by supplying the war effort, the prison camps just represented another avenue for the same behavior. Prison camps also required guard units, of course, and at most locations those guards were provided by state units as a part of the state's recruitment quota. Thus, governors could secure wartime positions for supporters that allowed them to volunteer but remain local, contributing to the war effort without facing the hardships and dangers associated with campaigns in the field.

For the Confederate states, there was less attraction for housing the POW camps. A prison camp might attract a liberating force, which would undoubtedly devastate the region, and it might also inspire local slaves to engage in rebellion. In the first two years of the war, the vast majority of Union prisoners were held in the vicinity of Richmond, with a handful of remote camps to hold POWs taken in other theaters of the war. The ability for governors to provide guard units was a minor incentive, but the financial rewards were considerably lower, both because the Confederate government paid less and because inflation made Confederate dollars significantly less alluring even in 1862. Prison camps might create a few opportunities for support personnel and sutlers, but it was equally likely that they would cost individual states money, and consequently there was much less political push upon the Confederate War Department to spread prisons throughout the countryside.

Sutlers were private merchants who paid a commission to the government for the privilege of selling articles to POWs. They quickly developed a reputation for offering poor-quality goods at heavily inflated prices, particularly as wartime scarcity made many items unavailable. Nevertheless, they were the only option for survival at many camps in both the North and South.

Although prison life could never be accurately described as pleasant, in 1861 the situation was better than all of the years that followed.[17] Individual exchanges on a rank-for-rank basis obtained the freedom of some prisoners, especially officers with political connections, but could not hope to empty the prisons of their unfortunate denizens. Thus, word of the exchange cartel brought a welcome relief to the POWs on both sides, particularly as the prisons began to empty during the summer and fall of 1862. By the time the summer campaigns were in full swing, the prisons had virtually emptied of enemy captives, although the Union's parole camps still held thousands of troops awaiting exchange. While the exchange system functioned, most of the prison camps ceased operations, or were turned to a different purpose. When the system faltered, most authorities assumed they could simply be reopened until the impasse ended, and did not react quickly to growing signs of an impending disaster. Of course, many camps had experienced overcrowding before, and various ailments had triggered spikes in the mortality rate included in the monthly returns supplied by each camp. By mid-summer of 1863, the problems had gone beyond alarming and balanced on the verge of a crisis, while enemy captures continued unabated. The major campaigns of that pivotal year pushed the functional camps to the bursting point, and forced Hoffman and Winder to seek alternate plans for where to house their charges.

In the Union, many of the camps that reopened in 1863 and 1864 had to expand their available housing in a quick and cheap fashion. This meant the newly-constructed barracks tended to use green wood, which contracted as it dried, leaving gaps throughout the buildings. As more prisoners filled them beyond capacity, the support systems of the camps became overwhelmed.[18] Water supplies proved especially vulnerable, as latrine and hygiene facilities became inadequate and led to massive contamination problems. Nowhere in the North was this problem worse than at Elmira, New York. The camp, commanded by Hoffman's West Point classmate Colonel Seth Eastman, was a former training depot with an intended maximum capacity of 5,000. Within a few months of operation, twice that number filled the camp to bursting, and the sluggish creek that supplied the camp became a festering swamp of fetid water. A few engineering improvements might have created enough water flow to sweep away the filth, but Eastman did nothing to address the problem beyond hoping for heavy rains to accomplish the task.[19] Another poorly-conceived prison put into operation during the lapse in exchanges was located at Point Lookout, Maryland. This compound of 40 acres offered only surplus tents of all varieties, surrounded by a 15-foot stockade wall, to house its inhabitants. Its location on the Potomac River made security a paramount concern, thus the guard personnel had orders to shoot any prisoners who approached a dead-line near the wall. Not surprisingly, its survivors reported the deplorable conditions in grisly detail, as a camp designed for 10,000 short-term occupants quickly swelled to over 22,000 inhabitants.

Conditions in the Confederacy managed to be even worse than the Union camps by late 1863. When General Ulysses S. Grant assumed command of the Union armies in early 1864, it was clear that he intended a major push toward Richmond. The Confederate capital was already having trouble maintaining its prison population, civilians, and the heavy military presence. In late 1863, Winder ordered his subordinates to scout out potential prison locations deep in the Confederate interior. He reasoned that a single large prison stockade might relieve Richmond of its POW problems and at the same time improve the Union prisoners' disastrous living conditions. Concentrating the prisoners elsewhere would also require fewer guards, freeing up thousands of men desperately needed in the front lines. In 1862, Winder had begun transferring POWs from the tobacco warehouses of Libby Prison to the open-air stockade on Belle Isle, in the James River. At this camp, Union prisoners had almost no shelter, little fuel for warmth and cooking, and extremely meager rations. Only the exchange program prevented a catastrophe, and Winder only kept the prison open for lack of other options. He hoped to transfer the prisoners out of Belle Isle at the first opportunity, reasoning that their lot could not fail to improve at virtually any other location. In February, Winder's son Richard began construction at a suitable location deep in the interior of Georgia, near the tiny town of Andersonville.[20]

Winder's idea for the creation of massive prison camps far distant from the battle lines had a degree of practicality that might have resulted in more humane conditions, under the right circumstances. Unfortunately, Confederate officials placed such great stock upon security that they devoted little thought to any aspect of the prisoners' maintenance beyond the need to prevent escapes. As a result, when Andersonville began to accept prisoners in early 1864, it consisted only of a walled stockade encompassing just under 17 acres. The first prisoners to arrive actually had plenty of space and although the interior had been clear-cut, the prisoners could still unearth tree stumps to burn for cooking rations. The area enclosed by the rough-hewn logs had enough room for the proposed 10,000 prisoners, although no effort had been made to dig latrines or set up any hospital facilities before the captives began to arrive. Tragically, when camp commanders throughout the Confederacy heard of the existence of the new prison, they immediately began to ship their POWs to the location, effectively making them somebody else's problem. The camp commandant, Henry Wirz, begged Winder to stop the shipments, but the prisoners just kept arriving, almost on a daily basis, until the stockade walls were full to the point of bursting. Eventually, Wirz received permission to enclose an additional ten acres, but the larger stockade did little to solve the terrible conditions at Andersonville.

THE PRISONERS' PROGRESSION

For most prisoners of war in any conflict, there are many common experiences. Almost all POWs suffer from fear regarding their future as captives, including the terrifying moment when surrender is offered but has not yet been accepted. There is an element of fright that the enemy might continue to engage in violence rather than agreeing to be burdened by captives. Even when the surrender has been accepted, there is no guarantee that prisoners will not be mistreated, and placing themselves entirely at the mercy of the captor is a major risk. There is typically a disorienting period as the new captives are transferred to a holding position, where they might be subjected to interrogation and a personal search for items of value or contraband. More travel often follows, terminating in the arrival at a semi-permanent housing facility that will serve as the POWs' quarters until they escape, are exchanged, die, or survive until the end of the war. The unfortunate captives had to make a very rapid transition from soldiers on the battlefield, who faced certain danger but also had the opportunity to act in response to that danger, to relatively helpless prisoners, dependent upon their captors for food, shelter, and medical care. Most found that the guards at POW camps did not have the mutual respect that is often shared across the battlefield, and instead engaged in displays of bravado despite never having heard the sound of the enemy's guns.[21]

A significant portion of prisoners taken during the war did not have to face the prospect of personally surrendering to an enemy during the heat of battle. Instead, they were simply informed that their commander had surrendered to the enemy, and they should stack their arms and march into captivity. Sometimes, as at the capitulations of Fort Donelson and Vicksburg, the surrender came after a prolonged siege, and did not surprise the troops. In other cases, such as the capture of Harpers' Ferry, the enemy attack came so rapidly that the captives had no time to mentally prepare for their new status as POWs. Occasionally, an army was ground down in the field through attrition, and simply lost the ability to offer any substantial resistance. For the exhausted troops of the Army of Northern Virginia, the 1865 surrender at Appomattox came as a relief, as they frankly had nothing left to give to their cause.

Once the surrender had been offered and accepted, new POWs faced an uncertain future. Some received an immediate battlefield parole, and after staff officers tabulated the rolls of prisoners, they were released to return home, where they awaited exchange or the end of the war. For those not paroled by the enemy, the march into captivity was typically characterized by confusion, insufficient rations, and little or no medical treatment for any wounds or illnesses they sustained before capture. The norm was a forced march toward the nearest rail hub, with captives held in an open field, surrounded by guards, whenever a rest period occurred. These marches represented the best opportunity for a successful escape that most captives saw during their imprisonment. The front lines were not too far away, making a return to friendly units more feasible. The captors had little experience guarding troops, and often a poor idea of exactly how many were even being held. No secure facilities were likely to be available, although sometimes it was possible to cram the new prisoners into a warehouse or a barn, which might be more easily secured.

Within the prison environment, the new POW must attempt to learn the expected behaviors of captives. This includes not only the routines set by the captor that pertain to movements, issuance of rations, and other regulations, but also the norms of the POW population. Every prison has its own characteristics and culture, and experienced prisoners offering to guide the new arrivals might not be providing such services for strictly altruistic reasons. Thus, prisoners are often wise to be wary, and typically cling to any comrades from their units who surrendered together. Of course, such safety nets might not exist, and under the right stressors, even formerly close comrades might turn upon one another.

The more unpleasant conditions became in a prison, the more likely its inhabitants would become obsessed with thoughts of exchange. After all, no government could willingly leave its troops to languish and die in captivity, if its leaders understood the horrors faced by its loyal soldiers. To convey their hopelessness, POWs wrote letters to family, friends, military leaders, and politicians, begging for release through an exchange cartel. On January 8, 1879, during a meeting of the Corporal Skelly Post of Gettysburg, Pennsylvania, W.T. Ziegler delivered remarks on his time at Andersonville Prison. Captured at Petersburg, Ziegler entered the prison in July 1864 and remained there through its darkest period. However, he concentrated his talk on the month of December, when conditions had improved, and he addressed the emotional and psychological dimensions of captivity. On more than one occasion he told the group of war veterans, "those of you who were not there, cannot imagine our condition." Ziegler recounted a cold and gloomy Christmas day when hunger and despair caused his friend Harry Coon to cry out "from the bitterness of his heart: 'O, that I was dead! O, that I could die! I must, for I can endure it no longer!'"[22] Escaped and paroled prisoners approached newspaper publishers with tales of the atrocities in the prisons of the enemy, hoping to increase the pressure upon authorities to conclude an exchange agreement. Stories with the salacious details proved the most popular; the enemy could not be portrayed too harshly for most newspaper editors. Such stories influenced public opinion, and probably contributed to the initial exchange negotiations, although they could not force the government's hand when the cartel collapsed. Regardless, rumors of impending exchanges circulated constantly in every prison, North and South, with most prisoners clinging to hope of exchange when all other sources of salvation had long since faded to nothing.

SURVIVING TO THE END

The majority of prisoners managed to survive their captivity, whether it was until parole, exchange, or the final release brought about by the end of the war. For those

Regulators vs. Raiders

The desperate situation at Andersonville drove many of the prisoners to turn upon one another, robbing and killing them for their meager possessions. Gangs of prisoners banded together for self-protection and to prey upon weaker captives. Robbing new arrivals became a commonplace activity, as they were the most likely to have ample supplies of money and other valuables. Unless the newcomers entered the compound surrounded by comrades from their own units, they were likely to be attacked, and those who resisted might be beaten or killed. As new prisoners arrived, the call of "Fresh Fish! Fresh Fish!" could be heard throughout the camp, alerting the predatory gangs that a new batch of victims had come into the prison. By the summer of 1864, a particularly vicious gang of soldiers from New York and Pennsylvania had become the unchallenged masters of the prison population. Their leader, William "Mosby" Collins, dubbed the gang the "Mosby Rangers," although most prison accounts simply refer to them as the "Raiders." These prisoners dominated the camp for several months, setting themselves up in far more comfortable accommodations at the expense of their starving and dying comrades. They took the fruits of their depredations to the camp guards, with whom they could trade cash, valuables, and even uniform buttons for extra food and luxuries. Prisoners who attempted to resist the Raiders were considered lucky if they only wound up naked and beaten bloody, as many who protested were simply killed, either on the spot or by the later arrival of a designated hit squad.

The victimized prisoners decided they had tolerated as much abuse from the Raiders as they could bear. A large volunteer posse, calling themselves the Regulators, wielded whatever weapons could be improvised and attacked the Raiders' camp. After a short-pitched battle, they captured the ringleaders, and requested permission from the Andersonville commandant, Captain Henry Wirz, to hold a trial. 24 Raiders were brought to the court to be tried for murder and robbery. The prisoners' jury sentenced the six worst offenders to execution. The remaining 18 had to run a gauntlet of angry prisoners, passing between 2 lines of fellow soldiers who beat each man as he passed. Three of the runners later died from injuries sustained in the ordeal. Upon hearing the verdict, Wirz provided materials to construct a gallows, allowing the six sentenced to death to be hanged at once. Their bodies were deliberately buried separately from the other dead prisoners interred in the camp cemetery, and their graves still stand apart today, a grim reminder of how low some prisoners could sink in a place like Andersonville. The Regulators continued to patrol the camp for the remainder of its operation, serving as a police force to mitigate some of the worst conditions of Camp Sumter.

prisoners in the Northern camps, the end of the war tended to find them in at least stable conditions, and able to slowly make their way back to their homes in the South once they agreed to take an oath of allegiance to the United States. Most did not refuse the oath, once it was clear that the prospects of Confederate survival had been eliminated. Even those bitter few who steadfastly refused to swear any such allegiance were released by the end of the summer of 1865, in part because the government simply had no interest in continuing to hold them, and in part because they did not represent a significant threat to resume the struggle. In the Confederate camps, the word of Union victory spread slowly. If there were Union troops in the vicinity, they arrived to accept the surrender of any guards that had not fled their post, and were usually followed by as many rations as the district commander could forward. In some locations, such as Camp Ford, Texas, the guards abandoned their duties and left the prisoners to fend for themselves, one last ignominy in the long line of offenses. The broken Federal prisoners at most locations required substantial assistance from their saviors to move toward freedom, and yet few hesitated to leave the confines of their camps. Most suffered lasting, debilitating effects from their time in captivity, often resulting in permanent physical and mental disabilities as a result of semi-starvation and long-term exposure to the elements.

The prisoner of war experience did not need to be such a terrible situation. Previous and subsequent American wars demonstrated that caring for large masses of prisoners could be done, even without substantial advanced planning, if commanders placed any degree of emphasis upon its necessity. Unfortunately, in the words of historian Roger Pickenbaugh, "Hoffman's passion for economy and Stanton's passion for revenge proved a problematic combination for Confederate prisoners."[23] While both sides in the conflict on occasion attempted to unilaterally declare some of their own paroled troops as exchanged, usually in reaction to the behavior of the enemy, neither side chose to unilaterally release its captives after the exchange cartel collapsed. As a result, the unfortunate wretches who languished in captivity served as political pawns in a political struggle. While many of the men who died in captivity did so of diseases that they would have faced in their own military organizations, the fact remains that neither the Union nor the Confederacy did much to preserve the lives and health of their captives, and thus both are worthy of castigation after the fact.

NOTES

1   Bernhard Domschcke, *Twenty Months in Captivity: Memoirs of a Union Officer in Confederate Prisons*, trans. Frederic Trautmann (Rutherford, NJ: Fairleigh Dickinson University Press, 1987), 38.

2   John James Geer, *Beyond the Lines; Or, a Yankee Prisoner Loose in Dixie* (Philadelphia: J.W. Daughaday, 1864), 81.

3   Lonnie R. Speer, *Portals to Hell: Military Prisons of the Civil War* (Mechanicsburg, PA: Stackpole Books, 1997), 35–38, 45–46.

4   M.C. Meigs to William Hoffman, October 7, 1861, *OR*, II:3:49; W. Hoffman to E.M. Stanton, March 13, 1862, *OR*, II:1:81–82.

5   W. Hoffman to M.C. Meigs, October 22, 1861, *OR*, II:3:54–57.

6   W. Hoffman to Jas. A. Mulligan, March 7, 1862, *OR*, II:3:361.

7   Benton McAdams, *Rebels at Rock Island: The Story of a Civil War Prison* (DeKalb: Northern Illinois Press, 2000), 203.

8   L.P. Walker to John Winder, August 8, 1861, *OR*, II:3:700; James Phelan to Jefferson Davis, August 28, 1861, *OR*, II:3:712–713.

9   Arch Fredric Blakey, *General John H. Winder, C.S.A.* (Gainesville; University of Florida Press, 1990), 207.

10 Ibid., 202, 207.

11 Isaiah H. White, "Sanitary Report of C.S. Military Prison Hospital, Andersonville, Georgia, for the Quarter Ending June 30, 1864," *OR*, II:7:426–427.

12 Henry W. Bellows to William Hoffman, June 30, 1862, *OR*, II:4:106; W. Hoffman to E.M. Stanton, December 3, 1863, *OR*, II:6:632–636.

13 Lucien J. Barnes, "General Orders No. 12," Jefferson City, MO, April 11, 1862, *OR*, II:3:443–444; Richard Owen to W. Hoffman, May 4, 1862, *OR*, II:3:518–519; W. Hoffman, "Circular," July 7, 1862, *OR*, II:4:152–153; W. Hoffman, "Circular," April 20, 1864, *OR*, II:7:72–75.

14 Domschcke, 39.

15 James R. Hall, *Den of Misery: Indiana's Civil War Prison* (Gretna, LA: Pelican Publishing, 2006), 35–40.

16 William O. Bryant, *Cahaba Prison and the Sultana Disaster* (Tuscaloosa: University of Alabama Press, 1990), 37.

17 Henry W. Bellows to William Hoffman, June 30, 1862, *OR*, II:4:106.

18 W. Hoffman to E.M. Stanton, December 3, 1863, *OR*, II:6:632–636.

19 Michael P. Gray, *The Business of Captivity: Elmira and its Civil War Prison* (Kent, OH: Kent State University Press, 2001), 27.

20 Richard Winder to John H. Winder, February 17, 1864, *OR*, II:6:965, 976.

21 Lyle Adair, *They Have Left Us Here to Die: The Civil War Prison Diary of Sgt. Lyle Adair, 111th U.S. Colored Infantry*, Ed. Glenn Robins (Kent, OH: Kent State University Press, 2011), 20.

22 W.T. Ziegler, *Half Hour with an Andersonville Prisoner: Delivered at the Reunion of Post 9, G.A.R., at Gettysburg, Pennsylvania, January 8, 1879* (n.p.: J.M. Tate, 1879), 1–12.

23 Roger Pickenpaugh, *Captives in Gray: The Civil War Prisons of the Union* (Tuscaloosa: University of Alabama Press, 2009), 221.

The Culture of Captivity

The Confederate victory at First Bull Run on July 21, 1861 included the capture of 50 Union officers and 1,000 enlisted men. The Confederates also snared U.S. Congressman Alfred Ely of New York, a spectator at the battle. Most of the Union captives were first sent to the capital city of Richmond and confined in a series of converted tobacco warehouses that became known as Libby Prison. Confederate authorities turned municipal jails and other buildings into prisons as well. General John H. Winder, provost marshal of Richmond in the summer of 1861, appointed Lieutenant David H. Todd, brother of first lady Mary Todd Lincoln, as commandant of the prisons. Todd was assisted by Sergeant Henry Wirz who later became commandant of Andersonville Prison. As historian Stephen Berry has remarked, "together the two made a terrifying pair." However, Todd was the first to incur the wrath of Union prisoners and an indignant Northern public. By August, just two months into his tenure as commandant, Todd was relieved of duty after allegations surfaced that he had stabbed a prisoner and on another occasion had kicked the corpse of a Union prisoner and left it on a city street overnight.[1] Unfortunately, this bizarre opening chapter was merely the prelude to a more horrifying Civil War prisons narrative that extended far beyond the city of Richmond and the First Bull Run prisoners.

MEETING BASIC NEEDS

In most prisons, a new arrival's first considerations were food and sleeping arrangements. To ease the distribution of rations, most enlisted camps organized captive soldiers into groups of 100 men, commanded by a sergeant, to draw, divide, and cook rations. Each such company was further divided into squads or messes, usually of approximately 10 men, to share utensils and cooking duties. If a large mass of prisoners arrived at one time, they formed new companies and squads. Those who arrived singly or in small groups were simply incorporated into existing units, taking the place of men who had died, been transferred, or managed to secure release through escape or exchange. This arrangement mirrored the typical rationing system for armies in the field, and worked relatively well for the quick disbursement of rations. Each squad created its own system to share the labors of cooking and cleaning, according

Libby Prison

Libby Prison, in Richmond, Virginia, was one of the first prisons opened by the Confederacy, shortly after the Battle of First Bull Run. After the Seven Days' Battles in June 1862, it was designated as an officers-only prison. About the same time, the Confederates established Belle Isle Prison for enlisted men on a sliver of an island in the James River. Libby Prison was simply three interconnected tobacco warehouses, know as East, Middle, and West. Prisoners occupied the top two floors of the three-story structures. Their living areas were sparsely furnished and bars covered opened windows. The buildings were like ovens during the hot Richmond summers and the cold winds swept through the quarters in the winter. A hospital was located on the first floor of East, the guards resided on the first floor of West, and the prison kitchen was located on the first floor of Middle. The estimated prisoner capacity of the three-building prison was 1,000.

In the fall of 1863, the prison population exceeded 4,000. The overcrowded rooms were covered in filth and emitted foul-smelling odors. Scurvy, diarrhea, dysentery, and pneumonia debilitated many prisoners but the death rate was relatively low. The prison was the target of intense Northern criticism. Libby Prison was the scene of one of the most famous escapes of the war as well as one of the most elaborate rescue raids. After the war, one of the buildings was moved to Chicago where it became a museum.

to the preferences of its members. The small group of men frequently pooled their resources and bartered with other prisoners to improve their fare. At Andersonville in late January 1865, seven mess mates sold their molasses rations for 30 cents and purchased 2 quarts of meal with the profits. A week later, they had accumulated two additional quarts of beans and had a little "feast."[2]

Mess squads also tended to sleep near one another, either sharing tents and barracks or huddled together on the open ground. Most accounts of prison life make mention of the authors' squad mates, and reference to the close bonds formed by shared hardships. In some locations, squads came from the same units, or the same regions. At other prisons, membership was entirely random, leading to some interesting relationships. Regardless of how a group of men came together, mess mates forged close bonds as they attempted to overcome the travails of imprisonment and sometimes an individual's survival depended on the loyalty of his mess mates. At a make-shift temporary prison in Thomasville, Georgia, Private W.B. Smith, 14th Illinois Volunteer Infantry, narrowly avoided death when a tree limb struck him in his right side, breaking three ribs and puncturing his lung. His "comrades" carried him to their quarters and Sergeant Will Close, one of Smith's "best friends" and a former mess mate, "took off the only pair of drawers he had, made a bandage six or seven inches wide." With the assistance of Smith's mess mates, Close patched the wounded prisoner as best he could. Smith was unconscious for two days and as he later recalled, "during the time I was insensible my messmates kindly drew and took care of my rations for me." They also sheltered Smith from the rain and sleet with their limited resources.[3]

There was no such thing as a typical ration at any Civil War prison; "it changed continuously, including the number of days it had to last." Early in the war, the rations issued to Confederate prisoners at Camp Douglas, Illinois, "consisted of ¾ of a pound of bacon, or one and ¼ pounds of beef, ounce and ⅓ pounds of white bread or one and ¼ pounds of cornbread, ⅒ of a pound of coffee, one and ½ ounces of rice or hominy, ⅙ of a pound of sugar, a gill [¼ pint] of vinegar, one candle, one tablespoon of salt, and beans, potatoes, and molasses in small amounts." To feed the nearly 8,000 prisoners and guards at Camp Douglas, officials spent $1,000 a day for rations.[4] In late 1863, Confederate prisoners at Camp Morton, Indiana, received daily, "three quarters of a pound of bacon or a pound of fresh beef, good wheat bread, hominy, coffee, tea, sugar, vinegar, candles, soap, salt, pepper, potatoes, and molasses."[5] Approximately three months after Andersonville Prison opened in southwest Georgia, Union prisoners received either one pound of beef or one-third pound of bacon with irregular supplements of rice, beans, or peas. Meal and molasses were fairly common staples. However, as the prison population exploded in the summer of 1864 food supplies became dangerously low.[6] One Union prisoner at Libby Prison estimated the daily ration as "one fourth to one-half a loaf of bread and four to eight ounces of meat" along with rice soup. Although most could not afford to do so, practically every prisoner had access to a camp sutler, a civilian merchant authorized by the military to sell items to troops or prisoners. Prison economies fluctuated wildly as did currency exchanges. Union prisoners paid 12 cents a piece for eggs and $3 per pound for butter at Libby Prison while the men at nearby Belle Isle paid 40 cents per quart for meal, $1 for a pint of beans and 30 cents for a spoon of salt.[7] Mess mates at Rock Island Prison, in Illinois, contributed eight to ten cents "per day, to purchase butter and milk for breakfast and potatoes and onions for supper."[8]

Complaints about ration quality and quantity were common to all prisoners. In particular, many noted that when meat was issued, it was of the worst quality, and often spoiled. Flour tended to be coarse, and was soon replaced in the Confederate camps by unbolted corn meal. With no cooking facilities and a poor water supply at many camps, the prisoners' attempts to cook their scanty rations often rendered them nearly inedible. But men had to eat in order to survive and prisoners resorted to consuming rats, dogs, cats, snakes, and alligators just to stay alive. Sometimes the men became so desperate that they tried anything to curb their hunger pains. A group of men at a temporary camp in Blackshear, Georgia "split up pieces of fat pine wood into splinters" and boiled it until a resin rose to the surface, which they skimmed off the top and "chewed it for gum." As one prisoner recalled, "this was evidently an injury to us, and in many instances was followed by severe pain."[9] No matter what they ate the men were rarely satisfied and ended each day stricken with hunger.

Camp authorities in both sections tried to provide at least some degree of cover from the worst of the weather, either in the form of wooden barracks, concrete or brick buildings, or tents. Shelter did not ensure comfort as Lieutenant Logan Williamson, 1st Regiment, Kentucky Infantry, recalled in a letter home to his family. Describing the scene at Point Lookout, Maryland, in April 1864 Williamson wrote:

we have had very stormy weather since coming here being situated on the bay . . . the wind is troublesome to persons living in tents. There is hardly a night passes without someone's tent blows down and the inmates are drenched in rain before morning.[10]

Prison officials in the North built rudimentary barracks at many locations, although the focus upon economy made for ramshackle construction in most cases. Out of fear that prisoners might escape, some camp commandants ordered that the floorboards be removed to discourage tunneling. As a result, the barracks were often muddy and filthy, such was the case at Camp Douglas, Camp Morton, and Fort Delaware.[11] The poorly-sealed buildings tended to be very drafty and humid, and rarely did the prisoners have enough fuel to keep them well heated. As a result, they crowded together for warmth, creating optimal conditions for the transmission of communicable diseases. In the North, the harsh winters added to the captives' misery. Confederate prisoners housed in barracks at Rock Island Prison, located on a strip of land in the Mississippi River between the cities of Davenport, Iowa and Rock Island, Illinois, faced "record-breaking" temperatures in December 1863. An early frost hit the area in late August and two inches of snow fell on October 22. By December the adjacent River Bend had frozen. The plummeting temperatures, which fell below zero for several days, caused schools to close for two weeks and the trains to stop running for several days. Temperatures were so frigid that guards did not report to their posts.[12] Some Union camp commanders managed to convince Hoffman of the need to build better facilities, and even managed to pry money out of the normally tight-fisted commissary.

Figure 3.1 Ration distribution at Andersonville Prison. Photo courtesy of Andersonville National Historic Site.

Confederate authorities converted structures such as tobacco warehouses in Richmond, Virginia, and Cahaba, Alabama, into prisons for captured Union soldiers. Those buildings tended to be dark, poorly ventilated, and overcrowded. Nevertheless, their mortality rates were substantially lower than the open stockades, despite being in operation for much longer periods of time. The sweltering Southern summers posed a great danger to Union prisoners, and camps with little or no shelter left captives subject to extreme heat, a situation that was exacerbated by inadequate water supplies. In the worst Confederate camps, the POWs could only dig holes in the ground for cover, or had to rely upon materials they possessed at the time of capture. The situation at Camp Lawton, Georgia illustrated how Union prisoners acclimated themselves to their surroundings. As one federal soldier observed:

> The huts were built in all manner of shapes, some had walls of logs, with a covering of timber, and over these a good layer of sand. Some had walls of turf, again others were cut into the ground perhaps two feet and then covered, sometimes pine slabs, sometimes with sand, and some were simply thatched with pine boughs, while others were bare sheds.[13]

The ability to adapt to one's environment required resiliency and creativity.

DEATH AND DISEASE

Remarkably, one out of every seven Civil War soldiers became a prisoner of war and of that number one out of every seven died in captivity. The likelihood and consequences of captivity struck the North and South in profoundly different terms. The North boasted a vastly superior manpower advantage and mobilized 2.2 million troops of which 194,743 (1 out of 11) became prisoners of war. The South mobilized fewer than 890,000 men with 214,865 (1 out of 4) becoming prisoners of war. Although there were more Confederates held in captivity, a larger number of Union men died in enemy prisons. Of the 56,194 prisoners who died in captivity, 30,218 were Union soldiers. Historian James McPherson has calculated that the death rate for Union prisoner was 28 percent "higher than for Confederate prisoners in the North." He further maintains that "Confederate prisoners were 29 percent less likely to die in Yankee prisons than to die of disease in their own army, while Union prisoners were 68 percent more likely to die in Southern prisons than in their own army."[14]

In the nineteenth century, some common illnesses were fairly well understood, and even certain preventive measures were attempted. For example, Civil War surgeons understood that smallpox could be transferred between people through close contact, although they did not understand the precise mechanism. Inoculations against smallpox existed for a century prior to the war, and consisted of harvesting scabs from victims and injecting small bits into healthy people who had never contracted the disease. The newly-inoculated patients were then placed into quarantine long enough for the disease to run its course. Some died, but most survived the experience, usually with scars to prove their hard-earned immunity. At the very least, this approach prevented a surprise outbreak of the disease, as once troops had survived their initial encounter with smallpox, they retained their immunity for life. As a matter of course, the Union Army tried to inoculate any troops that had not previously endured the process or survived the disease. The Confederate government, in contrast, did not attempt universal inoculations, and thus most Confederate troops had no immunity when the disease first appeared in the prison camps. Once the symptoms appeared, sick prisoners were often sent to quarantine facilities, but treatment for the full disease revolved primarily around trying to halt its spread and treat the symptoms enough to keep the victims alive.[15]

Scurvy was another relatively well-known disease. For decades, the British Royal Navy had issued doses of lime juice to sailors on long voyages, to combat the effects of vitamin C deficiency. By the Civil War, medical personnel understood that fresh fruits and vegetables could combat the disease, and even prisoners had some concept of how to treat it. Unfortunately, fresh produce was often unavailable, and when it could be located, it was often cost-prohibitive. Instead, dried vegetables were usually supplied, under the assumption that they would work equally well to combat the disease, but the drying and rehydrating processes destroyed most of the key components, resulting in an unappetizing staple with little nutritious value. Potatoes sometimes supplied the necessary vitamin C, but the soldiers typically peeled and fried their potatoes, removing or destroying the most useful portion of the tuber. Scurvy normally manifested with swollen extremities, bleeding gums, and poor night vision. Advanced cases might include teeth and hair loss and an inability to stand or walk. Scurvy killed few POWs in the Civil War, but it weakened immune systems and made its victims far more susceptible to other diseases.[16]

By far the biggest danger to POWs, from a medical standpoint, were the rampant effects of dysentery and diarrhea, common to almost every camp for most of the year. Both were present in field armies, and to a certain degree, an expected part of camp life. Surgeons had little advice for controlling either problem, and the solutions offered varied widely, according to local practices. Some called for dietary changes, eating easily digestible food that would not magnify the problem. Unfortunately, in many locations, little variety was available for the ailing prisoners' diet, and in some cases, the recommended dietary changes actually made the problems worse. In some areas, surgeons recommended drinking as much water as possible, which might offset the dehydrating effects of both conditions, but given the contamination found in the water supplies of many of the camps, drinking large quantities of fetid water probably made things worse. The uncontrollable bouts of sickness and resulting fecal matter added to the sanitation problems at many camps.[17]

Medical care in Union and Confederate prison camps varied somewhat, but neither side's medical personnel and supplies could keep the mortality rate from creeping upward, particularly as the exchange system broke down. In the North, the absolute demand for monetary savings prevented the issuance of significant amounts of medicine, and the needs of Federal troops in the field overrode the concerns of providing care to Confederate prisoners. Many camps did not have a trained surgeon, and instead had only a handful of assistant surgeons to oversee the health of thousands of prisoners. Nurses were drawn from the prison population, and could do little in any event beyond mild palliative care. In the South, the Union blockade produced severe medicine shortages and made a bad medical problem even worse.

In *Andersonvilles of the North*, historian James M. Gillispie examines prison policy and living conditions at the North's nine major camps. Specifically, he relies on the seldom used and regretfully neglected *Medical and Surgical History of the War of the Rebellion* to study prison illnesses, recovery rates, and death rates at Alton, Illinois; Camp Douglas; Camp Morton; Rock Island; Johnson's Island, Ohio; Camp Chase, Ohio; Point Lookout; Fort Delaware; and Elmira, New York. This sample group includes the prison with the highest death rate (Elmira), the largest population (Point Lookout), and the lowest death rate (Johnson's Island). He studies the treatment and effects of diarrhea/dysentery, pneumonia, and "eruptive fevers" (smallpox) at the nine camps and compares the outcomes to those achieved by the Confederates in the treatment of their own soldiers at Chimborazo Hospital, "the South's largest medical center." Gillispie discovered that in only one instance, Elmira, did the Northern camps have an appreciable difference (slightly better or slightly worse) than the Confederates in combating human sickness.[18] Still, such problems as poor sanitation, inadequate housing, shortages of fresh water, and incompetent prison officials caused the deaths of thousands of prisoners on both sides.[19] At Elmira, the death rate was 24 percent (2,961 deaths) and Alton, Rock Island, Camp Chase, and Camp Douglas recorded death rates between 13–15 percent with 1,508, 1,960, 2,260, and 4,454 deaths respectively. The death rates at Fort Delaware and Camp Morton were between 9–10 percent, 1,763 and 2,460 deaths respectively. Although 40,000 Confederates passed through the gates at Point Lookout, only 3,584 died, a 9 percent death rate, and at Johnson's Island 235 men died, a 3 percent death rate.[20] Irregular record keeping by Confederate prison officials makes it more difficult for historians to compile precise statistics for death rates. Despite significant overcrowding at Cahaba Prison, approximately 225 Union prisoners died, a death rate between 3–5 percent. Based on the only set of returns submitted by Camp Lawton, the death rate was not quite 5 percent.[21] At Danville, Virginia, 1,297 Union men died, and 3,700 at Salisbury, North Carolina. Andersonville Prison produced the most horrifying death rates of any Civil War prison. Of the nearly 45,000 men who entered the prison 12,930 died, a death rate of 29 percent.[22] These startling statistics are just part of a very complex story regarding Civil War prisons, and students must also understand the scope and variance of the captivity experience.

OFFICER CAMPS

Although there were exceptions to the rule, both North and South, officers generally fared better as prisoners of war than enlisted men. In a short article for *Century Magazine*, former Johnson's Island prisoner, Lieutenant Horace Carpenter, 9th Louisiana Infantry, concluded his reflections on his 16 months in captivity at that prison with the following admission:

> I have conversed and compared notes with men who had a story of
> imprisonment to tell, and am satisfied that, as compared with the

> enlisted men at Point Lookout, Elmira, Rock Island, Camps Morton, Chase, and Douglas, the officers at Johnson's Island merely tasted purgatory; the [enlisted] men went beyond that.

Lieutenant Alonzo Cooper, 12th New York Cavalry, made a similar confession in his memoir *In and Out of Rebel Prisons*, which chronicled the 10 months he spent in 6 Confederate prisons. "Being an officer, I suffered but little in comparison with what was endured by the rank and file, our numbers being less, our quarters were more endurable and our facilities for cleanliness much greater," he wrote, "besides, we were more apt to have money and valuables, which would, in some degree, provide for our most urgent needs." Cooper identified the major differences that officers held over enlisted men. He mentioned money that could be used to purchase items from a camp sutler.[23] At Johnson's Island, some of the officers were wealthy enough to hire enlisted men to cook for them and to wash their clothes. Often, officers received care packages from family and friends and sometimes were visited in prison by surrogates acting on behalf of their families. Officer camps were less crowded, which generally translated into better sanitary conditions. In some instances, officers were afforded a generous freedom of movement as their captors allowed them to leave the prison during the day and venture into town on the condition that they would return at a designated time.[24]

On two separate occasions, the Confederacy operated an officer prison camp in Macon, Georgia. Camp Oglethorpe was located in the center of the city on the site of the old state fair grounds. The 12 acre tract had been converted to a parade and camp ground for state troops in 1844. Therefore, a few modest buildings and horse stalls dotted the landscape when Union soldiers captured at the Battle of Shiloh arrived at Camp Oglethorpe on May 4, 1862.[25] The 800 prisoners received adequate rations for the first two months. During May, they drew "one pound of flour or meal per day; three quarters of a pound of pork; some rice, sugar, molasses, [and] rye for coffee." In late June, an additional 500 officers arrived from a prison in Montgomery, Alabama and the additions taxed the supplies at Camp Oglethorpe. Corn meal was substituted for flour and it "was of the coarsest kind, having often pieces of cob in it, and whole grains of corn, and this unsifted." Because of the scarcity of baking utensils, the men prepared their meals "at almost all hours of the day or night." The cooking scene dismayed some prisoners such as Lieutenant F.F. Kiner, 14th Iowa Infantry. "It really looked pitiable to see hungry men, young and old, hold an old piece of tin or iron over a smoking fire, with a batch of coarse corn dough upon it, trying to bake it," reflected Kiner, "and perhaps when done, it was so sad, or burnt, and smoked, that it was not fit for a dog to eat. But what could we do? We had no better." The Iowan grew somewhat indignant when describing the maggot-infested meat rations they received and suggested that "any decent man or woman in the North would feel ashamed to offer [it] to a dog." Kiner estimated that "one-third" of the pork ration was unfit for use. Nevertheless, the prisoners occasionally sold the rancid meat to the citizens of Macon and used the proceeds to buy such items as "sweet potatoes, tomatoes, onions, peaches," and vegetables from the camp sutler. This advantage that many officers held improved their lives immeasurably.[26]

Camp Oglethorpe lacked adequate shelter for its prisoners and many men simply sought refuge under the trees. The largest building in the compound served as the hospital and had a capacity of 100 patients. There were only two doctors, both of whom were viewed favorably by the prisoners. Medicines were sent to Camp Oglethorpe based on availability rather than need, which meant sometimes the sick were properly treated but once the supplies were exhausted the men had to act on their own behalf. Prisoners with money could purchase medicine in the city; some raised money by selling their rations. Others relied on medicinal remedies concocted from roots and tree bark. Kiner estimated that approximately 300 of the 800 captured at the Battle of Shiloh died at Camp Oglethorpe. Because of a scarcity of official prison reports, historians have not approximated the camp's death toll, and one of the few studies on the prison finds Kiner's figures "difficult to believe." The healthy prisoners occupied their time in a variety of pursuits such as playing marbles, pitching horse shoes, and exercising. The "most popular" and "most profitable" pastime was making bone jewelry. Prisoners formed rings, breast pins, and watch seals out of beef bones and sold them to the men and women of Macon, earning several thousand dollars. In early October 1862, virtually all of the officers at Camp Oglethorpe were paroled and the prison remained sparsely populated until the spring of 1864 when Union officers captured at various locations arrived in considerable numbers.[27]

Shortly after Johnson's Island Prison opened in April 1862, the Union military designated it as a place of confinement for Confederate officers, although small contingents of enlisted men were held there throughout the war. Situated in Lake Erie just off the shores of Sandusky, Ohio, Johnson's Island housed one of the war's most unique prison populations. Colonel Isaiah George Washington Steedman described his fellow prisoners as follows:

> These men were from the best classes of the southern people; they were men of education and property. The great majority of them were young and in the prime of life. Hence a better clan of men considered in any aspect, has never been, or never will be assembled again, in the same anomalous situation.

Originally, the prison covered 14.5 acres but was expanded to 16.5 acres in August 1864. There were 12 housing barracks roughly 120 feet long by 25 feet wide and most of these buildings had attached mess halls. A building similar in size to the living quarters operated as the hospital.[28]

Early in the war, rations were plentiful and Confederates dined on bacon or beef, chicory coffee, rice or hominy, and bread. The camp sutler sold cabbage, Irish potatoes, butter, eggs, various sauces, dried fruit and cheese. Some prisoners received opulent packages from home. In April 1864, the wife of Captain Wesley Makely, 18th Virginia Cavalry, sent him a box containing the following items:

> 2 shirts calico, 4 collars, 2 pairs yarn socks, 4 pair cotton also, 1 pair gauntlets, 2 bundles for Lt's somebody, 1 ham, 4 bolonies, 2 cans tomatoe, 1 can peaches, 1 jar pickled onions, 1 can blackberry wine, 1 bottle Hosteters bitters, 2 boxes sardines, 1 bottle horseraddish, 3 pies, some smoked herring, oranges, lemons, sugar, nuts, 1 pound cake.

She mailed a second box of comparable items a month later. Obviously, not every prisoner at Johnson's Island had access to this type of assistance, and all of the prisoners, including Makely, suffered through a grueling several months in the fall of 1864 when Colonel William Hoffman ordered a reduction in rations and placed restrictions on sutler operations. The prisoners began to hunt rats in order to fight their hunger, catching 25 to 100 each night in each building. The rats sold for one dollar a piece. Makely resisted as long as he could but he became so weak from a lack of food that he finally relented. He admitted to his wife, "they taste very much like a young squirrel and would be good enough if called by any other name."[29]

Despite the fluctuations in ration quality, the death rate at Johnson's Island, 3 percent, was the lowest of any prison camp in the North or South. The Confederate prisoners certainly had to battle the cold Midwestern winters and the psychological consequences of captivity, but the underlying story at Johnson's Island was one of survival. The men were resourceful and creative in occupying their minds. Some prisoners were adept at making jewelry and crafted a variety of pieces. They used the hard rubber from buttons, precious metals, and shells to make necklaces, watch chains, combs, crosses, and earrings. The prisoners also read, played chess and baseball, composed poetry, produced artwork, and formed a theatrical group known as the Rebellonians. The prisoner minstrels sometimes performed shows lasting as long as three hours. Letter writing was an essential activity for many of the men at Johnson's Island. In one of the best studies of the cultural dimensions of a Civil War prison, historian David R. Bush examined the correspondence of Confederate prisoner Captain Wesley Makely and his wife Catherine. Captured shortly after the Battle of Gettysburg, Makely spent 19 months at Johnson's Island and wrote scores of letters to his wife. Because of the close censorship of letters at Johnson's Island, prisoners could only discuss personal information and were limited to one page of letter-length paper; this regulation was amended to a length of no more than 28 lines. The exchange of each of the Makelys' communiqués took between two and four weeks, but Catherine learned of her husband's whereabouts, his health, his general state of mind, and his needs. Wesley learned of his family's well-being, including that of his young daughter, and hometown news. Most important, the letters created a sense of connectedness amid war and captivity.[30]

AFRICAN-AMERICAN PRISONERS

When President Abraham Lincoln signed the Emancipation Proclamation, he made the destruction of slavery a second war aim and authorized the enlistment of black soldiers. Black units performed admirably and courageously when given the opportunity to step onto the field of battle. Beginning with the "first significant assault by black troops in the war" at Port Hudson, Louisiana in late May 1863, and including such notable performances at Milliken's Bend, Louisiana in June 1863, the Battle of Olustee (Florida) in February 1864, and during the Petersburg Campaign in Virginia, African-Americans demonstrated their "potential and effectiveness as combat soldiers." However, these men who risked their lives in battle faced equally hazardous possibilities if they were captured by or surrendered to the enemy.[31] Some of the most vicious and deadly instances transpired at: Olustee, Plymouth, North Carolina; Poison Spring, Arkansas; Fort Pillow, Tennessee; and Petersburg. At Fort Pillow, the death rate (those killed) among African-American troops was significantly higher than the death rate among white Union troops, 64 percent to 31 percent.[32] The Confederates took 168 white Union troops captive but only 58 blacks were seized. Ultimately, the treatment of captured black soldiers, according to historian Thomas J. Ward, "varied tremendously throughout the war, depending on the time, the place, and the commander into whose hands they fell."[33]

Adding to the uncertainty was the Confederacy's attempt to distinguish between Union soldiers who were runaway slaves and those who were freemen when the war began. During the fighting in and around Charleston, South Carolina in July 1863, Confederate forces captured slightly more than 100 members of the 54th Regiment Massachusetts Volunteer Infantry. As the military leaders and the War Department debated the fate of the black prisoners, South Carolina governor Milledge L. Bonham demanded that they be turned over to him because he intended to put them on trial for violating the state's laws regarding slave insurrections. His request was granted but for unknown reasons Bonham received only 24 prisoners. Concerned about any potential political backlash or retaliation against Confederates held in Northern prisons, the Davis administration urged Bonham to exercise caution. The governor's investigation into the prewar status of the black prisoners determined that only four were ex-slaves. The confused episode reached a point of resolution when a state court ruled that it, "as a civilian court . . . lacked jurisdiction to try the cases of individuals alleged to have committed offenses as soldiers in the forces of the enemy." Bonham eventually turned all of the black captives over to Confederate prison officials.[34]

Sometimes captured black soldiers were impressed as Confederate military laborers or reenslaved. After fighting near Athens, Alabama in September 1864, the Confederates sent nearly 600 African-American prisoners to Mobile, Alabama where they were forced to work on the city's coastal fortifications. Private Joseph Howard, 110th USCT, later testified that they were "searched" and "robbed . . . of everything," even the buttons on their clothes. They were forced to perform hard labor and if they "lagged, or faltered, or misunderstood an order," then they "were whipped and abused." They were fed "corn-meal and mule meat, and occasionally some poor beef."[35] In mid-October, the city's *Advertiser and Register* listed the names of 575 members of the 106th, 110th, and 111th USCT and informed any of the men's owners that they were eligible for compensation. No evidence has surfaced of any corresponding claims in the Mobile case; however, slaveholders were successful periodically in arguing that individual black prisoners were their former slaves. Confederate prison commandants, such as Captain Henry Wirz at Andersonville, released several black prisoners to local planters.[36]

Historians are at a disadvantage when studying the prisoner of war experience of black soldiers because of a lack of Confederate records and the limited number of African-American accounts. It appears that the Confederates held black prisoners in at least nine camps: Andersonville, Salisbury, Florence, Charleston, Danville, Libby, Castle Thunder, Cahaba, and Huntsville, Texas. A U.S. House of Representatives report, completed in 1869, concluded that 776 African-American soldiers were taken as prisoners of war and of that number 79 died in captivity. Many historians, however, believe the number who were captured and died in captivity "exceeded . . . official estimates."[37] At Andersonville, black prisoners, taken during the Battle of Olustee, arrived in piecemeal fashion in the spring of 1864. They, and in some cases their white officers, had been held in Tallahassee, Florida just long enough for them to regain some of their health to complete the trip to Andersonville. About 70 African-Americans made the journey and once inside the prison they "congregated" in an isolated area near the south gate. The Confederates denied them medical treatment but otherwise they received the same meager rations, lived in the same deplorable conditions, and died at the same rate as their white counterparts.[38] In some instances, black prisoners faced a seething resentment from white Union prisoners. By September 1864, after having spent a year in captivity, Private William Tritt, 21st Wisconsin Volunteer Infantry, had become convinced that Lincoln's emancipationist policies were having a direct impact on their continued imprisonment. While confined in Florence, South Carolina, Tritt noted in his diary, "Much complaint is made against our government on account of the Negro soldiers undermining our exchange. No language is too bad to use in some mouths." He noticed that "much fear" had gripped the prison population concerning the prospect of "staying over the winter" and he complained bitterly, "Old Abe and the niggers are all that's in the way" of our exchange. Just south of Tritt, in Savannah, Georgia, Private M.J. Umsted, 13th Iowa Volunteer Infantry, came to a similar conclusion when he realized "here we have to stay. And pine away through the prime of life all for the Sons of Africa."[39] Although historians have struggled to develop a detailed record of the African-American prisoner of war experience, they have made several important observations. Ira Berlin suggests, "black soldiers came to realize that, while they might have more to gain in the war than whites, they also had more to lose." Joseph Glatthaar contends that the Confederate policy toward black troops and their white officers "had a positive effect on relationships within the USCT" because "the possibility of execution by surrendering . . . demanded a degree of interdependence . . . that rarely existed in white volunteer units."[40] These different perspectives illustrate the complexity of the black prisoner of war story.

ESCAPES

Every prisoner of war contemplated escape; thousands made an attempt but only a few were successful in reaching friendly lines. During the first years of the war, exchanges and paroles transpired on a regular basis, which lessened the incentives for escapes. The implementation of the Dix–Hill Cartel created an expectation among the prisoners that their release was forthcoming and they continued to cling to this hope even after the exchange system collapsed. Regardless of the level of optimism over the possibility of release, prisoners faced a series of imposing obstacles and considerable risks if they chose the escape option. They had to bypass armed guards and fortified prison facilities as a dangerous first step only to have trigger-happy pursuers accompanied by recovery dogs chase them as they attempted to navigate "hundreds of miles of hostile territory."[41]

Throughout the war both sides plotted daring raids to liberate their prisoners. The location of Johnson's Island in northwest Ohio, in close proximity to Lake Erie and the Canadian border, made it a frequent target of elaborate escape schemes. Most of the plans involved some

According to the *Official Records*, 1,210 Confederates escaped from Union prisons. The largest number of escapes occurred at Camp Douglas (310) and a facility in New Orleans (231).

combination of Southern sympathizers in Canada, Confederate military personnel, escaped prisoners, and Northern Copperheads. Rumors circulated in the summer of 1862 that Southern sympathizers in Canada were contemplating an assault on the prison, prompting Union military officials to send additional troops from Camp Chase, Ohio to enhance security. This particular liberation plan never came to fruition.[42] The Confederates tried again, however, in early 1864. The leaders of this latest effort were Captains Charles H. Cole and John Yates Beall. Cole had served with cavalryman Nathan Bedford Forrest and had recently escaped from Johnson's Island, fleeing to Canada. Beall was an acting master in the Confederate Navy. The sophisticated plan

> involved commandeering a couple of passenger boats . . . waiting for Cole to send up a flare signal from the *Michigan*, where he, under the guise of a Philadelphia banker, would attend a dinner party, seize control of the ship, and have its big guns turned on prison headquarters with the demand to surrender the island.

Cole was arrested on the day the plot was to unfold. During his interrogation, Cole disclosed the names of several prominent individuals associated with the scheme such as James C. Robinson, the Democratic candidate for governor of Illinois in 1864. Cole remained imprisoned until February 10, 1866. Beall carried out his part of the mission, commandeering two passenger ferries, but the absence of a signal from Cole forced him to abort this rescue attempt. Afterward, Beall remained in the area conspiring and assisting prisoners. Eventually, he was captured and hanged as a spy on February 24, 1865.[43]

In early 1864, President Abraham Lincoln and Secretary of War Edwin Stanton approved a plan to attack the Confederate capital and free the prisoners at Libby Prison and Belle Island. General Judson Kilpatrick commanded the operation and Colonel Ulric Dahlgren, son of Admiral John A. Dahlgren, headed a detachment. The plan called for Kilpatrick to lead 3,500 cavalrymen into Richmond from the north while Dahlgren moved against the city from the south with 500 men. The raid began on February 28. On March 2, Kilpatrick penetrated the Richmond defenses, but he did not locate Dahlgren within the Confederate capital and withdrew to regroup. Confederate forces had been alerted to the raid and had mobilized. They ambushed Dahlgren east of the city and the colonel died in the attacks. A young boy serving with the Richmond Home Guard found on Dahlgren's body a set of handwritten orders that sanctioned the burning of Richmond and the assassination of President Jefferson Davis and his cabinet. The orders were subsequently published in Southern newspapers. Controversy ensued until General George Meade convinced

General Robert E. Lee that the orders were not officially authorized. Historians have yet to determine, conclusively, whether the orders originated with Kilpatrick, Dahlgren, or Stanton.[44]

In hindsight, the timing of the Kilpatrick-Dahlgren raid seems curious given that one of the most spectacular escapes of the entire war occurred at Libby Prison just one month earlier. In January and February, 1864, Colonel Thomas E. Rose led a group of men who dug a tunnel, measuring 16 inches in diameter, 50 to 60 feet in length, and fell 8 to 9 feet below the ground's surface. Their work consumed several weeks as the prisoners, working in shifts, excavated the earth with clam shells and knives and painstakingly removed loads of dirt in a wooden spittoon box. On the night of February 9, slightly more than 100 prisoners exited through what legend dubbed The Great Yankee Tunnel. Search parties discovered 2 drowned prisoners in the nearby James River and eventually captured 48 men; 59 others reached Union lines.[45]

The number of successful escapes, one where the prisoner actually reached friendly lines, was small, and one need look no further than the Confederacy's most populated prison camp, Andersonville, for proof of the difficulty of the flight to freedom. The prison's morning reports indicated that a total of 328 men escaped from the southwest Georgia prison, but as historian Robert S. Davis discovered, "considering that, with some 40,000 different inmates, Andersonville's escape rate comes to only 8 per 1,000 men." Moreover, a closer examination of the records revealed that Andersonville recovered 181 escapees, and that of the remaining 147, more than 100 were recaptured and assigned to new prison camps. Davis concludes that "no more than two dozen men" escaped from Andersonville and reached Union lines. He pointed to the prison's isolated location, prison informants, the poor health of the prisoners, and the lack of assistance offered by the Southern civilian population as factors that thwarted successful escapes. As for the prevalence of tunneling, Davis feels that most prisoners undertook the work as a symbolic show of defiance and as an emotional and even physical outlet from the drudgery of their captivity.[46]

GALVANIZED REBELS AND YANKEES

As the burden of captivity pressed down on the captives, some Union prisoners, who did not want to risk the consequences of escape, took unusual steps to relieve their despair. Most prison camps lacked the military personnel necessary for routine operations. In order to fill this void, camp authorities offered Union prisoners of war the opportunity to work in such capacities as hospital stewards, woodcutters, cooks, or undertakers. Some men were even willing to fight for the Confederate army rather than remain in captivity. In exchange for this so-called privilege, the prisoners had to pledge an oath that they would not attempt to escape and would demonstrate a loyalty to the Confederate cause. The men who accepted this offer and swore their allegiance to their former enemy became known as Galvanized Rebels. The exact number of men who became Galvanized Rebels cannot be accurately determined because the Confederate prisons did not submit monthly population returns. The exception to that rule was Andersonville prison, but even in those cases where population reports existed, the classifications, "paroled, released, or exchanged," were imprecise and often generated confusion.[47]

The number of prisoners who accepted the Confederate offer startled many Union inmates. On January 24, 1865, the day after arriving at Andersonville prison, Sergeant John Ely, 115th Ohio Volunteer Infantry, noted that "some 200 took the oath and went into the C S Army." Approximately one month later, Private John Duff, 101st Pennsylvania Infantry, observed a second wave of defections at Andersonville as "about 125 of our men took the oath."[48] The Confederate recruiters were also successful at Millen, Georgia and Florence, South Carolina. Regarding the former, Private James Vance, 5th United States Cavalry, wrote in his diary: "through the past week [the last week of October 1864] the Rebs have been busy getting our men to enlist in their army. 700 went out." As for the latter, Corporal William W. Seeley, 150th Pennsylvania Volunteer Infantry, whose diary entries rarely exceeded two lines, pointed out that "about 1,000 prisoners took the Oath of Oleagience" on September 19, 1864. The practice of Union prisoners taking the Confederate oath of allegiance was so prevalent and disheartening for some prisoners that they even recorded rumored information about defections at other camps. On September 28, 1864, while serving as a prisoner at Florence, South Carolina, Private William Tritt, 21st Wisconsin Infantry, mentioned news of a "report of 400 Yanks taken the Confederate Oath at Charleston, South Carolina." Tritt had been a prisoner there two weeks earlier.[49]

The numbers recorded by the Union diarists appear to be fairly accurate when compared to the intermittent reports submitted by Confederate prison officials. On October 12, 1864, Colonel W.D. Pickett reported the activities for the 4 previous weeks at the prison in Florence, South Carolina, indicating that 807 men took "the oath of allegiance and enlisted in the service of the Confederate States." If these figures are accurate, then roughly 6 percent of the 13,169 prisoners at Florence became Galvanized Rebels. Pickett had actually "inspected the recruits" and found "they are mostly foreigners, and are generally good-looking men, and I doubt not will make good soldiers." Interestingly, Pickett speculated that "several hundred more foreigners can be enlisted, and if you take Western men, 1,500 or 2,000 more can be enlisted." If these projections had been reached an additional 12 to 16 percent of Florence's prison population would have taken the Confederate oath of allegiance.[50] The defection rate at Camp Lawton in Millen, Georgia was slightly lower than at Florence. In a brief report, the camp commander, Captain D.W. Vowels, indicated that 349 of a total of 9,698 prisoners took the Confederate oath during late October and early November of 1864. This number fell just short of 4 percent of the camp population.[51]

On one level, the Union prisoners understood why their comrades succumbed to the temptation posed to them by the Confederates, drawing a correlation between the scarcity of rations and poor weather conditions. The weather, however, was not always a contributing factor in the decision to take the Confederate oath. At Andersonville in late February 1865, Duff noted that Confederate recruiters were circulating throughout the camp, but on this occasion it was "a fine morn" and "all medicine to be drawn outside each day." Adair also recalled that February 26 was a "clear and pleasant . . . day. It looks very much like Spring." Yet two days later, the

Confederate recruiters "got quite a number from among the prisoners." Ely also remembered that the weather was improving and that the prisoners were drawing "more cooking vessels" and rumors of an impending exchange seemed more reliable than in the past. Yet the sergeant confirmed that a "good many" Union prisoners were still "entering in the C.S. Service."[52]

Whatever motivated the Galvanized Rebels to make their dramatic decisions, the remaining prisoners often viewed them with hatred and condemnation. In October 1864 when Umsted learned that several hundred prisoners at Camp Lawton had taken "a false oath to the Rebel form of a government," he remarked, if those "men were inside this stockade I think that the Union loving men inside this camp would give them their just dues by hanging them."[53] At least one Southern civilian looked upon the Galvanized Rebels with a similar disdain. Grace Brown Elmore, a member of a prominent South Carolina secessionist family, encountered a group of the oath takers in Columbia, South Carolina on December 4, 1864. She wondered how trustworthy these men could be given that they were fighting against the Confederacy just "a few months" earlier. "I can excuse the foreigners, and have some pity for them," she remarked, "but the Yankee who has taken the oath I despise if possible even more than those who remain true to the government for which they have fought and which they have sworn to protect." Galvanized Rebels and Confederate soldiers convalesced in the same hospital in Columbia, but Elmore refused to knowingly assist or comfort the former. "More than once" she had the "satisfaction" of her hospital work "destroyed" by mistakenly giving something to a Yankee oath taker whom she believed was a Confederate soldier.[54] The Galvanized Rebel represented a unique aspect of the Union prisoner of war experience. Perhaps these men were selfish or lukewarm supporters of the Federal war effort from the beginning, or opposed to the emancipationist aims adopted by President Lincoln, or maybe they believed that the breakdown of the exchange system meant that their county and government had abandoned them to die in Confederate prisons.

Early in the war, the North balked at the notion of allowing Confederate prisoners to take the oath of allegiance to the United States and transform themselves in Galvanized Yankees. The opposition stemmed from the Lincoln administration's refusal to accord the Confederacy official status as a belligerent, a move that would have granted prisoners a legal status as enemy combatants. The passage of the Dix–Hill Cartel removed that barrier but a group of Confederate prisoners created a rather bizarre dilemma for officials at Camp Morton. What if they did not want to be exchanged? Several hundred Tennesseans posed that very question during the summer of 1862. They seemed motivated by a desire to avoid returning to the Confederate army, which was the scenario most likely to occur following their release. The prisoners had been in contact with Andrew Johnson who had been appointed military governor of Tennessee after the fall of Nashville in February 1862.[55] He had also received word from prisoners at Camp Douglas who offered to take the oath of allegiance to the United States and return to Tennessee as long as they were not forced back into Confederate lines. A significant part, but not all of Tennessee, was under Union control at that time and Johnson felt the prisoners possessed the potential to "exert a great moral influence [in the state] in favor of the perpetuity of the union." He therefore supported the Camp Morton petitioners and requested that the War

Department release them on the stated terms.[56] The War Department agreed and the Union government furnished their transportation from Indianapolis to Nashville. They departed Camp Morton on August 22. Most of the 300 oath takers had been at the prison for 6 months.[57]

Despite the lack of a formal policy regarding Galvanized Yankees, a handful of enterprising recruiting officers managed to enter several Northern camps and present their pitch to the Confederate prisoners. In June 1863, 50 Tennesseans held at Camp Morton enlisted in the 71st Indiana Infantry and another 155 joined the 5th Tennessee Union Cavalry. An Illinois regiment inducted a handful of Confederate prisoners from Camp Douglas two months earlier. At Fort Delaware, Galvanized Yankees were formed into Ahl's Independent Battery, an artillery unit that manned the guns overlooking and protecting the prison. By summer 1863, camp commanders, burdened by overcrowded prisons, pressed the War Department to adopt an official policy for enlisting Confederate prisoners. Secretary of War Stanton seemed receptive to the idea when he permitted a small group of captives to take the oath of allegiance in late June. However, a large number of oath takers "deserted at the first opportunity," causing Stanton to reverse his position in late August. Still, the War Department did not completely abandon the proposition and renewed interest in the matter drew President Lincoln into the deliberations in January 1864. He composed a four-part questionnaire in order to identify those prisoners who wished to be exchanged and those who desired to take the oath of allegiance. Each prisoner was examined individually and the questioner posed all four questions.[58]

1. Do you desire to be sent South as a prisoner of war for exchange?
2. Do you desire to take the oath of allegiance and parole, and enlist in the Army or Navy of the U.S., and if so which?
3. Do you desire to take the oath and parole and be sent North to work on public works, under penalty of death if found in the South before the end of the war?
4. Do you desire to take the oath of allegiance and go to your home within the lines of the U.S. Army, under like penalty if found South beyond those lines during the war?

After hearing all of the questions, prisoners were required to answer only one and to sign their name in a ledger book next to their recorded reply.[59]

As the number of oath takers increased, General Ulysses S. Grant expressed his firm opposition to the use of "former Confederates against Confederates" on the field of battle. He permitted Galvanized Yankees to be "employed as civilians in the quartermaster department" or for "minor guard duties." Not until the fall of 1864 did Grant acquiesce to the inclusion of former Confederates into the U.S. Army, but only on the condition that they be used against Native Americans on the western frontier.[60] This proviso partially explains why Confederates were willing to take the oath. As late as February 1865, just a few months before the war ended, 1,400 Confederate prisoners at Camp Douglas indicated their desire to become Galvanized Yankees. Their decision coincided with the release for formal exchange of 1,500 of their comrades from the same Illinois prison.[61] At Camp Morton in February 1865,

1,500 Confederate prisoners from the states of Missouri, Kentucky, Tennessee, Arkansas, and Louisiana, approximately 45 percent of the camp's entire population, rejected formal exchange, preferring to remain in prison until the war was over. The secretary of war granted their request.[62] Although Confederate prisoners at Camp Chase were informed that no one would be released for exchange against their wishes, Northern recruiters raised two companies of Galvanized Yankees, some 200 men, in March 1865. Their term of enlistment was for three years and they received no bounties.[63]

Overall, more than 6,000 Confederate prisoners agreed to become Galvanized Yankees. They were recruited primarily from Point Lookout, Rock Island, Alton, Camp Douglas, Camp Chase, and Camp Morton. They were organized into six regiments and were known officially as the United States Volunteers. When the war ended and the citizen-soldiers of the U.S. Army mustered out and returned home, the U.S. Volunteers went west for frontier duty. The six regiments received different assignments. The 2nd and the 3rd Regiments "escorted supply trains along the Oregon and Santa Fe trails" and "rebuilt hundreds of miles of telegraph line destroyed by Indians between Fort Kearney [Nebraska] and Salt Lake City [Utah]." The 5th and 6th performed similar duties while the 1st Regiment defended settlements along the "bitterly contested Minnesota frontier" against attacks from the Sioux. From September 1864 to November 1866, the Galvanized Yankees "were engaged in numerous skirmishes" and endured "Indian attacks, starvation, and blizzard marches." For the most part, they performed admirably, although in their post-frontier service lives they were not claimed by Confederate or Union veterans groups.[64]

THE JOURNEY HOME

The Union prisoners who left Andersonville on April 4, 1865 traveled an unusual path to freedom. The previous day the men reported to Captain Wirz's headquarters where they were paroled, the guards dispatched, and they "were at liberty to run around." The prisoners received 4 days rations on April 4 and boarded a train for Albany, Georgia, some 50 miles south of Andersonville, where they camped for the night. Prisoner Lyle Adair marveled at how "Jonnie Reb and Yankee one and all" bathed together in one of the area's largest natural springs. With no train connection between Albany and Thomasville, Georgia, the men embarked on a 3-day march covering approximately 60 miles. The journey was physically painful for many. "Although the blood flowed from wounded feet at every step . . . [it] was by far preferable to the loathsome prison," Adair recorded in his diary, "yet I bore it willingly for Liberty was dawning in the distance." The prisoners stayed in Thomasville for a day before they learned that they were being sent back to Andersonville because federal officials could not agree on the exact location for exchange, debating between Savannah, Georgia and Jacksonville, Florida. They arrived at Andersonville on the morning of April 13. The reversal of fortune weighed heavily on the men. "All hope has banished," Adair confessed, "we are not living but only drawing out a miserable existence. And *death* seems to be the only words of relief." Their torment appeared to end on the evening of April 17 at which time they boarded a train for Macon,

Georgia with Savannah as their final destination. A Union cavalry raid on Macon forced another adjustment and the men headed south once again to Andersonville.[65]

Frustrated by the chaos, Captain Wirz informed the prisoners that he was sending them back to Thomasville and if federal authorities refused to solve the logistics of the exchange then he would simply turn them loose. The men retraced their march to Thomasville, buoyed by the confidence that they would soon obtain their freedom. They moved slowly but steadily and on April 23 they rejoined Union lines in Baldwin, Florida. "The joyful hurrah that went up from the prisoners made the surrounding forest ring," Adair remembered. The now former prisoner rested and recovered at nearby Jacksonville, Florida for nearly two weeks, having their every material and nutritional need met. On May 10, the contingent of Andersonville survivors boarded a transport steamer and sailed to Annapolis, Maryland where they entered a parole camp on May 14.[66]

Not every released Union prisoner made it to a parole camp. In March 1865, the Alabama River overflowed from torrential rains and flooded the Cahaba Prison. The natural disaster helped to accelerate the depopulation of the prison. For roughly a month, the men were released in stages and sent west to Vicksburg, Mississippi. Along the route, men from Camp Oglethorpe and Andersonville joined them and they entered Camp Fisk, a U.S. parole center, where they waited anywhere from two weeks to a month before boarding steamboats to return to their homes in the border states and the Midwest. On the evening of April 24, 1865 nearly 2,300 civilian passengers and former prisoners boarded the USS *Sultana*. The exact number on board has never been determined because the muster rolls were not completed prior to departure. Most sources agree that the *Sultana* passenger total exceeded, by five to six times, the boat's certified limit. The overcrowding was but one problem. Upon arriving at Vicksburg the boat's engineer discovered that the vessel's boilers were leaking badly and repairs were hastily made. Tempting fate, the *Sultana* pushed on to Memphis, Tennessee. After a brief stop on the evening of April 26, the boat continued northward and at around 2 a.m. one of the boilers exploded, toppling the smokestack and causing massive structural damage to the boat. Some former prisoners were killed instantly as a result of the explosion. Those who survived the initial blast were forced to jump over board. Approximately 800 survivors were rescued, but in excess of 1,500 former prisoners either drowned or died in the wreckage of the *Sultana*. The timing of the accident contributed to the tragedy. Coming less than two weeks after President Lincoln's assassination, the nation's attention was riveted elsewhere, and the worst riverine disaster in U.S. history went largely unnoticed.[67]

Release did not always translate into happy endings for former prisoners and their families. Jason Roberts returned to his Indiana home on a stretcher. Having contracted scurvy, he lost all of his teeth. Chronic diarrhea and rheumatism caused continued physical suffering. Roberts also displayed erratic behavior and his wife sensed "a wild angry look in his eyes." He threatened his neighbors, abused his children, and he became fixated on religious topics. Finally, his wife committed him to the Indiana Hospital for the Insane in February 1866 as a result of his chronic mania. The Pension Bureau reviewed Roberts' application for benefits and concluded, "he seemed all right mentally, until he began to tell his prison experience, & then he got excited, & wild in his Conversation. It will be seen from the evidence of

Mrs. Roberts that the man is insane."[68] Less dramatic but equally heartbreaking, Eliza Starbuck lamented the changes to "Cousin Seth" caused by his confinement in Libby Prison. Before the war, Seth possessed a "vigorous young body," but his physical prowess could not help him overcome the trauma of captivity. As he spoke to his cousin about his experiences, she detected a sadness in his "quiet voice which had the curious hint of finality." She wondered "if the twinkle would ever have come back to those deep-set gray eyes! Or was everything [to remain] 'different'?" When he recalled the day that fellow prisoner Arthur Rivers died in his arms, there was clearly a haunted glaze in his eyes. Seth himself passed away soon after his return home, which caused Eliza deep regret.[69]

Some men, particularly officers, survived their confinement as reasonably healthy men. Such was the case of Calhoun Clemson, grandson of John C. Calhoun. Colonel Clemson spent two years in captivity at Johnson's Island. When he returned to South Carolina, he looked "very handsome, & well," according to his sister Floride. She did note that "he stoops dreadfully," a condition likely attributable to a spinal ailment diagnosed before the war. Otherwise, Floride described her brother as possessing "a very fine" and "well portioned" figure, with "bright brown" hair, and "white, & well shaped" teeth. Numerous visits from family and friends, who brought food, clothing, and money, allowed Clemson to maintain his health and energy level during his imprisonment. Based on the letters Clemson sent to his sister from Johnson's Island, Floride observed "I never saw any one improve more than he has in spelling, writing, & style." She also learned that he had been reading "a great deal." With respect to her brother's character, Floride admitted, "I do not see that he has changed much . . . except that he is graver. He is very profane which I regret & had roughened in his everyday manners, although when he chooses he is quite elegant & stylish." After the war, Clemson resumed his life as a gentleman planter, but died in a railroad accident in 1871 at the age of 30.[70]

Jesse Malachi Howell departed Point Lookout before the war ended and traveled to Columbia, South Carolina where he resided temporarily with the family of Grace Brown Elmore. Although she observed no physical disabilities, she pitied the young man. "What a sad return is his," she confided in her diary, "no home to go to, no brother or sister to greet him, all gone, the last laid in the grave not a month ago." Howell benefitted from the kindness of friends in the North, but he told Elmore "how brutally" the Confederate prisoners were treated by their guards, "especially when those guards were negroes." He claimed men "were shot down like dogs" and were "cursed and insulted" by their captors. He described Point Lookout as a place of "total disregard of life, the utter absence of all humanity." The stories infuriated Elmore; her "heart burned" and she was filled with "hate and bittern scorn." In her estimation, "the Yankees are a perfect outrage to everything noble in the nature of man, they are a blot upon the whole creation."[71] The anger expressed by Grace Elmore regarding the prisoner of war issue was not unique. Moreover, this type of animus did not emerge at the close of the war. In fact deep sectional enmity formed over the prisoner of war issue shortly after the first captives were taken. Likewise, the press and politicians, primarily those in the North, tapped into the currents of hatred and used such mechanisms as congressional investigations and even a presidential election to sow the seeds of discord.

POLITICIZING THE PRISONERS

The Union debacle at Bull Run delivered into Confederate hands the first sizeable contingent of Federal prisoners. With their capture, the Northern press began clamoring for prisoner exchanges, ignoring the concerns of the Lincoln administration that such negotiations would confer to the Confederacy a type of diplomatic recognition. The *Herald*, *Times*, and *Tribune* of New York were among the three most outspoken papers in the North, and their reporting not only raised public awareness about the plight of the captured, but fueled a rapidly developing sectional animosity over the prisoner of war issue.[72] The Northern press disseminated stories about poor and inadequate rations, filthy and unhealthy living conditions, and cruel and abusive treatment of federal prisoners. The coverage was not restricted to the Richmond prisons. Escaped or paroled prisoners from Camp Oglethorpe in Macon, Georgia and those from a series of makeshift facilities in Montgomery, Alabama spoke of similar hardships and indignities.

Northern editorialists offered several justifications for demanding formal exchanges. They argued that a failure to do so would have an adverse effect on soldiers' morale and hamper future enlistments and reenlistments. Furthermore, the Northern papers appealed to the administration on humanitarian grounds. In explaining the perceived suffering of Union prisoners of war, certain presses suggested that Southerners had been corrupted and dehumanized by the institution of slavery and could not be trusted to care properly for Union captives. A writer from New York referred to Southerners as "barbarians" and said they possessed "satanic spirits."[73] These characterizations helped shape Northern public opinion and by pushing for formal exchanges Northern papers kept the prisoner of war issue on the collective conscience of an anxious homefront.

As the war in the Western Theater unfolded in early 1862, Southerners responded to Northern accusations of brutality with allegations of their own. Newspapers in the Confederate capital of Richmond covered the prisons and prisoner of war issue extensively and with great passion. Moreover, news items from the city's three primary papers, the *Enquirer*, *Dispatch*, and *Examiner*, were reprinted in the South's other major newspapers. There was widespread agreement in the Richmond press on the need for exchanges. Likewise, the presses expressed outrage over the wretched state of the Northern prisons. Using the testimony of Confederate prisoners confined at Camp Douglas, Illinois, the *Examiner* informed readers of the damp and vermin infested conditions and alleged that more than thirty Southerners froze to death in the prison. The Confederate captives also claimed that Northern guards robbed them of their valuables, their warm clothing, and their gear. The evidence, as interpreted by Southern papers, pointed to deliberate abuse by Northern prison officials and led to calls for retaliation against Union prisoners. The *Examiner* demanded "Lex Talionis" or an "eye for an eye."[74]

On May 6, 1864, the Joint Committee on the Conduct of War began a review of alleged Confederate mistreatment of Northern prisoners, who a few weeks earlier had arrived at an Annapolis, Maryland parole camp.

The prisoners had been held in several Richmond-area prisons, including Libby Prison and Belle Isle Prison. For the previous three weeks, the committee had

The Joint Committee on the Conduct of the War was created in December 1861 to investigate Union military failures in the summer and fall of 1861. Two of the most prominent members of the committee Benjamin Wade of Ohio, who was also the chairman, and Zachariah Chandler of Michigan, were Radical Republicans.

investigated Confederate atrocities committed against the Union garrison at Fort Pillow, Tennessee, amassing evidence—some of which was inaccurate—that accused Confederates of murdering soldiers after they surrendered, mutilating corpses, and setting survivors on fire or burying them alive. They reported their findings to the executive branch. As the president and his cabinet contemplated retaliatory actions for the Fort Pillow massacre, the committee undertook the work of interviewing the men recently released from the Confederate prisons. Private Howard Leedom, a 17-year-old from the 52nd New York Infantry summarized for the committee the events of his 5-month ordeal following his capture in late November 1863. Assigned to Belle Isle Prison, Leedom soon displayed signs of a serious case of frostbite. He testified that his "good shoes" had been confiscated by his captors and he had been given "an old pair of shoes, all cut and split open." He added that the Confederates had taken his blanket and "a pair of buckskin gloves," but offered no replacements. His tent leaked as well. When asked by the committee how badly his feet were frozen, Leedom replied, "Well, my toes are all off one of my feet now." A surgeon then removed the private's bandages so that the committee members could see "the stumps" of his toes. Leedom addressed the issue of rations, stating that he did not get enough to eat and meat was distributed "may be once a day; may be once a week—just as they happened to have it." The committee heard similar stories of callous disregard and extreme privation from nine other released prisoners, and four Union surgeons and two Union chaplains, who were caring for the convalescing soldiers, gave corroborating testimony based on their interactions with the released men.[75]

The committee drafted separate reports on the Fort Pillow massacre and the treatment of Union prisoners, but published their findings in a single volume, charging "the one being, in their opinion no less than the other, the result of a predetermined policy." In scathing language, the committee condemned high-ranking Confederate officials for their malicious handling of Northern captives. The congressmen maintained that despite three weeks of recuperation the former captives still "present literally the appearance of living skeletons" and suggested that "some of them are maimed for life." The prisoners had been "deliberately and persistently" mistreated. The rations provided to the men were, in the opinion of the committee, "totally insufficient in quantity to preserve the health of a child, even had it been of proper quality, which it was not," and their clothing and shelter had been likewise insufficient. The committee also accused Confederates of "mercilessly" shooting and killing Union prisoners "when they failed to comply with all the demands of their jailors, sometimes for violating rules of which they had not been informed."[76]

Simultaneous with the committee's work, newspapers circulated vivid and incriminating stories pointing to a deliberate policy of starving Union prisoners. The *Christian Advocate*, a weekly paper published in New York by the Methodist Episcopal

Church, declared: "There can now scarcely be a doubt that the rebels have determined to kill or disable our men who may fall into their hands." The poet Walt Whitman, whose work in Union field hospitals exposed him to the horrors of war, was stunned by the physical appearance of the released prisoners. "Can these be *men*," Whitman wrote, "these little, livid brown, ash-streaked, monkey-looking dwarfs?" Ultimately, President Lincoln decided against retaliation for the Fort Pillow massacre, but the official investigation and the public response gave political cover to Secretary of War Edwin Stanton who ordered the reduction, by 20 percent, of rations to Confederate prisoners. The linking of the Fort Pillow massacre and the abuse endured by Union prisoners painted Southerners as a backward and barbaric people and deepened the outrage of the Northern public. In this regard, the Republican-dominated Joint Committee on the Conduct of the War succeeded, as historian Bruce Tap has argued, in casting the South as a deeply-flawed society and in generating support for a "comprehensive reconstruction program" in the region following the war's end.[77]

Nevertheless, it was Northern Democrats who interjected the prisoner of war issue into the presidential election of 1864. The party adopted a six-resolution platform that emphasized through various examples the erosion of civil and individual liberties under Republican rule. The fifth platform resolution dealt directly with the prisoner exchange:

> Resolved, That the shameful disregard of the Administration to its duty
> in respect to our fellow-citizens who now are and long have been
> prisoners of war and in a suffering condition, deserves the severest
> reprobation on the score alike of public policy and common humanity.

Although the Republican party platform expressed its "thanks" for the "patriotism" and "valor" of the men of the army and navy, it did not specifically address the prisons question in any of the 11 platform resolutions. The Republicans, however, affirmed their commitment to their anti-slavery agenda in several instances and vowed to protect the rights of "all men employed in its armies, without regard to distinction of color," and pledged to retaliate against "the Rebels now in arms" if they violated the laws of war. Ultimately, the so-called peace plank in the Democratic platform, which "demand[ed] that immediate efforts be made for a cessation of hostilities, [so that] peace may be restored on the basis of the Federal Union," muted a more thorough discussion of how the respective political parties differed on the exchange question.[78]

Meanwhile, the United States Sanitary Commission conducted its own investigation of the prisoner of war issue soon after the congressional probe and published its findings in late 1864. The Sanitary Commission's investigative committee interviewed privates and non-commissioned and commissioned officers who had been held in Confederate prisons as well as

The United States Sanitary Commission, a civilian humanitarian organization, was formed in the summer of 1861. Its primary purpose was to provide medical care and material comforts to Union soldiers, and it included both male and female workers.

U.S. Army surgeons who had treated the men since their release. It discovered instances where prisoners were robbed, slowly starved, and left exposed to the elements, and uncovered cases where the sick were neglected and where prisoners were sometimes shot and killed.

The Sanitary Commission rejected Confederate claims that the rebel government lacked the necessary supplies and provisions to care adequately for Northern captives, calling such an excuse an "embarrassment," and it blamed the poor hospital conditions on Southern indifference to the fate of Northern soldiers. Whereas the Joint Committee on the Conduct of the War looked solely at the plight of Union prisoners, the Sanitary Commission included a review of the North's handling of Confederate prisoners of war. It received depositions from Union surgeons regarding the care and confinement of Confederate prisoners at Fort Delaware Prison, David's Island Prison, New York, and Johnson's Island Prison, Ohio, and interviewed captives at these same camps. Corporal William Farmer, 24th Georgia Infantry, stated: "I have needed nothing since captured, having been supplied at the landing by the Sanitary Commission. I have had plenty to eat; no difference has been made since my capture between the wounded prisoners and the Federal wounded." Private William H. Ferguson, 11th Mississippi Infantry, felt that he had been "kindly treated" since his capture, his leg wound had received proper medical attention, and he had "not been, and never" saw any of his comrades "robbed or otherwise ill-treated by the Union men." Interestingly, the 20 Confederate witnesses were questioned mostly about the conditions in their army before capture. Artilleryman George Roler of Virginia expressed a common refrain when he asserted, "We had plenty of rations from [our] Confederate Government . . . clothing plenty all winter."[79] The intent of the Sanitary Commission was clear: to advance an argument that Southern men fared as well in Union prisons as they had in the Confederate army.

The bitter criticism of the Confederacy's handling of Union prisoners prompted Southerners to launch a spirited rebuttal, one covered extensively in major newspapers. Based on a detailed study of Confederate responses to Northern denunciations, Elizabeth C. Bangert has concluded that "by far, the largest category of prison stories in the Richmond papers can be classified as the 'Denial and Blame' articles." In explaining the high death toll in Confederate prisons and hospitals, the Richmond papers pointed to the Union army's practice of leaving behind on the field of battle its own seriously wounded soldiers. Once in captivity, these vulnerable men became victims of the "sin and depravity" of their fellow comrades. The papers alleged that Yankee prisoners stole food and clothing from one another and left the weak and infirmed to die without rendering any assistance. The *Examiner* also estimated that 75 percent of Union soldiers were foreign-born mercenaries who were uneducated, uncivilized, and lived like filthy animals. By dehumanizing the enemy captives, the Southern press attempted to portray the prisoners "as unworthy of proper care."[80] Although the Confederate government played the primary role in the initial stoppage of the exchange system by refusing to release black prisoners, the Southern press and public placed the responsibility for the breakdown squarely on the shoulders of the Lincoln government. When an outbreak of yellow fever threatened Union prisoners in Charleston, South Carolina, Catherine Ann Devereux Edmondston, the niece of Episcopal bishop and Confederate General Leonidas Polk, declared: "Their blood be on Lincoln's head! He it is who has power to exchange them & for a peice [sic] of petty policy refuses to do so."[81] Thus, Southerners held that the suffering of Union prisoners was largely self-inflicted, that the North subverted the exchange cartel, and that only innocent Confederates were subjected to an immoral and tormented captivity.

From the beginning of the war, the Northern press leveled accusations of prisoner neglect and abuse against the South and laid the foundation for what historian William Hesseltine termed a "war psychosis." In the months following the breakdown of the general exchange, the inflammatory press accounts and prisoner testimony convinced the general public that the Confederate government had intentionally adopted policies to deliberately harm Union captives. Consequently, the citizenry condoned and in some cases called for a Northern policy of retaliation, which was ultimately carried out by Commissary General of Prisoners William Hoffman when he ordered the reduction of rations (June 1864) and the suspension of sutler services (August 1864) in Union prisons.[82] Although Hesseltine looked only at the North, the psychosis afflicted the South as well. The press, the Richmond papers in particular, cultivated a deep-seated hatred of the opposing government, the Northern people, and the Union men in Confederate prisons.[83] Hoffman's retaliatory orders combined with the ragged and frail condition of many released prisoners inflamed the passions of the beleaguered Confederacy. Catherine Edmondston embodied the raw emotionalism felt throughout the South when she remarked, "the details they give of the horrors" of Northern prisons "freeze ones [sic] blood with horror one moment & the next makes it boil in our veins with indignation."[84]

Under the rules of war, prison officials bore the responsibility for meeting the basic needs of their captives. But policy and practice often diverged during the Civil War and prisoners were forced to adjust to and cope with unbearable conditions in order to survive. For the most part officers faced less daunting challenges and received more external assistance than enlisted men. More than any other group, African-Americans experienced the uncertainty of captivity as they confronted the specter of black flag surrender policies, reenslavement, and disdain from white Union prisoners who held them responsible for the breakdown of the exchange system. Although some men successfully escaped from their captors and made it to friendly lines, the majority of prisoners could not overcome prison security, their own poor health, and a hostile civilian population. The number of men who became Galvanized Rebels and Galvanized Yankees was high enough to provoke outrage both during and after the war. As the prisoners returned home, they sometimes found readjustment difficult, but more so they continued to be part of the politics of captivity. Clearly, Northern and Southern newspapers influenced the public's understanding of the prisoner of war issue and fomented bitterness and divisiveness. While neither side could rightfully claim the moral highground regarding its treatment of enemy captives, the North's military victory afforded it the power to prosecute and punish Confederates for prison atrocities. The arrest and trial of Andersonville commandant Captain Henry Wirz for war crimes, "helped assure that the bitter memories of the treatment of prisoners of war remained as strong throughout Reconstruction as during the Civil War itself."[85]

NOTES

1   Stephen Berry, *House of Abraham: Lincoln & The Todds, A Family Divided By War* (New York, Houghton Mifflin, 2007), 83–89.

2   Lyle G. Adair Diary, January 26, 1865, February 2, 1865, Andersonville National Historic Site, Andersonville, Georgia, hereafter ANHS.

3   W.B. Smith, *On Wheels and How I Came There: Giving the Personal Experiences and Observations of a Fifteen-Year-Old Yankee Boy as a Soldier and Prisoner in the American Civil War* (New York: Hunt & Eaton, 1893), 263–264.

4   George Levy, *To Die in Chicago: Confederate Prisoners at Camp Douglas 1862–65* (Evanston, IL: Evanston Publishers, 1999), 57, 87.

5   Hattie Lou Winslow and Joseph R.H. Moore, *Camp Morton 1861–1865: Indianapolis Prison Camp* (Indianapolis: Indiana Historical Society, 1995), 101.

6   Ovid L. Futch, *History of Andersonville Prison.* Revised edition (Gainesville: University Press of Florida, 2011), 21.

7   Roger Pickenpaugh, *Captives in Blue: The Civil War Prisons of the Confederacy* (Tuscaloosa: University of Alabama Press, 2013), 77, 78, 95.

8   Roger Pickenpaugh, *Captives in Gray: The Civil War Prisons of the Union* (Tuscaloosa: University of Alabama Press, 2009), 186.

9   Smith, *On Wheels and How I Came There*, 257–258.

10 Logan Williamson to Madison P. Jones, April 12, 1864, Madison P. Jones Letters, Special Collections, Auburn University Libraries, Auburn, Alabama.

11 James M. Gillispie, *Andersonvilles of the North: The Myths and Realities of Northern Treatment of Civil War Confederate Prisoners* (Denton: University of North Texas Press, 2011), 123, 133, 192.

12 Benton McAdams, *Rebels at Rock Island: The Story of a Civil War Prison* (DeKalb: Northern Illinois University Press, 2000), 45–46.

13 John K. Derden, *The World's Largest Prison: The Story of Camp Lawton* (Macon, GA: Mercer University Press, 2012), 75.

14 James McPherson, *Ordeal By Fire: The Civil War and Reconstruction* (New York: Alfred A. Knopf, 1982), 451.

15 For an interesting discussion of smallpox in the Civil War context see, Carole Emberton, "The Minister of Death," http://opinionator.blogs.nytimes.com/2012/08/17/the-minister-of-death/?_r=0 (accessed July 2, 2014).

16 Alfred Jay Bollett, *Civil War Medicine: Challenges and Triumphs* (Tuscon, AZ: Galen Press, 2002), 332, 347.

17 For a discussion of dysentery in the Civil War context see Terry L. Jones, "Brother Against Microbe," http://opinionator.blogs.nytimes.com/2012/10/26/brother-against-microbe/ (accessed July 2, 2014).

18 Gillispie, *Andersonvilles of the North*, 4.

19 *OR*, II:8:997–1003.

20 For death rates see Michael P. Gray, *The Business of Captivity in the Chemung Valley: Elmira and Its Civil War Prison* (Kent, OH: Kent State University Press, 2001), 153–154. For death tolls see Lonnie R. Speer, *Portals to Hell: Military Prisons of the Civil War* (Mechanicsburg, PA: Stackpole Books, 1997), 323–340.

21 Glenn Robins, *They Have Left Us Here to Die: The Civil War Diary of Sgt. Lyle Adair, 111th U.S. Colored Infantry* (Kent, OH: Kent State University Press, 2011), 27, 36.

22 Speer, *Portals to Hell*, 323–340.

23   Horace Carpenter, "Plain Living at Johnson's Island," *Century Magazine* (March 1891): 717; Alonzo Cooper, *In and Out of Rebel Prisons* (Oswego, NY: R.J. Oliphant, 1888), v.

24   David R. Bush, *I Fear I Shall Never Leave This Island: Life in a Civil War Prison* (Gainesville: University Press of Florida, 2011), 228.

25   Morton R. McInvale, "'That Thing of Infamy', Macon's Camp Oglethorpe During the Civil War," *Georgia Historical Quarterly* 63 (Summer 1979): 279–280.

26   F.F. Kiner, *One Year's Soldiering: Embracing the Battles of Fort Donelson and Shiloh, and the Capture of Two Hundred Officers and Men of the Fourteenth Iowa Infantry, and Their Confinement Six Months and a Half in Rebel Prisons* (Lancaster, PA: E.H. Thomas Printer, 1863), 100–109.

27   Ibid., 111–120. See also McInvale, "'That Thing of Infamy'," 282.

28   Bush, *I Fear I Shall Never Leave This Island*, 8, 228.

29   Ibid., 25, 62, 87, 149, 152.

30   Ibid., 19–20, 60, 126–127, 205, 228.

31   John David Smith, Ed., *Black Soldiers in Blue: African American Troops in the Civil War Era* (Chapel Hill: University of North Carolina Press, 2002), xv–xvii.

32   Gregory J.W. Urwin, *Black Flag Over Dixie: Racial Atrocities and Reprisals in the Civil War* (Carbondale: Southern Illinois University Press, 2005); John Cimprich, *Fort Pillow, a Civil War Massacre, and Public Memory* (Baton Rouge: Louisiana State University Press, 2011); Kevin M. Levin, *Remembering the Battle of the Crater: War as Murder* (Lexington: University Press of Kentucky, 2012).

33   Thomas J. Ward, Jr., "Enemy Combatants: Black Soldiers in Civil War Prisons," *Army History* (Winter 2011): 33.

34   Ibid., 35. See also Pickenpaugh, *Captives in Blue*, 191–193.

35   Ira Berlin, Ed., *Freedom: A Documentary History of Emancipation, 1861–1867* (New York: Cambridge University Press, 1982), 591–592.

36   Ward, "Enemy Combatants," 37.

37   Walter L. Williams, "Again in Chains: Black Soldiers Suffering in Captivity," *Civil War Times Illustrated* 20 (May 1981): 38, 41.

38   Marvel, *Andersonville*, 41–43.

39   William J. Tritt Diary, September 19, 25, 1864; M.J. Umsted Diary, October 2, 1864, both in ANHS.

40   Berlin, *Freedom*, 570; Joseph T. Glatthaar, *Forged in Battle: The Civil War Alliance of Black Soldiers and White Officers* (New York: The Free Press, 1990), 203–204.

41   Pickenpaugh, *Captives in Gray*, 160.

42   *OR*, II:4:37.

43   Speer, *Portals to Hell*, 235–238.

44   Joseph Wheelan, *Libby Prison Breakout: The Daring Escape from the Notorious Civil War Prison* (New York: Public Affairs, 2010), 195–200.

45   Ibid.

46   Robert S. Davis, "Escape from Andersonville: A Study in Isolation and Imprisonment," *Journal of Military History* 67 (October 2003): 1067, 1072–1073.

47   *OR*, II:8:1004.

48   John Ely Diary, January 24, 1865, ANHS; John Duff Diary, February 28, 1865, ANHS.

49   James Vance Diary, October 30, 1864, ANHS; William W. Seeley Diary, September 19, 1864, ANHS; William Tritt Diary, September 28, 1864, ANHS.

50   *OR*, II:7:972–974.

51   Ibid., 7:1113–1114.

52 Duff Diary, February 16, 1865, Adair Diary, January 23, February 26, 1865; Ely Diary, February 23, 28, 1865.
53 Umsted Diary, October 29, 1864.
54 Marli F. Weiner, Ed., *A Heritage of Woe: The Civil War Diary of Grace Brown Elmore, 1861–1868* (Athens: University of Georgia Press, 1997), 82.
55 Winslow and Moore, *Camp Morton 1861–1865*, 58–60.
56 *OR*, II:4:457–458.
57 Winslow and Moore, *Camp Morton 1861–1865*, 58–60.
58 D. Alexander Brown, *The Galvanized Yankees* (Urbana: University of Illinois Press, 1963), 64–66. For information on Fort Delaware see Dale Fetzer and Bruce Mowday, *Unlikely Allies: Fort Delaware's Prison Community in the Civil War* (Mechanicsburg, PA: Stackpole Books, 2000), 111.
59 *OR*, II:7:823.
60 Brown, *The Galvanized Yankees*, 12–13, 68–70.
61 Levy, *To Die in Chicago*, 316.
62 Winslow and Moore, *Camp Morton 1861–1865*, 134.
63 Roger Pickenpaugh, *Camp Chase and the Evolution of Union Prison Policy* (Tuscaloosa: University of Alabama Press, 2007).
64 Brown, *The Galvanized Yankees*, 1–10.
65 See daily entries in Adair Diary, April 1–16, 1865.
66 Ibid., April 17–28, 1865.
67 Alan Huffman, *Sultana: Surviving the Civil War, Prison, and the Worst Maritime Disaster in American History* (Washington, D.C.: Smithsonian, 2009).
68 Eric T. Dean, *Shook Over Hell: Post-Traumatic Stress, Vietnam, and the Civil War* (Cambridge, MA: Harvard University Press, 1999), 84–85.
69 Mary Eliza Starbuck, *My House and I: A Chronicle of Nantucket* (Boston: Houghton Mifflin, 1929), 202–204.
70 Charles M. McGee, Jr. and Ernest M. Lander, Jr., Eds., *A Rebel Came Home: The Diary and Letters of Floride Clemson, 1863–1866* (Columbia: University of South Carolina Press, 1989), 9–10, 41, 43, 51, 76, 88–89, 163.
71 Weiner, Ed., *A Heritage of Woe*, 78–79.
72 Elizabeth C. Bangert, "The Press and the Prisons: Union and Confederate Newspaper Coverage of Civil War Prisons," M.A. Thesis, College of William and Mary, 2001, 46–47; William B. Hesseltine, *Civil War Prisons: A Study in War Psychosis* (Columbus: Ohio State University Press, 1930), 9–11.
73 Bangert, "The Press and the Prisons," 48, 54.
74 Ibid., 116–117, 120–121.
75 The committee's report appears in Frank Moore, *Rebellion Record: A Diary of American Events*, 8 vols., (reprint, New York: Arno Press, 1977), 8:80–98.
76 Ibid., 8:80–98.
77 Bruce Tap, *Over Lincoln's Shoulder: The Committee on the Conduct of the War* (Lawrence: University Press of Kansas, 1998), 201–208.
78 Donald Bruce Johnson, compiler, *National Party Platforms, Volume 1 1840–1956* (Urbana: University of Illinois Press, 1956), 34–36; Stephen W. Sears, "McClellan and the Peace Plank of 1864: A Reappraisal," *Civil War History* 36 (March 1990): 57–64; William C. Harris, "Conservative Unionists and the Presidential Election of 1864," *Civil War History* 38 (December 1992): 298–318.

79   United States Sanitary Commission, *Narrative of Privations and Sufferings of United States Officers and Soldiers while Prisoners of War in the Hands of the Rebel Authorities* (Philadelphia: King & Baird, 1864).

80   Bangert, "The Press and the Prisons," 118, 144, 153–159.

81   Beth G. Crabtree and James W. Patton, Eds., *"Journal of a Secesh Lady": The Diary of Catherine Ann Devereux Edmondston, 1860–1866* (Raleigh, NC: Division of Archives and History, 1979), 622.

82   Hesseltine, *Civil War Prisons*, 172–176.

83   Bangert, "The Press and the Prisons," 158–159.

84   Crabtree and Patton, *"Journal of a Secesh Lady,"* 542.

85   Benjamin G. Cloyd, *Haunted by Atrocity: Civil War Prisons in American Memory* (Baton Rouge: Louisiana State University Press, 2010).

CHAPTER 4

The Politics of Captivity

As reports of the horrible conditions in Southern prisons began to reach the North, carried by escapees, parolees, and exchanged troops, they excited the passions of the Northern populace. They also proved a major attraction for radical newspaper editors, who published the most excoriating accounts with little regard for the plausibility or accuracy of the stories provided. Soon, the assumption that Confederate officials overseeing the prison system were deliberately harming their charges became the norm in the Union. This belief made Federal troops less willing to surrender in the field, particularly after 1863, when it became clear that the exchange system had completely collapsed. Calls soon emerged for a strict policy of retaliation, in the belief that only a response in kind would drive the Confederacy to improve its treatment of prisoners. Further, calls for vengeance against specific Confederate targets soon began, with Brigadier General John H. Winder singled out as the man most responsible for the conditions. President Jefferson Davis and General Robert E. Lee were also suggested as culpable individuals who should be punished at the war's end.[1] Winder deprived the growing mob of its opportunity for revenge when he died on February 21, 1865, during an inspection tour of Florence, South Carolina. Mary Chesnut remarked upon Winder's passing in her diary, noting on February 10, 1865:

> Yesterday, General Lovell dined here—and then they went to poor old Winder's funeral. Well Winder is safe from the wrath to come. General Lovell suggested that if the Yankees ever caught Winder, 'it would go hard with him—the prisoners complain of him you know.'[2]

Davis and Lee survived the conflict, but both had substantial numbers of supporters in the North. Thus, to test the idea of prosecuting Confederate officials for their wartime transgressions, Secretary of War Edwin M. Stanton looked for an easy first case. Ideally, he wanted to find a target that could be tried for grievous crimes and would certainly be convicted. In the spring of 1865, there was no man in the Confederacy more loathed than the commandant of the most notorious prison in the South, Captain Henry Wirz. If he was placed on trial for the murder of Union prisoners, it might set the precedent Stanton craved.

The need to punish the Confederate leaders rose precipitously after the assassination of President Abraham Lincoln on April 14, 1865. Rather than entrusting the case of the Lincoln conspirators to a civilian court, newly-installed President Andrew Johnson ordered a military tribunal, led by Major General David Hunter. Four of the defendants received death sentences, three got life in prison, and one minor figure received a six-year sentence. Their only appeal, to Johnson, fell on deaf ears, although he pardoned the surviving defendants as one of his last official acts in 1869. On July 7, 1865, Mary Surratt, Lewis Powell, David Herold, and George Atzerodt were publicly hanged in the Old Arsenal Penitentiary. The executions were met with enthusiasm by the public, and signaled the willingness of the citizenry to punish anyone for treachery against the nation.

Punishing a murderous conspiracy for the assassination of a president may have been relatively easy to accomplish, but holding enemy officials responsible for wartime activities might prove another matter. Although General Orders No. 100 established responsibilities for the treatment of enemy forces and civilians by Union troops, it could not be construed as any form of international law, and its provisions certainly did not extend to Confederate leaders. In theory, anyone who took up arms against the U.S. government could be tried for treason, but trying to enforce such an idea would either entail conducting thousands of trials or renewing the fighting, neither of which appealed to the public. For a nation exhausted by war, conducting treason trials on such a scale was unfathomable. However, placing the leaders of the insurrection on trial might slake the nation's thirst for vengeance. Men who had served in the U.S. military and resigned their commissions to join the Confederacy, or those who held high political positions in the renegade government, represented the obvious targets for such trials.

THE TRIAL OF HENRY WIRZ

Wirz's tenure at Andersonville brought him to the attention of virtually all of the prisoners there, most of whom believed he deliberately inflicted the terrible conditions upon them. They considered him a cruel, foul-mouthed, cold-blooded man who delighted in tormenting his charges. By all accounts, he swore frequently, and his strong German accent undoubtedly limited any perceptible compassion in his voice. He yelled at guards and prisoners alike, although his physical problems made any direct acts of violence highly unlikely. The constant pain from his injured arm probably did little to improve his demeanor. Yet, it seemed that he might be placed on trial not for specific actions, but rather because he was a disagreeable man who stood for all of the evils of the POW system. When Andersonville closed, Wirz intended to take his family to Europe, but he was still in Georgia when Captain Henry Noyes visited his home and informed him that Major General James H. Wilson, the district commander, had ordered his arrest.

Stanton moved quickly to create his military courts. He appointed Major General Lew Wallace, a trained lawyer, to head the nine-member tribunal, which included six more general officers and two colonels. Wallace can hardly be considered an impartial judge; not only did he have a strong reputation as a fiercely anti-Southern

The Chronology of Henry Wirz

November, 1823:	Born in Zurich, Switzerland.
1849:	Emigrates to the United States.
1861:	Enlists in Company A, 4th Battalion, Louisiana Volunteers from Milliken's Bend, LA.
May 31, 1862:	Wounded in right arm at Battle of Seven Pines.
June 12, 1862:	Returns to duty, cited for bravery and promoted from sergeant to captain.
August 26, 1862:	Assigned to command Richmond military prison.
September 26, 1862:	Acting adjutant general of Confederate Provisional Army, sent to Montgomery to obtain Federal POW records, then assigned to command prison at Tuscaloosa, AL.
October, 1862:	Receives permission for convalescent leave in Europe, President Davis orders Wirz to establish contacts in Paris and Berlin during his journey.
1864:	Returns to Confederacy, resumes his service.
March 27, 1864:	Assigned to command prison at Andersonville, Georgia.
May 8, 1864:	Reports difficulties in performing duties at prison.
June 9–10, 1864:	Discovers plot to attack guards and overthrow camp. Ends work details outside of stockade, threatens to use canister shot against prisoners in event of mass escape.
May 7, 1865:	Arrested by Captain H.E. Noyes.
May 10, 1865:	Arrives in Washington, D.C., confined in Old Capitol Prison.
August 23, 1865:	Placed on trial for war crimes against Federal Prisoners.
October 31, 1865:	Found guilty of atrocities, sentenced to death.
November 10, 1865:	Hanged at Old Capitol Prison, buried at Washington Arsenal.

partisan, he was also well aware of Stanton's desire for a conviction. For a political general like Wallace, the esteem of the secretary of war might prove essential, and could lead to a commission in the postwar regular army.

Two charges were presented against Wirz. The first was conspiracy to torture, injure, and murder Union POWs at Andersonville. This charge named Davis, Lee, Winder, James A. Seddon, and Howell Cobb as co-conspirators, although none of them were ever prosecuted. Although Davis spent two years under house arrest at Fort Monroe, arriving at about the same time as Wirz's confinement in Washington, D.C., he faced little chance of being placed on trial. The second charge included

Lew Wallace resigned his commission on November 30, 1865. He eventually served as the territorial governor of New Mexico, where he dealt with the infamous outlaw Billy the Kid, and wrote the highest-selling novel of the nineteenth century, *Ben Hur*.

13 specifications of murder and associated crimes. In each specification, Wirz was blamed for the death of an unnamed Union soldier, on an unspecified date, either through direct action or by ordering his subordinates to kill the unknown victims. The claims were very specific about Wirz's actions, but extremely vague about any other aspect of the charges, and unsupported by anything other than verbal testimony.[3]

Being held in close confinement at the Old Capitol Prison, Wirz had little opportunity to conduct a vigorous defense. In the nineteenth century, defendants never testified at their own trials, whether in military or civilian courts, as doing so was considered a violation of the Fifth Amendment prohibition against self-incrimination.[4] Thus, Wirz needed legal representation if he hoped to fight any of the charges. Military prisoners had two options for counsel: they could hire private lawyers, or they could rely upon the military officer presenting the case. Strangely, this would force a single officer to act as both prosecutor and defender, a dangerous gamble in such a high-profile case. To try the case, Stanton hand-selected Colonel Norton Chipman of the judge advocate general's office, a fierce partisan determined to convict and hang Wirz. Luckily for the destitute Wirz, the well-respected Washington firm of Hughes, Denver, and Peck offered to take his case. However, the firm had little experience in courts-martial, and this put the defense at a decided disadvantage for the duration of the trial. Wirz's lawyer requested a postponement of the proceedings, on the grounds that the defense had only one day to prepare a case. Wallace refused to allow any delay, and Hughes resigned in protest, stating his belief that the court had no intention of following legal procedures. The withdrawal left Chipman in charge of both sides of the case, causing him to request a delay to review Wirz's defense file. Wallace immediately granted the pause, only a day after rejecting the same request from Hughes. Before the trial resumed, Louis Schade and Otis Baker offered to serve as defense counsel, allowing Chipman to return to his preferred role as prosecutor. Because the trial was held in a military court, Wirz's lawyers had no power to compel the appearance of witnesses for the defense. They had to submit the names of proposed witnesses to Chipman, who could then issue the necessary subpoenas if he accepted their utility. Wirz contacted a number of potential supporters through his lawyers, and several travelled to Washington in anticipation of providing testimony. Chipman blocked the appearance of dozens of such witnesses, and refused to issue subpoenas to order the appearance of other witnesses that Wirz requested.

Wirz attempted to answer the charges against him without entering a plea. He first argued that he had been paroled by Wilson, and thus should not be confined, much less prosecuted. When this failed, Wirz and his legal team began questioning the existence of the military court and its right to conduct a trial when civil courts were available. He considered this unconstitutional, and also argued that he had not violated any existing military laws.[5] Unsurprisingly, Wallace overruled each of these arguments, as well as Wirz's last claim that as a Confederate officer he was entitled to discharge under the terms of General Joseph E. Johnston's surrender. He also attacked the specifications presented, on the grounds that they were too vague to be defensible, an effort that also failed and forced him to finally plead not guilty to all charges.[6]

Over the next 9 weeks, the court heard testimony from a total of more than 250 witnesses, most of them former captives in Andersonville. Chipman's case began with an effort to show that Andersonville stood in a region with ample agricultural resources, suggesting that the poor rations at the prison could have been improved.[7] Of course, as a captain, Wirz had authority neither to impress resources from the citizenry, nor to divert them from other destinations. Chipman also demonstrated the availability of lumber for shelters and fuel, and the large supply of local labor that could have improved the water supply problems in the prison. Many of the prosecution witnesses refused to accuse Wirz of the acts described by the specifications, and agreed he did the best he could for his captives. Still believing that Wirz failed to utilize the resources available near the prison, Chipman then pivoted to an attempt to prove the conspiracy charges. He created links from the prison to Davis, essentially absolving Wirz of responsibility for the conditions and making him simply the tool of the Confederate president.[8] Many observers of the trial came to believe that Wirz might save himself by accusing higher officials of ordering the mistreatment of Union captives, in particular Davis and Lee.

In the third phase of the trial, Chipman's case tried to prove the specifications of murder against Wirz. Some prosecution witnesses testified to the awful conditions at the prison, but made no direct accusations against Wirz. Some offered only hearsay regarding Wirz's actions, on the assumption that if enough prisoners circulated the same story about Wirz, it must be true.[9] Unconscionably, all defense accusations against the admissibility of hearsay were overruled. Many witnesses accused Wirz of robbery and murder, with named victims who did not appear on the prison roster, or the death rolls, often on dates when Wirz was absent from the prison.[10] Their testimony was admitted without regard for any defense protests. Perhaps the most egregious example of perjured testimony came from Felix de la Baume, ostensibly a POW at Andersonville who fought in the 39th New York Infantry. He supplied an eyewitness account of Wirz's worst behavior, including murder, and bolstered his tales with drawings of what he described. In reality, de la Baume was a false name, the witness was actually Felix Oeser, a deserter from the 7th New York Infantry. He had reenlisted under a new name and been captured in Virginia before being sent to Andersonville. While the trial continued, Oeser was outed by a reporter and admitted he had lied on the stand.[11] Rather than striking his testimony, Chipman referenced it in his closing arguments, and Oeser was never prosecuted for his desertion or perjury.[12] His testimony was not the only damning evidence, and in all likelihood, Wirz was doomed to conviction from the start of the trial. Nevertheless, writers attempting to defend Wirz after the fact have harped upon the questionable veracity of the witness.[13]

The defense attempted to call more than 100 witnesses, but Chipman's objections whittled the list to only 32. When the defense called Robert Ould, the Confederate commissioner of exchange, Chipman visited his hotel and revoked his subpoena. Under the terms of his parole, Ould was forced to immediately return home, preventing his testimony at court.[14] Any defense witnesses who offered examples of Wirz's compassion received an immediate challenge from Chipman, on the grounds of irrelevance or leading questions. The vast majority of the objections were sustained, making the defense unable to offer any substantial evidence contrary to the prosecution's case. At times, Wallace chose to directly question defense witnesses, rather than leaving it to Chipman. At the end of its case, the defense was required to submit a written summation, to be read without inflection by one of the clerks of the court.[15] Wirz correctly summed up the difficult challenge that he faced:

> As to the charge of murder: the specifications accuse me of no less than thirteen distinct crimes of this grade; three by shooting with my own hand, one by jumping and stamping upon a prisoner, three by torturing prisoners in stocks and chain-gang, four by ordering sentries to fire upon prisoners, one by having a soldier torn in pieces, and one by beating a soldier with a revolver. The name, regiment, date, or circumstances are not, in a single instance, stated in the specifications, and in the whole mass of testimony there are but two cases of this character that there is any possibility of fixing with any definiteness. In these two cases I am prepared to make my defence, and I hope to do so satisfactorily and completely.
>
> It cannot be expected, neither law nor justice requires, that I should be able to defend myself against the vague allegations, the murky, foggy, indefinite, and contradictory testimony, in which these other so-called murders are enwrapped.[16]

After hearing Wirz's defense, Chipman then presented his closing argument, spending two days reminding the court of the horrors of Andersonville and recounting the most damning testimony even when it had already proven false.

The final phase of the trial involved the appearance of two surgeons, called to determine if Wirz was even capable of the acts described in the accusations. Both concluded that Wirz's arm prevented him from significant physical exertion, and made any assault upon a Union POW highly unlikely.[17] Chipman argued that Wirz might have been healthier at Andersonville a year earlier, even though the wound was sustained in 1862, but in reality, he had no need to bother. The outcome of the trial had never been in doubt. After only two hours of deliberation, the court returned a guilty verdict for all but three of the specifications, as well as a death sentence.[18]

The date of execution was set for November 10, just two weeks after its proclamation. Military tribunals had no formal appeals process, although a convict could request that a sentence be overturned by the secretary of war or the president. Any appeal to Stanton would undoubtedly fail, but Wirz sent Johnson a letter asking for mercy. Johnson had little interest in sparing Wirz, and never responded to the request.[19] According to Schade, emissaries from Stanton approached Wirz the night before his execution and offered to commute the sentence if he implicated Davis in the tragedy of Andersonville. Wirz refused the offer and instead resigned himself to the gallows.[20]

Stanton controlled the spectator list for the execution, to be held at the Old Capitol Prison. He admitted only sympathetic reporters and fervent Republicans to the proceedings. Wirz went to his death without seeing any of his family, who were prohibited from visiting him in prison. When the gallows trap released, the noose failed to break his neck, leaving him to slowly strangle while being taunted and jeered by the crowd.[21] Strangely, Stanton ordered an autopsy of the body, despite the obvious

Figure 4.1 The execution of Henry Wirz. Photo courtesy of Library of Congress.

According to one eyewitness, as Wirz stood on the gallows, Major Russell read the death sentence, and then informed Wirz that he "deplored this duty." Wirz's last words were: "I know what orders are, Major. I am being hanged for obeying them."

cause of death. The medical examination conclusively proved that his arm injury would have prevented any exertion. Having denied his family the return of the body, Stanton ordered that Wirz be buried at the Washington Arsenal, next to one of the Lincoln conspirators.[22]

PRISONER MEMOIRS

The survivors of Civil War prisons worked diligently to create a written record of their personal sufferings as well as histories of the places of their confinement. Their accounts appeared in newspapers, pamphlets, journal or magazine articles, and as book-length treatments. Northern captives published a much larger body of prison literature than their Southern counterparts but all writings shared certain themes. Each attempted to portray the inhumanity of their captors and to describe their battles against boredom, loss of hope, the weather, starvation, disease, and death. Most important, the vast majority of writers believed that "they were pawns of the federal and Confederate governments" and "very few narratives fail to show the prisoners' violent hatred for the other side, Union or Confederate, with the ultimate judgment that the captors wanted to murder their prisoners."[23] The volume of prison literature flowed unevenly in the years following the war with the best and most accurate evidence coming from an analysis of Northern publication rates. Using the *Periodical Index* and Poole's *Index*, historian William Hesseltine has estimated that from 1862 to 1866, 54 books and articles were published by former Union prisoners and an additional 20 books and articles during the next 5-year interval. No books were published in the years, 1871, 1873, 1875, and 1877. An uptick occurred between 1878 and 1881, when 12 books and articles were published. This "resurgence of prison literature" resulted in the publication of 90 books and articles from 1882 to 1901. The trend continued until 1921. Each period of productivity provides insights into the motivations of the writers and the content of the narratives.[24]

Michael Corcoran and W.H. Merrell, both of whom were captured at First Bull Run, released two of the first prisoner of war accounts, each in 1862. Corcoran's *The Captivity of General Corcoran, The Only Authentic and Reliable Narrative of the Trials and Sufferings Endured During his Twelve Month's Imprisonment in Richmond and Other Southern Cities* bore the imprint of an officer. Corcoran spent time in several Confederate prisons and his rank afforded him a modicum of consideration from his Confederate captors. He found Castle Pinckney, Charleston, South Carolina "a hundred times more preferable" than the Richmond, Virginia prisons, although he did not seem the least bit surprised when the Confederates pilfered through the trunk bearing his personal possessions during one of his prison transfers. After a foiled escape, Corcoran recounted one of "the most cruel" and "vindictive" acts committed by a Confederate guard during his year in confinement, "he came into the room where, with my companions, I was seated in conversation, and, in a pompous tone, informed me that he had come to lock me up in a cell by myself." Many prisoners endured far greater cruelties than temporary isolation, but officers, in particular, took great offense at the crass and undignified way that they were handled by their guards. He wrote to and received letters from family and friends. He occasionally dined on "fine ham" and drank coffee. Throughout his memoir, Corcoran downplayed the harsh conditions of imprisonment. Instead, he stressed the bonds of brotherhood that formed between the prisoners, citing the formation of the Richmond Prison Association and the Castle Pinckney Brotherhood. The purpose of these prison societies, according to Corcoran, was "to improve our minds, pass away our time, and amuse ourselves." Corcoran also used his memoir to celebrate the Union cause. He confessed that "dying for one's country" on the field of battle "is glorious" but considered "languishing in the dungeon's of your country's enemy, almost within hearing of the booming guns of the struggling armies, . . . a most awful fate." Corcoran concluded his memoir with a solemn, patriotic pledge:

> But ere I lay down my pen, let me assure the reader of these pages that
> I have again taken up the sword, and will never sheath it until victory
> perches upon the National Banner of America, or Michael Corcoran is
> numbered among those who returned not from the battlefield.[25]

In contrast to General Corcoran's text, Merrell's *Five Months in Rebeldom, or Notes from the Diary of a Bull Run Prisoner at Richmond* painted a harsher portrait of captivity and presented the perspective of an enlisted man. Initially confined to a Confederate prison hospital, Merrell complained of the crowded conditions that forced some infirm prisoners to sleep on the floor. Meal time was an "irregular and melancholy farce," the corporal explained, the living areas were "filthy," and the Union men were "emaciated" and "miserably clothed." Merrell, however, reserved his most severe condemnation for the prison guards. He accused them of committing "the most gratuitous and unprovoked outrages" against Union prisoners and recounted one incident where a guard used the flat edge of his sword to strike an "invalid soldier" in the face and another where a guard used the butt-end of his musket to hit a prisoner in the head. As for the officer in charge of the guard detail, Merrell referred to him as a "ferocious and vindictive monster," who the prisoners viewed with "the deepest horror and detestation." Merrell concluded his slim narrative with the same patriotic bravado expressed by Corcoran. He suggested that the released prisoners form a special regiment and be given "the right of line in the next great battle." Merrell stated that "the boys have several *small* accounts to settle with the Southern (bogus) Confederacy and *a few deaths to avenge*." He added that "if they would not make the rebels bite the dust, it would be because they could out-run them."[26] Aside from the martial flair of these accounts, Corcoran and Merrell set a vindictive tone in their works, one that never faded in subsequent additions to the genre.

Southern accounts of captivity in the North were far less numerous in the years immediately after the war. Fewer financial resources and fear of federal retribution during Reconstruction meant Confederate prisoners of war remained largely silent about their experiences in Northern prison camps. Anthony Keiley and Joe Barbiere were exceptions to the general rule. Although Keiley recounted the terrible conditions, the poor rations, and the brutish behavior of the Union guards, he clearly stated his intentions for writing *In Viculus or the Prisoner of War*. "Through books, newspapers, magazines, military commissions, congressional legislation, proclamations, reports, [and] novels," Keiley charged, "the North is not only writing the story of the late war, but the *character* of its late enemies" as well. The Virginian intended to set the historical record straight and to expose "the crimes committed [by the North] in the name of Liberty!" Based on his personal observations at Point Lookout, Keiley challenged the credibility of the Confederate prisoners who testified for the U.S. Sanitary Commission in 1864. They were Galvanized Yankees, "prisoners who had applied for permission to take the oath, or . . . prisoners who had little offices in the pens, which they would lose on the whisper of anything disagreeable," Keiley revealed. He considered their testimony as given "under duress." He also disputed the statements made to the commission by Superintendant of Army Nurses Dorothea Dix. She contended that the Confederate prisoners were well-fed. Keiley retorted, "Common gallantry forbids the characterization of this remarkable extract in harsher terms than to say that it is untrue *in every particular*."[27]

Aside from Point Lookout, Keiley was confined briefly at Elmira. He resented, in particular, the doctors who worked in the prison's hospitals. He found them ignorant of anything pertaining to medicine and called head surgeon, Major Eugene Sanger, "a brute." They deprived Confederate prisoners of necessary medicines and essential nourishment and what angered Keiley the most was that the North possessed abundant resources. He compared the calamity of Elmira to the one at Andersonville, arguing that they shared similar death rates, but insisting that the Union blockade of the South prevented the Confederate authorities from meeting the material needs of its prisoners. In Keiley's mind, the North had no such excuse, and he branded the Wirz trial an enormous "mass of

> Anthony Keiley served as mayor of Richmond, Virginia from 1871 to 1875. President Grover Cleveland nominated him as ambassador to Italy and to Austria but both countries refused to officially receive him. The rejection scandal became known as the "Keiley Incident."

lies" that could have easily been disproved in a fair or just hearing. Interestingly, Keiley displayed some sympathy or respect for Northern prisoners of war. When describing the "wretchedness" of imprisonment, Keiley did not regard the "loss of liberty" or the disappearance of material comforts as the nadir of captivity. For him, "the great overshadowing agony of imprisonment" was being cut off intellectually and emotionally from society. He quoted Lord Byron's "The Giaour" to convey his point, ". . . the dreary void, the leafless desert of the mind, the waste of feelings unemployed."[28]

In *Scraps from the Prison Table at Camp Chase and Johnson's Island*, Joe Barbiere used his memoir to excoriate the North for its handling of Confederate prisoners and defended the Southern treatment of Union captives. He quoted a Confederate prisoner who survived the harsh winter of 1862 at Camp Douglas as saying "if those who now sleep on the shores of Lake Michigan could tell the story of their sufferings, Andersonville would appear as a paradise in comparison." Barbiere accused an African-American guard of killing and wounding five men at Point Lookout and he stated that the guards at Fort Delaware routinely hung men by their thumbs for two or three hours at a time "for the slightest infraction of prison rules." He was appalled by the charges, trial, and execution of Henry Wirz as well as the post-war imprisonment of Jefferson Davis. Barbiere conceded that men on both sides had experienced "grievous sufferings" while in enemy hands, but he maintained that taken as a whole "Northern prisoners in the hands of the Confederacy were treated more leniently." Ultimately, Barbiere challenged the people of the South to hold the "lying" historians of Andersonville accountable and to remember their falsehoods were "written, to hide the cruelties, practiced by our enemies upon Confederate prisoners."[29] Writers such as Keiley and Barbiere spoke not only of their individual captivity experience but gave voice to thousands of former Confederate prisoners of war who lacked the ability or the means to tell their story. As two of the first memoirists, they also sought to assert a type of Southern hegemony over the Civil War prisons controversy by promoting a version of history that absolved the Confederacy for the deaths of Union prisoners while holding the North directly responsible for the deaths of Southern prisoners.

PRISONS AND THE BLOODY SHIRT

The third and final U.S. Congressional investigation of Confederate treatment of Union prisoners of war occurred in 1869. Given the two previous congressional reports, the release of the Wirz trial transcript, and the publication of more than 50 books and articles by Northern captives, one must question why Congress felt an additional inquiry was necessary, especially one that resulted in slightly more than 1,200 pages of text. In fact, the committee anticipated that very question and offered several explanations in the first few pages of the formal report. The committee was concerned that

> the transient and somewhat fugitive histories based on the personal experiences and observations of the authors, which have appeared from time to time, though truthful in character and interesting in narrative, can hardly be trusted to convey to future generations in living and permanent form the horrors of southern prison life.

Based on this fear, the committee sought to establish a "comprehensive history," one "stamped with the national authority." The committee also wanted to refute the Southern claim that Union prisoners suffered because of the Confederacy's "destitution and want of supplies" and moved to defend "the loyal administration of Abraham Lincoln, and the army and navy" against accusations that they caused unnecessary suffering among Confederate prisoners. Finally, the committee intended to show that the "indescribable horrors" of Southern prisons were "the inevitable results of slavery, treason, and rebellion," which future generations should view with "shame and detestation."[30]

Generally speaking, the lengthy report offered no new evidence or interpretations. The committee identified 21 of "the most prominent" prisons, but Andersonville consumed the committee's attention. The final report covered, in great detail, such topics as rations, medical care, shelter, water quality, shooting of prisoners, whippings, the dead line, the treatment of the dead, and even incorporated testimony from the Wirz trial. The committee drew three conclusions regarding Andersonville:

> First. That the sufferings of the Union prisoners at Andersonville have never been equaled in intensity, duration, and magnitude in modern times.
> Second. That the causes that led to these sufferings were not accidental or inevitable in their origin, but were deliberately planned, and were the direct results of human agency, ingenuity, malice, and cruelty.
> Third. That the responsibility of these horrors cannot be restricted to the immediate agents in charge of the prisoners, but rests, with irresistible weight, on the higher officials of the confederate government, with whose knowledge and consent they were perpetrated.

The committee also blamed the Confederacy for the breakdown of the prisoner exchange program. It praised the Lincoln administration for supporting the rights of captured African-American soldiers and condemned Southern officials for allowing paroled prisoners from Vicksburg to return to Confederate lines before they were formally exchanged.[31] Historian Benjamin Cloyd has concluded that the report constituted a Republican effort "to press their rhetorical advantage in order to define the memory of the conflict and thus win the peace as well."[32]

The waging of the peace had just begun for Congressional Republicans. The impeachment and near removal from office of President Andrew Johnson and the ratification of the Fourteenth Amendment had occurred directly prior to the final congressional investigation of the treatment of Northern prisoners of war. War hero Ulysses S. Grant was elected president in the fall of 1868 and Congress ratified the Fifteenth Amendment in February 1870. By 1870, all of the former states of the Confederacy had been readmitted to the Union under the rule of Republican coalitions of scalawags, carpetbaggers, and African-Americans. The Northern version of the prison controversy justified Republican Reconstruction policies, particularly a provision in the Fourteenth Amendment which excluded former Confederate officeholders from election or appointment to any federal or state office as well as the Fifteenth Amendment, which was to ensure black male suffrage. Moreover, the Force Acts of 1870–1871 "enabled the president to use the power of the federal government" to dispatch the U.S. military, impose martial law, and suspend the writ of habeas corpus in order to combat "Ku Klux Klan-inspired voter intimidation," political murders, and terror campaigns. This legislative thrust demonstrated the need for Republican vigilance in reshaping Southern society.[33]

Although President Grant's reelection in 1872 was never seriously in doubt, he continued to receive enthusiastic support from powerful politicians, religious leaders, and civil rights activists as well as an endorsement from *Harper's Weekly* cartoonist Thomas Nast. According to Nast biographer Fiona Deans Halloran, the cartoonist's "work in 1872 was more plentiful, more pointed, and much more focused on national politics."[34] A fervent admirer of Grant, Nast sketched a cartoon, "Let Us Clasp Hands Over the Bloody Chasm," in September 1872 that attacked the reconciliationist positions of Democratic presidential candidate Horace Greely. In the cartoon, Greely stands near a guard tower at Andersonville Prison reaching into the stockade, which is filled with grave markers. On the stockade wall hangs a sign bearing a skull and crossbones and carries an ominous message: "Who Ever Entered Here Left Hope Behind." Nast reminded voters of the evil deeds of the Confederacy and the Democrats willingness to forgive these heinous acts and to form a political alliance with those who tried to destroy the union.[35] Without question, Republicans seized onto the prison controversy and used it to their political advantage during Reconstruction.

Throughout the era of Reconstruction and well into the period known as the Gilded Age, Republican politicians employed a political tactic, which their opponents labeled "waving the bloody shirt." Considering themselves the party that won the war, Republicans intended to stay in power by recalling the great sacrifices that were made on the field of battle to save the union and destroy slavery. As part of the political strategy, Republicans resurrected the injustices committed by the Confederacy and linked them to the Democratic Party. One of the ablest practitioners of "waving the bloody shirt" was Robert Ingersoll, a Republican from Illinois. Ingersoll raised the 11th Illinois Cavalry in December 1861, fought at Shiloh in April 1862, and nine months later was captured by General Nathan Bedford Forrest near Lexington, Tennessee. He was held as a prisoner for a mere three days before being

> James Blaine served in the U.S. House from 1863 to 1876 and the U.S. Senate from 1876 to 1881. He was U.S. Secretary of State on two occasions, briefly in 1881 and from 1889 to 1892.

released on a parole of honor. Ingersoll resigned his commission before he was formally exchanged. Although he personally could not speak of the travails of captivity, he used the suffering of others to persuade voters and to justify Republican policies. Speaking before a group of Union veterans in Indianapolis, Indiana, Ingersoll associated the inhumanity of Confederate prisons with the Democratic Party:

> Every enemy this great republic has had for twenty years has been a Democrat. Every man that shot Union soldiers was a Democrat. Every man that denied to the Union prisoners even the worm-eaten crust of famine, and when some poor, emaciated Union patriot, driven to insanity by famine, saw in an insane dream the face of his mother, and she beckoned him and he followed, hoping to press her lips once again against his fevered face, and when he stepped one step beyond the dead line the wretch that put the bullet through his loving throbbing heart was and is a Democrat.

Ingersoll also referenced Andersonville and Libby Prison at the 1876 Republican national convention during a speech in which he nominated James G. Blaine for president.[36]

Blaine proved with his own variant of "waving the bloody shirt" to be a rigid partisan and turned to the tactic with great intensity to counter the Democratic Party's resurgence in the late 1870s.

THE AMNESTY DEBATE

The congressional elections of 1875 gave the Democratic Party control of the U.S. House of Representatives. Southern members of the Democratic majority included 60 former Confederates. On the state level, Democrats controlled all of the old Confederacy except for Louisiana, South Carolina, and Florida. These gains were significant in view of the upcoming presidential election of 1876. Against this political context, Democratic Congressman Samuel Randall of Pennsylvania introduced an amnesty bill into the U.S. House during the first session of the 44th Congress when it convened in December 1875. The legislation would remove the political disqualifications, which had been set by the Fourteenth Amendment, from all remaining Confederates. The very same bill had passed the Republican-controlled House of Representatives in the 43rd Congress before dying in the Republican-dominated Senate. An unsuspecting Randall received opposition to the reintroduced bill from former Republican Speaker of the House James G. Blaine of Maine. Blaine, who supported the bill in the previous congress, drafted an amendment that would have eliminated the political disqualifications from all former Confederates with one lone exception—Jefferson Davis. Blaine targeted the former Confederate president in an attempt to split Northern and Southern Democrats assuming those in the North would support his amendment for fear of political consequences at the polls, while Southerners would vote against the amendment. The debate over Blaine's amendment commenced on January 10, 1876. This blatant partisan posturing reopened the Civil War prisons controversy as congressmen clashed over the history and legacy of the war's two most infamous prisons, Andersonville and Elmira.[37]

To justify his amendment and its focus on Davis, Blaine charged that the Confederate president had "knowingly, deliberately . . . and willfully" authorized the "gigantic murders and crimes at Andersonville." The congressman compared "the hideous crime of Andersonville" to the Spanish Inquisition and other European atrocities. Blaine believed that Davis had within his power as president the ability to prevent the tragic outcome at Andersonville, and he surmised, "that there is not a government, a civilized government . . . that would not have arrested Mr. Davis . . . tried him for maltreatment of the prisoners of war and shot him within thirty days." The congressman also disputed claims by Confederate prisoners that they had been mistreated while in Northern prisons. Blaine's speech was interrupted several times by offended and outraged congressmen. Representative Samuel Cox of New York followed Blaine and from the floor of the House criticized Republican Reconstruction policies and accused his colleague of hypocrisy. The New York Democrat correctly pointed out that Blaine had previously supported the amnesty bill. William Kelly, a Republican from Pennsylvania, followed Cox. He proposed that he likely would have supported the execution of Davis in 1865 but he reminded his colleagues that the U.S. government had the former president in its possession and had released him without charging him with war crimes. Now, Kelly appealed, was the time for the two parties to move forward. Benjamin Hill of Georgia rose to follow Kelly but the House adjourned for the day.[38]

When the House resumed the debate on January 11, Hill lambasted Blaine, defended the Confederate record at Andersonville, and berated the North for its failures at Elmira. The Georgian concentrated his remarks on what he determined were the two primary points in Blaine's speech: Davis' culpability for the Andersonville record and the reasons for the Andersonville tragedy. Hill recounted the Wirz trial. It lasted 3 months, entailed 160 witnesses for the prosecution, and in Hill's opinion, accepted perjured or falsified testimony. But no evidence was presented implicating Davis, despite, as Hill contended, a deal was extended to Wirz by a Republican cabinet member. The offer: Wirz's sentence would be commuted "if he would implicate Jefferson Davis with the atrocities at Andersonville." Having dismissed Blaine's first allegation, Hill turned to the second and presented "the real

facts about Andersonville." He stated that Union prisoners received the same rations as Confederate soldiers and the captives were allowed to purchase additional supplies from a camp sutler. Hill viewed the lack of medicine, rather than the quantity of rations, as a greater cause of the

Benjamin Hill served as a Confederate Senator from 1861 to 1865. After the war, he served in the U.S. House from 1875 to 1877 and the U.S. Senate from 1877 to 1882.

suffering at Andersonville and he blamed the Northern blockade of Southern ports for the scarcity of medicines. "Whatever horrors existed at Andersonville, not one of them could be attributed to a single act of legislation of the Confederate government or to a single order of the Confederate Government," Hill maintained. He further argued that "every horror of Andersonville grew out of the necessities of the occasion, which necessities were cast upon the Confederacy by the war policy of the other side." Satisfied with his defense of Davis and the Confederate management of Andersonville, Hill brought into the discussion the North's record at Elmira.[39]

The Georgia representative read into evidence a letter that he attributed to a former Elmira hospital surgeon. With this testimony, Hill accused the Elmira officials of improperly clothing Confederate prisoners during the "unusually severe and rigid" winter of 1864–1865. A polluted water supply and an overcrowded prison contributed to the spread of smallpox and attempts to vaccinate the prisoners, with contaminated needles, led to an outbreak of syphilis and other skin rashes, Hill charged. He noted too that the respective death rates at Andersonville and Elmira were virtually identical, which they were at 29 percent and 24 percent respectively, but he ignored the vast disparity between the Andersonville death toll which was 12,920, and Elmira's which was 2,961. Hill then visited the causes for the breakdown of the prisoner exchange system, placing the fault squarely on the shoulders of the federal government. As he presented his case, Representative Blaine interrupted Hill and read a resolution passed by the Confederate Congress. The resolution had been passed in the aftermath of Lincoln's Emancipation Proclamation and called for the execution of those officers captured while leading African-American troops. The introduction of African-Americans into the Union military was a major factor in the breakdown of the prisoner exchange system. Although a Confederate senator at the time as well as the chairman of the judiciary committee, Hill claimed that he had no recollection of the resolution.[40]

Unfazed by the challenge, Hill continued to advance claims that the North was responsible for the breakdown of the prisoner exchange system and for rejecting a Confederate offer permitting the North to send surgeons and supplies to the aid of Union captives in Confederate prisons. He brought to light General Ulysses S. Grant's role in the exchange breakdown. He cited the general's August 1864 communiqué to Union Commissary of Exchange Benjamin Butler, in which Grant stated:

> it is hard on our men held in Southern prisons not to exchange them, but it is humanity to those left in the ranks to fight out battles. Every man released on parole or otherwise becomes an active soldier against us at once.

Hill concluded his remarks with an appeal for political reconciliation and national pride. "There are no Confederates in this house, there are now no Confederates anywhere; there are no Confederate schemes, ambitions, hopes, desires, or purposes here. But the South is here, and here she intends to remain," Hill declared. To those "who seek still to continue strife," the Georgian promised, "to you we make no concessions."[41] Ultimately, the amnesty bill, as originally presented by Congressman Samuel Randall, went down in defeat, although the measure received 175 votes in favor to 97 votes against, with 18 abstentions. The simple majority was not sufficient to overturn the Fourteenth Amendment's required two-thirds majority for removing political disqualifications from former Confederates.[42]

PENSIONS

Historians have struggled with the accuracy and reliability of Civil War prisoner memoirs because the authors have confessed to intentions other than an objective account of captivity. A.O. Abbott in *Prison Life in the South* admitted that one of his purposes was "to throw . . . light upon the question, what shall we do with the Negro?," an insinuation that Abbott supported Republican Reconstruction policies that advocated civil rights and voting rights for African-Americans.[43] Those who helped Robert Kellogg publish his memoir, *Life and Death in Rebel Prisons*, championed the book's potential to "raise a storm of indignation . . . through the entire South," but they bemoaned their profit margins and inserted in the text a call for traveling book salesmen. Publishing costs—paper, binders' cloth, gilding—and government taxes had increased to a level that the company was selling many books at "less than cost," causing a loss of $6,000 over the past four to five years. They felt $2.50 was a reasonable and fair price for Kellogg's book.[44] Jesse Hawes, author of *Cahaba: A Story of Captive Boys in Blue*, hoped that "when the facts are known Cahaba must go down in history as worse in a great many respects than Andersonville or any other military prison of the Confederacy."[45] The two memoirs that reached the widest contemporary audiences and have attracted intense scrutiny from modern historians are John McElroy's *Andersonville: A Story of Rebel Military Prisons* and John Ransom's *John Ransom's Diary*. Both works coincided with the first substantive revision to the federal pension system.[46]

The U.S. government established a pension system for Civil War soldiers in 1862. To qualify, a soldier had to incur a disability "by reason of wounds received or disease contracted while in the service of the United States, and in the line of duty." The monthly rate for full disability ranged from $8 per month to $30 per month. Rank determined the rate of payment for full disability with officers receiving a higher pension than enlisted men; a separate payment scale existed for partial disability. If the veteran died from service-related causes, then his widow or dependent mother, sister, or children (under the age of 16) were entitled to pension benefits at the full disability rate.[47] No payment was issued to a veteran for injuries or diseases not connected to military service even if he became indigent and was unable to work. There were no special provisions for prisoners of war; they followed the same guidelines and requirements of all veterans. Under this system, the federal government paid a yearly average of $26.5 million in pension claims from 1866 to 1878, with nearly 225,000 names on the pension roll by 1878. Only minor changes in the pension system occurred between its inception in 1862 and 1878. At no time during that period were Confederate veterans eligible for federal benefits.[48]

Congress made a major modification to the pension system in 1879 with the passage of the Arrears Act. This legislation still required pension payment to be the result of service-related disability and did not alter rates. It did, however, establish "a common starting point" for all pensions. Specifically, the act permitted current pensioners or those who had an old or new claim approved by July 1, 1880 to receive a back payment from the soldier's original discharge date, which in most cases was 1865. For example, a veteran discharged in 1865 who had a claim approved in 1872 would be eligible for seven years of back pension pay. In some circumstances, the Arrears Act awarded some veterans a lump-sum payment of $1,000. The act also eased the standard of proof for service-related disability and accepted evidence "based on ex parte affidavits rather than on military records alone." As a result, an applicant needed only to secure a sworn statement from a former military officer to include in the pension application. The changes led to "a stampede on the Pension Bureau." In 1880, new claims, which did not include re-filed petitions, totaled almost 140,000, a number higher than the "previous five years combined." Within 5 years, an estimated $180 million had been paid out as a consequence of the Arrears Act. John Ransom filed his pension claim in the fall of 1879.[49]

Aside from financial gain from book sales, Ransom wanted to assist former prisoners in their quest for pensions. He made the rather bold declaration that his book was "essentially different from any other" published by one of the war's participants. Ransom included a list of the Andersonville dead, which he thought would be "valuable in many pension cases and otherwise."[50] In addition, the first edition of the book reprinted "the text of a congressional bill intended to provide pensions for ex-prisoners." Thus, Ransom hoped to generate sympathy for prison survivors seeking federal pensions. This outcome required the former prisoner of Andersonville to paint his time in captivity in the worse possible light. He had previously published some of his experiences in his hometown newspaper using diaries that he had kept while a prisoner of war. Those diaries were subsequently destroyed in a fire but Ransom assured his readers that the refashioned account was essentially the same as the one he compiled 15 years earlier during the war. Much of his memoir even followed the daily-entry diary format. Historian William Marvel, a diligent student of Andersonville, characterized Ransom's book as "partly [based] on memory, partly on published material, and partly on imagination." In fact, Marvel documented a number of instances where Ransom's diary entries were inaccurate or had been fabricated.[51] Marvel suspects that Ransom "doctored his diary entries to satisfy the demands of the pension department, especially in light of the diary's other inconsistencies." He even suggests that "there appears to have been no original diary to amplify and Ransom's book warranted no more trust than the myriad diatribes that are best represented by John McElroy's lyrical, mythical memoir."[52]

Marvel's judgment may sound harsh, but historian James McPherson expresses a cautious approach to the use of postwar memoirs constructed for public audiences in his study of the motivations of Civil War soldiers. Aside from the problems of "faulty memory" or viewing an experience with "hindsight," McPherson warns that postwar memoirists, depending on their intent, had a tendency to either magnify or gloss over certain events, a person's character, or an individual's decision-making processes.[53] Historians tend to agree that uncensored letters and diaries are more reliable as primary sources than first-hand accounts produced for publication. This is especially true of prisoner of war memoirs.

Because federal pensions were not extended to Confederate veterans, Southern states acted singularly or individually to care for veterans, most notably through

John McElroy

John McElroy was born on August 25, 1846 in Greenup County, Kentucky and later moved to St. Louis, Missouri where he apprenticed in the printing business. Only 16 years old in 1863, McElroy enlisted with the 16th Illinois Cavalry. On January 3, 1864, he was captured near Jonesville, Virginia and was quickly transported to Richmond. Subsequently, he was held at Camp Lawton (Millen), Florence, and Blackshear, Georgia, but most of his 15-month imprisonment was spent at Andersonville.

Shortly after the war, McElroy began to write prison sketches for the *Toledo Blade*. Unsure of how readers would respond to his sensational accounts, McElroy received more than 3,000 letters from former Andersonville prisoners praising his depiction of captivity. The affirmation convinced him to publish a book, *Andersonville: A Story of Rebel Military Prisons*, in 1879. McElroy had a clear aversion to both slavery and secession that colored his views of the Confederacy. McElroy told a story of unimaginable horror, suffering, and depravation. He painted prison officials and guards as sadistic fiends capable of any form of human depravity. He cast Southerners in general as ignorant and unskilled. He singled out General John Winder for being primarily responsible for prisoner suffering. In addition, he reviled Captain Henry Wirz and President Jefferson Davis for allowing the deplorable conditions to manifest and for precipitating the tragic outcome at Andersonville. Unlike John Ransom, McElroy did not shy away from exposing the heinous acts of the Raiders and he did not downplay the frequency to which Union prisoners accepted the Confederate oath and became Galvanized Rebels.

McElroy's Andersonville book was not his only literary achievement. He also published several other books: *The Red Arrow* (1885), which celebrated the First Division of the Fourteenth Army Corps, and *The Struggle for Missouri*, an anti-Confederate, anti-slavery history of the state's Civil War years. McElroy died on October 12, 1929.

programs to provide artificial limbs and the establishment of soldiers' homes. In several states the artificial limb effort evolved into a full-fledged pension system. Former prisoners of war were eligible for these types of state assistance. Starting in the late 1880s and early 1890s, Southern states, again acting individually, created a pension system similar to that enacted by the federal government, meaning it required proof of a veteran's service-related disability and provided support to widows and dependents. The Southern system, however, differed in appreciable ways. First, Southern pension laws did not factor in rank when determining pension payments, only the severity of the disability. Second, the dollar amount received by Confederate veterans, their widows, and dependents was far less than that awarded to Union veterans, their widows, and dependents, and the payment rate for Confederate widows was "lower than those to which their husbands would have been entitled should they have survived."[54] The implementation of a state-driven Confederate pension system did not lead to a stampede of applications as occurred with the passage of the Arrears Act of 1879. And even in generous states such as Georgia the passage and funding for veteran-related programs was often a long drawn-out affair. The state legislature authorized artificial limbs for life to Confederate veterans in 1877, but not until 1886 did Georgia award pensions to its Confederate veterans who suffered a war-related disability. Indigent veterans were granted pensions from the state in 1894.[55] Therefore, ex-Confederate prisoners of war, in contrast to their Northern counterparts, had less incentive to publish memoirs as a means to securing a lucrative pension award. Indeed, "by the 1890s, the average northern recipient was receiving $160 a year, while the average payment to Confederate veterans was $40." An outpouring of publications by former Confederate prisoners did not transpire during the 1880s and 1890s, although they did find new mediums for publishing their captivity narratives.[56]

During its inaugural year of 1876 the *Southern Historical Society Papers* (*SHSP*) designated the March and April issues to the topic of "Treatment of Prisoners." The 55 articles touched on virtually every aspect of the prisoner of war controversy and the editors of the periodical ended the discussion with a 6-point summation:

1. The laws of the Confederate Congress and the orders of the Confederate War Department required the humane treatment of Union Prisoners.
2. All individual instances of Union prisoner neglect or abuse occurred "without the knowledge" or sanction of the Confederate government.
3. Union prisoners received the same quantity and quality of rations as Confederate soldiers.
4. The mortality rates in Confederate prisons "resulted from causes beyond the control" of Confederate authorities, most notably the North's designation of medicines as "contraband of war" and the blockading of Southern ports.
5. The sufferings of Confederate prisoners were equal to or greater than the hardships of Union prisoners and were completely avoidable given the North's abundant resources.
6. The North bore the responsibility of the prison tragedy because it opposed the exchange cartel by orders of General Ulysses Grant and Secretary of War Edwin Stanton.[57]

These conclusions formed the foundation of the Southern interpretation of the prison controversy and by devoting two issues to this contentious issue the *SHSP* proved to be an ardent defender of the Confederate prison record. However, it is important to note that the prison controversy was a small part of the *SHSP*'s historical agenda. Under the direction of editor John William Jones, the *SHSP* focused on preserving Confederate history and rituals and on celebrating the valor of General Robert E. Lee's Army of Northern Virginia.[58] The 1880 edition of the *SHSP* (12 issues), which carried a three-part series on Fort McHenry Prison, contained two additional articles on the prisoner of war issue, but featured 18 articles on Gettysburg and seven on Lookout Mountain as well as two articles on Confederate flags.

VETERANS ORGANIZATIONS

The Grand Army of the Republic (GAR) was the dominant veterans organization of the Civil War generation both in terms of its membership size and political influence. Established in 1866, the GAR grew to 400,000 members by 1890, roughly one-third of all surviving Union veterans. The organization aggressively and constantly lobbied Congress concerning pension matters, endorsed political candidates, encouraged veterans' preference in appointment and hiring to federal jobs, and engaged in the censorship of school textbooks. It also operated as a "fraternal lodge, charitable society . . . [and a] patriotic group."[59] The GAR's original initiation ritual incorporated elements specific to the memory of the prisoner of war experience. First, the officer of the guard placed "a torn and otherwise disfigured government blanket" over the shoulders of the initiate "to represent the condition of a prisoner of war." Then, the initiate marched into a room staged with a funeral scene. In the center of the room was "a box six feet in length, three feet in width, and two in depth . . . labeled upon the lid, in a conspicuous manner, with the name and regiment of some soldier who died at Andersonville Rebel Prison." The initiate kneeled before the coffin display, placed one hand on the Bible, and swore his oath to the veteran organization.[60] Former prisoners joined the Grand Army of the Republic. Some served as officers of the various chapters known as posts, and they all benefitted from the organization's numerous activities.

By attending the meetings of the GAR, veterans were able to reminisce about their combat experiences and the meaning of the Civil War. Whether by "personal sketch, war lecture, written camp scene, [or] campfire performances," the members stressed the importance of "camaraderie" and shared sacrifice and rejoiced in the success of their efforts to save the union.[61] On January 8, 1879 during a meeting of the Corporal Skelly Post of Gettysburg, Pennsylvania, W.T. Ziegler delivered remarks on his time at Andersonville Prison. Captured at Petersburg, Ziegler entered the prison in July 1864 and remained there through its darkest period. However, he concentrated his talk on the month of December when conditions had improved and he addressed the emotional and psychological dimensions of captivity. On more than one occasion he told the group of war veterans, "those of you who were not there, can not imagine our condition." Ziegler recounted a cold and gloomy Christmas day when hunger and despair caused his friend Harry Coon to cry out "from the bitterness of his heart: 'O, that I was dead! O, that I could die! I must, for I can endure it no longer!'" To this "once proud" and vibrant man, Ziegler responded with "rough consolation." He advised his friend that he could not simply give up and die and that one day they would return home to Gettysburg. The timely arrival of rations helped the two men survive the Christmas day crisis. The broader struggle, however, required more than the meager rations the men received at Andersonville, and Ziegler shared his personal method for coping with imprisonment. Many nights he and his fellow captives laid on the ground for 8 to 9 hours before falling asleep, usually after 3 a.m. Amid their restlessness, they thought of home and hoped that their mothers were praying for them and that a merciful God would deliver them so that they could "protect" and "comfort" their mothers in old age. The men also dreamed of friends and home and lives of "comfort and plenty." Ziegler used his imagination to survive his ordeal. To those who perished at Andersonville, he honored them as the "martyred dead" and as an "everlasting reminder" of the cost of the Union victory.[62]

The United Confederate Veterans (UCV) formed in 1899, several decades after the GAR. With a modest state pension system in place in the former Confederacy, the UCV had as one of its primary purposes assisting and caring for sick and destitute veterans. The organization also performed fraternal and social functions by planning reunions and by attending and aiding in the burial of deceased members. The United Confederate Veterans acted as a historical agency, gathering documents and compiling military and political histories of the war. Although local Confederate veterans associations formed immediately after the war, the long delay in constituting a national group meant that a small portion of Confederate veterans were still alive to join the organization. The peak membership (active and inactive) for the UCV was 80,000 men. The influence and utility of the UCV "reached its zenith" in 1903, a mere 4 years after its founding. By 1910, it "had become a relic." Still, the UCV served an important social and historical purpose for former Confederates, including prisoners of war, but its contributions were far less than those afforded to Union veterans by the GAR.[63]

Unlike the GAR, which used Andersonville and the imagery and symbolism of captivity in its initial rituals, the UCV meetings "were non-secret, informal, without ritual . . . [and] often being open to guests and coupled with social affairs." The UCV sponsored several publications including the *Confederate Veteran* and the 12-volume *Confederate Military History* series. Established in 1893 and published monthly until 1932, the *Confederate Veteran* was clearly more focused on traditional military history and defending the Confederacy as a just and righteous cause while paying tribute to its leaders. The *Confederate Military History*, edited by Clement A. Evans and endorsed by the UCV, documented in 11 volumes the battles and campaigns of the war from the perspective of each Confederate state. The twelfth volume covered Confederate naval history. Ultimately, the major contribution of Confederate veteran organization to the prisoner of war controversy was the support it lent to the identification and care of the prisoner dead and the erection of monuments and memorials to their memory and legacy.[64]

As historian David Blight has written "no wartime experience . . . caused deeper emotions, recriminations, and lasting invective than that of [Civil War] prisons." Societal memories of the prison controversy constructed by both Northerners and Southerners during the war and the period of Reconstruction contained "a layer of real hatred."[65] When prisoners told their stories, either in the form of memoirs or through newspapers or magazines, they focused on a primeval struggle for survival, the barbarity of their captors, and the constant spectacle of death. The U.S. Congress conducted three separate investigations and generated a mountain of incendiary evidence against the Confederacy. The Northern version of events justified the Republican blueprint for reconstructing the postwar South, and party leaders used the prison controversy, most notably during the amnesty debate and in connection with pension reform, to garner political support for an even broader partisan agenda. Objectivity was never the intent of the victorious North nor did it motivate the defeated South. Confederate apologists accused the North of halting the prisoner exchange program and of instituting a policy of retaliation against Southern men in Union prisons that caused widespread suffering and the death of thousands, despite the resources to prevent such a tragedy. The politics of captivity, as practiced by both sides, greatly influenced how the Civil War generation understood and assigned meaning to the prison controversy.

NOTES

1   Charles W. Sanders, *While in the Hands of the Enemy: Military Prisons of the Civil War* (Baton Rouge: Louisiana State University Press, 2005), 295.

2   Mary Boykin Miller Chesnut, *Mary Chesnut's Civil War*, Ed. C. Vann Woodward (New Haven, CT: Yale University Press, 1981), 712.

3   "General Court Martial Orders No. 607," November 6, 1865, *OR*, II:8:784–792.

4   Gayla M. Koerting, "The Trial of Henry Wirz and Nineteenth Century Military Law" (Ph.D. diss., Kent State University, 1995), 34–35.

5   U.S. House of Representatives, *Trial of Henry Wirz*, 40th Congress, 2nd Session, 1866, Serial 1331, 10 (Hereafter cited as *Wirz Trial*).

6   Ibid., 13–17.

7   Ibid., 276.

8   Norton P. Chipman, *The Horrors of Andersonville Rebel Prison* (San Francisco: Bancroft, 1891), 65–76; *Wirz Trial*, 239–243.

9   Ibid., 61–69.

10   Examples abound throughout the trial records. Prominent examples are found in *Wirz Trial*, 155–156, 163–169, 323–325.

11   *New York Tribune*, November 26, 1865.

12   William Marvel, *Andersonville: The Last Depot* (Chapel Hill: University of North Carolina Press, 1994), 244–245.

13   The mythology of de la Baume has been a persistent issue in discussions of the trial. The Andersonville National Historic Site have verified his presence in the prison, and demonstrated that while he was certainly a deserter, he might not have perjured himself. See National Park Service, "Myth: The Mystery of Felix de la Baume," www.nps.gov/ande/history culture/felixdelabaume.htm (accessed July 2, 2014).

14   Edward Younger, Ed., *Inside the Confederate Government: The Diary of Robert Garlick Hill Kean* (New York: Oxford University Press, 1957), 228–231.

15   *Wirz Trial*, 701–711.

16   Ibid., 710.

17   Marvel, *Andersonville*, 246; *Wirz Trial*, 805–808.

18   Sanders, *While in the Hands of the Enemy*, 295.

19   *OR*, II:8:773–774.

20   Mildred Lewis Rutherford, *Facts and Figures vs. Myths and Misrepresentations: Henry Wirz and Andersonville Prison* (Athens, GA: United Daughters of the Confederacy, 1921), 27–30.

21   Dorothy Meserve-Kunhardt and Philip B. Kunhardt, *Twenty Days: A Narrative in Text and Pictures of the Assassination of Abraham Lincoln and the Twenty Days and Nights that Followed* (New York: Harper and Row, 1965), 54.

22   Marvel, *Andersonville*, 308.

23   Robert C. Doyle, *Voices From Captivity: Interpreting the American POW Narratives* (Lawrence: University of Kansas Press, 1994), 19.

24   William B. Hesseltine, *Civil War Prisons: A Study in War Psychology* (Columbus: Ohio State University Press, 1930), 247–248.

25   Michael Corcoran, *The Captivity of General Corcoran, The Only Authentic and Reliable Narrative of the Trials and Sufferings Endured During his Twelve Month's Imprisonment in Richmond and Other Southern Cities* (Philadelphia: Barclay & Co., 1862), 27–28, 40, 46, 47, 52, 64, 66, 85–86, 100.

26   W.H. Merrell, *Five Months in Rebeldom, or Notes from the Diary of a Bull Run Prisoner at Richmond* (Rochester, NY: Adams & Dabney, 1862), 25, 29, 62.

27   Anthony Keiley, *In Viculus or the Prisoner of War* (New York: Blelock & Co., 1866), 5, 66.

28   Ibid., 61, 62, 138–142.

29   Ibid., 288, 289, 291.

30   U.S. Congress, House, *Report on the Treatment of Prisoners of War by the Rebel Authorities*, 40th Congress, 3rd Session, 1869, Report No. 45, 6–7.

31   Ibid., 11, 22, 27–161, 324–335, 352–353.

32   Benjamin G. Cloyd, *Haunted by Atrocity: Civil War Prisons in American Memory* (Baton Rouge: Louisiana State University Press, 2010), 44.

33   Joan Waugh, *U.S. Grant: American Hero, American Myth* (Chapel Hill: University of North Carolina Press, 2009), 141, 145.

34   Fiona Deans Halloran, *Thomas Nast: The Father of Modern Political Cartoons* (Chapel Hill: University of North Carolina Press, 2012), 145.

35   The cartoon appears in *Harper's Weekly* September 21, 1872.

36   Robert Ingersoll, *Political Speeches of Robert G. Ingersoll* (New York: C.P. Farrell, 1914), 55–60, 157–187.

37   E. Merton Coulter, "Amnesty for all Except Jefferson Davis" The Hill-Blaine Debate of 1876, *Georgia Historical Quarterly* 57 (Summer 1973): 453–457.

38   Ibid., 457–462.

39   Benjamin Harvey Hill, *Senator Benjamin H. Hill of Georgia: His Life, Speeches, and Writings* (Atlanta, GA: T.H.P. Bloodworth & Co., 1891), 442–449.

40   Ibid., 449–460.

41   Ibid., 455–460.

42   Coulter, "Amnesty for all Except Jefferson Davis," 457.

43   A.O. Abbott, *Prison Life in the South: At Richmond, Macon, Savannah, Charleston, Columbia, Charlotte, Raleigh, Goldsborough, and Andersonville During the Years 1864 and 1865* (New York: Harper & Brothers, 1865), xiii.

44   Robert Kellogg, *Life and Death in Rebel Prisons* (Hartford, CT: L. Stebbins, 1865), 399.

45   Jesse Hawes, *Cahaba: A Story of Captive Boys in Blue* (New York: Burr, 1888), 461.

46   John McElroy, *Andersonville: A Story of Rebel Military Prisons* (Toledo, OH: D.R. Locke, 1879); John Ransom, *John Ransom's Andersonville Diary* (Philadelphia: Douglass Brothers, 1883).

47   William Henry Glasson, *History of Military Pension Legislation in the United States* (1900, reprint; New York: AMS Press), 73–74.

48   Stuart McConnell, *Glorious Contentment: The Grand Army of the Republic, 1865–1900* (Chapel Hill: University of North Carolina Press, 1992), 144.

49   Ibid., 146–150.

50   Ransom, *Andersonville Diary*, 8.

51   William Marvel, "Johnny Ransom's Imagination," *Civil War History* 41 (September 1995): 181–184.

52   Ibid., 182, 189.

53 James McPherson, *For Cause and Comrades: Why Men Fought in the Civil War* (New York: Oxford University Press, 1998), 11.

54 David S. Heidler and Jeanne T. Heidler, *Encyclopedia of the American Civil War: A Political, Social, and Military History*, 5 vols. (Santa Barbara, CA: ABC-CLIO, 2000), 1489–1490.

55 James R. Young, "Confederate Pensions in Georgia, 1886–1929," *Georgia Historical Quarterly* 66 (Spring 1982): 48.

56 James Marten, *Sing Not War: The Lives of Union and Confederate Veterans in Gilded Age America* (Chapel Hill: University of North Carolina Press, 2011), 17.

57 "Summing Up," *Southern Historical Society Papers* 1 (April 1876): 325–327.

58 Charles Reagan Wilson, *Baptized in Blood: The Religion of the Lost Cause* (Athens: University of Georgia Press, 1980), 123–124.

59 McConnell, *Glorious Contentment*, 94.

60 Grand Army of the Republic, *Proceedings of Enlistment & Muster of the Grand Army of the Republic* (Springfield, IL:, B. Richards, 1866), 4.

61 McConnell, *Glorious Contentment*, 177–182.

62 W.T. Ziegler, *Half Hour with an Andersonville Prisoner: Delivered at the Reunion of Post 9, G.A.R., at Gettysburg, Pennsylvania, January 8, 1879* (n.p.: J.W. Tate, 1879), 1–12.

63 William W. White, *The Confederate Veteran* (Tuscaloosa, AL: Confederate Publishing Company, 1962), 12, 32–45.

64 Ibid., 32; Cloyd, *Haunted By Atrocity*, 72.

65 David Blight, *Race and Reunion: The Civil War in American Memory* (Cambridge, MA: Harvard University Press, 2001), 152.

CHAPTER 5

Honoring Civil War Captives

With the end of the Civil War, prison lands in both the North and the South typically reverted back to the prewar owner. For example, the Enders family reclaimed the three buildings which comprised Libby Prison, selling one of the warehouses to the Southern Fertilizer Company. Castle Thunder, also in the Confederate capital, was returned to the heirs of the original owner, but a fire destroyed the building in 1879.[1] At Elmira, the Quartermaster Department sold thousands of leftover items to the general public such as 284 coal and wood stoves, 346 pounds of rope, 1,500 tin cups, 2,000 plates, and 37 bread baskets, and when the property leases expired "nothing remained except what had existed before the Civil War, an empty lot occupied only by Fosters Pond." The city, as historian Michael Gray suggests, really was in "the business of captivity."[2] Not every case transpired smoothly. Georgian Benjamin Dykes embarked on a 10-year crusade against the U.S. government regarding disputed land claims connected to the Andersonville Prison. He eventually sold 120 acres that surrounded the cemetery to the government.[3]

NATIONAL CEMETERIES

With some exceptions, the "care of many prisoner of war graves lapsed after the military abandoned the prison camps."[4] Local citizens often assumed the initial responsibility for maintaining the prisoner of war cemeteries, and individual families occasionally arranged to have a loved one exhumed and returned to their native region. Shortly after the war, the federal government established four national cemeteries at former Confederate prison sites and eventually assumed responsibility for all surviving Civil War prisoner of war cemeteries. However, the federal government placed a greater priority on tending to the Union dead, and the South's limited resources restricted its ability to tend to its war dead. Complicating matters was the spirit of acrimony and vindictiveness, on both sides, regarding the prisoner of war issue. Most important, as historian John Neff has argued "reconciliation would always run counter to the undeniable fact that many young men lay in graves because of the actions of the enemy, and no reunion, encampments, or political orations could deny that essential reality."[5] As a result, the memorialization and commemoration of Union and Confederate prisoner of war dead followed much different trajectories and timelines.

The National Cemetery System first originated during the Civil War. Between 1862 and 1864, congressional legislation created 27 national cemeteries, largely as a wartime measure that would provide an honorable burial for Union soldiers. The Quartermaster Department of the U.S. Army bore administrative responsibility for the National Cemetery System. Most often, the department opened burial grounds "at troop concentration points" where it could receive the hospital dead or in combat zones that were directly on or near the fields of battle.[6] By 1870, an additional 46 sites had been created, and by then the national cemeteries had assumed a more encompassing patriotic purpose. They linked the fallen to "the cause for which they died," established a "sense of obligation" and "indebtedness" between the living and the dead, and sought to preserve and communicate certain "values and ideals" to future generations. Indeed, one historian has called the creation of the national cemeteries "the single greatest expression" or endeavor by the federal government about the importance of the war and the survival of the nation. As a result of the Quartermaster Department's efforts, some 300,000 Union soldiers had been laid to rest by 1870, in more than 70 national cemeteries, at a total cost of over $3,000,000.[7]

Approximately 10 percent of Union war deaths occurred in Confederate prison camps, and in the aftermath of the Civil War these former places of infamy were transformed into sacred landscapes. The Quartermaster Department established national cemeteries at Danville, Virginia; Salisbury, North Carolina; Florence, South Carolina; and Andersonville, Georgia. Of these, the cemetery at Andersonville was by far the largest. Shortly after the war ended, an unlikely friendship formed between Clara Barton and a former Andersonville prisoner, Dorence Atwater. Barton had spent the final months of the war in Washington, D.C. working on behalf of military families by aiding them in their search for their missing husbands and sons. Atwater had served in Andersonville's prison hospital where he kept an official "Death Register" of the Union dead. Fearing Confederate duplicity, Atwater made a copy of the register, which he was able to sneak out upon his release. After some behind the scenes maneuvering to gain the support of several influential congressmen, Barton and Atwater earned the right to accompany Captain James M. Moore of the Quartermaster Department, along with 40 laborers, on an expedition to southwest Georgia to identify the Andersonville dead. The project began in late July. The main work entailed the replacement of the numerical identification posts, which had been set at each grave site at the time of internments, with new headboards containing the name, rank, unit, and date of death of the former prisoners. The Atwater death register contained the crucial biographical data that corresponded with the numbers carved on the identification posts. Of the 12,920 prisoners dead at Andersonville, 12,461 were positively identified, leaving only 451 marked as unknown.[8]

The 97 percent identification rate was an astonishing accomplishment given that nearly 40 percent of all Union war dead were buried in graves marked as unknown. If examining only the number of unknown prisoner of war dead the percentage is probably higher. In fact, 2,167 of 2,738 headboards at the Florence National Cemetery bore the inscription, "Unknown." At the former Salisbury prison site, the Quartermaster Department could only speculate as to the number of dead buried in the cemetery. Because prisoners were often buried with no headboard and a comprehensive burial list did not survive the war, estimates ranged from 1,800 to 11,700. One source claims 3,700 men died between October 1864 and February 1865 at the prison, which first opened in October 1861. Eventually, the federal government placed markers bearing the inscription unknown at the ends of more than a dozen burial trenches.[9]

Dorence Atwater

Dorence Atwater was born on February 3, 1845 in Terryville, Connecticut. At the age of 16, he joined the 2nd New York Cavalry. He was captured on July 7, 1863 at Boonsboro, Maryland just after the Battle of Gettysburg. He spent the next five months as a sickly prisoner on Belle Isle. Atwater was among the first prisoners to arrive at Andersonville in late February 1864. Having attended quality public schools prior to the war, Atwater developed exceptional penmanship. For this reason, General John Winder assigned him to the prison's surgeon's office where he kept the official roll of the dead. Atwater remained at Andersonville until February 1865 when he was transferred to Columbia, South Carolina. He was paroled later that month at Wilmington, North Carolina.

Even before his visit to Andersonville with Clara Barton in the summer of 1865, Atwater had been approached by the War Department about the death rolls. Secretary of War Edwin Stanton authorized a payment of $300 for the list. Atwater refused, claiming his only objective was to publish the list for the benefit of the families. He was warned that if he did so he could be subject to court martial. Atwater then requested a payment of $300 and a government clerkship for which he would loan the list to the War Department so that it could make copies. No final agreement was reached between the parties before the completion of the August expedition to Andersonville, although Atwater received $300 from the government and the War Department made copies of the list. Nevertheless Atwater still retained possession of the death rolls and refused to turn them over to the War Department. In a strange twist of events, Atwater, the former prisoner of war, was arrested by his own government on a charge of grand larceny and placed in the same prison as Captain Henry Wirz who was awaiting trial for war crimes. Atwater stood trial in September, was found guilty of theft, and was sentenced to 18 months hard labor at Auburn State Prison in New York. In early December, he received a pardon from President Andrew Johnson and was released.

Upon his release, Atwater published the death register. And aided by Barton's influence and his own unique character and abilities, Atwater was appointed to the U.S. Consul in the Seychelles Islands. He was later promoted to the position of U.S. Consul to Tahiti. While there he met and married Princess Moetia Salmon in 1875. Toward the end of his life Atwater moved to San Francisco where he died on November 26, 1910.

The dedication of the Andersonville National Cemetery was a low-key and informal affair. On August 14, 1865, Barton, Atwater, and the Quartermaster detail gathered in the cemetery and raised an American flag to mark the solemnity of the occasion. Conversely, President Abraham Lincoln delivered what became known as the Gettysburg Address at the dedication of the Soldiers' National Cemetery in November 1863, and such dignitaries as President Andrew Johnson, and generals Ulysses S. Grant and George McClellan attended the September 1867 dedication of the Antietam National Cemetery. Barton led the campaign to draw public attention to the Andersonville National Cemetery publishing an article in the *New York Tribune* in February 1866. The one-half page article recounted the back story of her recent trip to Georgia and the work they performed. She gave substantial credit for the trip's success to Dorence Atwater.

"The future of this historic spot," Barton informed the American people, "cannot fail to constitute a subject of deep and abiding interest . . . and it would seem fitting that it should be preserved as one of the sanctuaries of the nation." She was referring primarily to "the cemetery, around which the chief interest must gather." Barton also advised her readers that when they heard an Andersonville survivor speak of "his sufferings, how he fainted, scorched, drenched, hungered, sickened, was scoffed, scourged, hunted, and, persecuted," they must realize that "however defiantly he may have spoken, know that he has not told you all." There would come a time, Barton was certain, when a former prisoner or a faithful widow would petition their fellow citizens for assistance. At that moment, Barton hoped that Americans would embrace a Biblical attitude regarding priorities: "the poor you will always have with you, but him you have not always and withhold it not."[10] This reference was drawn from a story about Jesus and the reaction one of his disciples had when a woman anointed Jesus' feet with expensive perfume. An offended disciple argued that the perfume could have been sold and the proceeds used to help the poor. Jesus responded by saying the disciples could assist the poor after he concluded his earthly mission; his time with them was finite. Barton, in essence, had constructed a Messianic identity for the surviving prisoners, and as such, the American people owed an immediate allegiance to these men. In this lengthy piece, Barton did not once mention the name Henry Wirz.

The work of Barton and the quartermaster detail impressed John Townsend Trowbridge when he visited the Andersonville National Cemetery in 1866. Trowbridge, a New England journalist, spent four months in eight Southern states surveying the damaged landscape and interviewing former Confederates and freedpersons alike. As for the town of Andersonville, Trowbridge wrote, "The entire aspect and atmosphere of the place are ugly and repulsive." The abandoned prison site and the cemetery drew a different response. A white-washed picket fence surrounded the cemetery and at the entrance Trowbridge observed the following inscription above the archway:

> On fame's eternal camping-ground
> Their silent tents are spread,
> And glory guards with solemn round
> The bivouac of the dead

The words were from Theodore O'Hara's famous poem "Bivouac of the Dead." Trowbridge had noticed the same inscription at Spotsylvania, Virginia and felt it would be appropriate to place it "before every national soldiers' cemetery." Inside the cemetery fence, the four sections of graves were divided by two perpendicular avenues. An American flag marked the intersection of the avenues and the symbolism was not lost on Trowbridge. "Here, on the soil of Georgia above the graves of our dead," the New Englander proudly declared, "waves the broad symbol of the Nation's power and victory."[11]

Like Trowbridge, Sidney Andrews, an Illinois-based journalist, conducted a 14-week tour of Georgia, South Carolina, and North Carolina shortly after the war. He found the Andersonville National Cemetery to be well maintained and suitably adorned with markers accompanied by patriotic inscriptions reminding visitors of the supreme sacrifice paid by the nation's faithful servants. His commentary on the national cemeteries at Florence and Salisbury focused more on how the Union prisoners were buried by the Confederates and on the large number of unknown graves. Of Florence, Andrews related a conversation he had with a black carpenter who told the journalist that the captives were "chucked" into their graves "like muttons." Although some 2,300 graves were numbered, "many score [were] unnumbered," which angered Andrews. He knew "the Rebels kept a record of this potter's field" but the ledger had not been recovered and Andrews feared that it "never" would be found. At Salisbury, he learned from an elderly white man that the bodies of the dead Union prisoners had been thrown into long trenches by "the heartless Rebel guards," and he could see with his own eyes that "no headboards were used," and it was "impossible to tell where any particular soldier lies."[12] Even in cases where the federal government had assumed control of the prison cemeteries, a lingering hatred of the Confederacy persisted because of its treatment of Union prisoners of war.

Roughly a decade after Trowbridge reported on conditions in the postwar South, Anna Dickinson, a popular lyceum speaker, delivered a series of lectures in Virginia, North Carolina, South Carolina, Georgia, and Tennessee. The fiery Northern radical used her free time between speaking engagements to view some of the Civil War battlefields, prisoner of war camps, and national cemeteries. She also interacted with the Southern populace and discussed the issues of the day. The number of unknown soldiers (12,844) buried at Fredericksburg saddened Dickinson as did the number (5,691) at the Richmond National Cemetery, where she paused to reflect on the "long agony" and "slow torture" of those who perished at Libby Prison and Belle Isle. At Salisbury, the magnitude of the unknown graves overwhelmed Dickinson. She could not fathom a situation "where name & place could be so easily" recorded but that a register of dead prisoners had not been kept. Dickinson lamented that "not merely their *graves* unknown, but they themselves unknown even the mothers who bore them not knowing *where* and how ended their days." She blamed the shameless people of the town and their wretched Confederate government for allowing the prisoners to starve and die in the first place. After an emotional day, she returned to her hotel.

> I sat in my room like one in a dream—There was such a weight on my heart it almost crushed it—I could not go into the parlor where these people were, nor onto their streets—I hated them with such loathing as to make me craven at only having to breathe the same air with them.[13]

DECORATION DAY AND EMANCIPATION DAY

Decoration Day celebrations became an integral part of the commemorative heritage at national cemeteries. One of the first observances of Decoration Day (today known as Memorial Day) can be traced to May 1865 in Charleston, South Carolina where Confederates had converted a horse-racing track into a prison during the final stages of the war. More than 250 men died from "exposure and disease and were hastily buried without coffins in unmarked graves behind the former judge's stand." Concerned that the Union soldiers had not received a proper burial, nearly 30 African-Americans from a Charleston-area church constructed a 10-foot-high fence around the makeshift cemetery and "landscaped the graves into neat rows." On the arch above the entrance gate the freedpersons painted the words, "Martyrs of the Race Course." White missionaries and teachers working with freedperson's relief associations teamed with the city's African-American community to plan a day of commemoration. On May 1, a crowd estimated at 10,000, most of whom were former slaves, turned out to pay tribute to the Union prisoner of war dead. The procession was led by 3,000 black school children and they were followed by hundreds of black men and black women. All placed flowers, wreaths, and crosses on the grave sites. One *New York Tribune* correspondent described the scene as follows: "when all had left, the holy mounds—the tops, the sides, and the spaces between them—were one mass of flowers, not a speck of earth could be seen." An assortment of Union military officers, local black ministers, and white abolitionists delivered close to 30 dedication speeches. The festivities also included a picnic and a dress parade by "a full brigade of Union infantry," including members of various USCT regiments.[14]

Observed in various locales in the North and the South, Decoration Day quickly became a holiday of national commemoration, although Southerners developed a separate Confederate Decoration Day to honor their war dead.

In May 1868, General John A. Logan, commander-in-chief of the Grand Army of the Republic, issued General Order No. 11, which essentially established Decoration Day as a national day of remembrance. The response to Logan's order was manifold. The first year services were held in at least 27 states at more than 175 cemeteries and were attended by thousands of people. The following year the celebration grew to 31 states, involving more than 336 cities and towns.[15]

Decoration Day observances in the North often referenced Union prisoner of war dead. When C.S. Wilson addressed the "citizens and soldiers" of Corry, Pennsylvania on June 25, 1868 he reminded the audience of those individuals who had suffered and died at Andersonville and

> Many historians credit Georgian Lizzie Rutherford and the women of the Soldiers' Aid Society of Columbus with establishing Confederate Memorial Day. In early 1866, advocates called on Southerners to pay tribute to the Confederate dead on April 26, the date that General Joseph E. Johnston surrendered the Army of Tennessee to General William Sherman. Subsequently, many Southern states established April 26 as Confederate Memorial Day.

Libby prisons. They were, according to Wilson, the brave men who had saved the republic and were owed an eternal debt of gratitude. An observance at St. James Cemetery in Woonsocket, Rhode Island honored Richard O. Stratford, 1st Connecticut Calvary, who died while in captivity at the Florence Prison, but whose remains were returned and interred in Rhode Island. During a roll call of honor at a service in Coldwater, Michigan, Dr. J.H. Beech recognized Byron E. Bates, 8th New York Heavy Artillery, who died in Salisbury Prison, "a victim of one of the most horrid peculiarities of this unprecedented outbreak of treason." Decoration Day services often were held at national cemeteries, including Danville, Salisbury, Florence, and Andersonville.[16] African-Americans from a black Baptist church in Florence organized memorial services in 1895. Some 1,500 people paraded through the town and out to the cemetery where they strew flowers on graves and conducted patriotic and religious services.[17] During her stay in Raleigh, North Carolina, Dickinson inquired about how the tradition was celebrated at the Salisbury National Cemetery by asking "a very pleasant woman" whose husband was an architect and the woman was obviously a lady of social bearing and economic means. Dickinson was taken aback when the woman replied, "Oh! You mean Nigger's day." The Southern matron went on to explain that on Decoration Day African-Americans were the only people to place flowers on the graves of the Union dead and if "an oration is made, it has almost none but colored hearers."[18]

In addition to celebrating the preservation of the Union on Decoration Day, the federal presence at national cemeteries, particularly Andersonville, certainly encouraged African-Americans to commemorate the emancipationist legacy of the Civil War. During the Barton–Atwater visit, former slaves rushed to the scene "by scores, men, women, and children sometimes 100 in a day." They approached Barton and asked "if it were true that Abraham Lincoln was dead, and they were free," and "how Massa Lincoln's great paper read," and "what they ought to do." The freedpersons empathized with the former prisoners who "ran" from the blood-hounds and search dogs "like they did." They regretted that they could not alleviate the captives' suffering but during that time they faced harsh punishments if they consorted with, and risked even graver retribution, if they aided Andersonville prisoners.[19] These unscripted pilgrimages to Andersonville quickly transformed into more ritualized forms of commemoration.

In the fall of 1866, the American Missionary Association (AMA) established a school for freedpersons in the town of Andersonville, in an old storehouse previously maintained by the Confederate quartermaster, about one-half mile south of the national cemetery and near the railroad depot where the former prisoners disembarked before entering Camp Sumter. The AMA descended from "evangelical abolitionists" of the Congregational and Presbyterian denominations and supported the advancement of black civil rights.[20] Enrollment at the school soon exceeded 60 and a biracial Congregational Mission Church was also established in the town. On January 1, 1869, a biracial group of teachers, ministers, students, and friends from seven Northern states assembled to celebrate Emancipation Day. New Year's Day previously held agonizing memories for blacks because of its historic association with slave auctions. However, President Abraham Lincoln's formal signing of the Emancipation Proclamation on January 1, 1863 allowed blacks, in the words of historian

W. Fitzhugh Brundage, to invent "their own commemorative festivals."[21] The Andersonville Emancipation Day observance included ceremonies at the mission church, where the program included singing, scripture reading, prayers, a recitation of the Emancipation Proclamation, and a formal speech. The procession then marched from the church to the national cemetery "with slow and solemn" steps. They sang the "most appropriate and beautiful songs" as they traveled. As they entered the cemetery, they paused to reflect on the archway inscription from the "Bivouac of the Dead" before proceeding to six points in the cemetery where they placed wreaths around tablets bearing tributes to the fallen soldiers. The group gathered at the flag-staff in the center of the cemetery, reminiscent of the Barton–Atwater expedition, and hung their last wreath, but as Rev. Dr. H.W. Pierson explained: "It was no place for [a] speech. The surroundings were too solemn." The group decorated the graves of the "brave boys" who preserved the nation and freed the slaves. Afterward the biracial procession departed the cemetery and they returned to the train depot, assembled around the flag-staff, sang a chorus based on William Bradbury's "See the Flag, the Dear Old Flag," and concluded their Emancipation Day commemoration.[22]

The establishment of national cemeteries in the South and their continued maintenance by the U.S. military allowed white Northerners and former slaves the chance to celebrate the preservation of the Union. But these sites also served as a platform for celebrating the emancipationist legacy of the Civil War, especially for African-Americans who "steadfastly maintained a connection between Civil War prisons and the fight for racial equality." According to historian Benjamin Cloyd:

> these commemorations helped preserve the unique emancipationist legacy of the Civil War, as blacks celebrated the sacrifices of the dead Union soldiers not just as the heroes of a reunited America . . . but more precisely as martyrs to the cause of human freedom.[23]

CONFEDERATE CEMETERIES

Northerners and African-Americans commemorated the Union war dead, including prisoner of war dead, on a grand scale. However, civilian and military leaders insisted that no Confederates be interred in national cemeteries if they died while fighting Union forces on the field of battle. To afford these soldiers a proper burial, the various chapters of the Ladies Memorial Associations (LMAs) raised funds and oversaw the reinterment of Southern war dead into Confederate cemeteries. There were between 70 and 100 LMAs chapters in the states of Georgia, South Carolina, North Carolina, Mississippi, Alabama, and Virginia. Women of the LMAs in the 5 Virginia communities of Winchester, Fredericksburg, Petersburg, Lynchburg, and Richmond "reinterred the remains of more than 72,520 Confederates, nearly 28 percent of the 260,000 Confederate soldiers who perished in the war."[24] Perhaps the most unusual undertaking by a LMAs chapter transpired in 1880 in the town of Americus, located 10 or so miles from Andersonville, Georgia. The Americus chapter disinterred the bodies of the 115 Confederate guards buried in the Andersonville National Cemetery and reburied them in the city's Oak Grove Cemetery. In an official report, the women of the Americus chapter explained their decision:

> in the latter part of the seventies, when the government began to
> improve the cemetery at Andersonville, building a wall around it and
> making many other changes, the graves of the Confederates, who had
> died there during the war, were thereby thrown out in the woods, and
> left in a very neglected condition.

The dramatic statement contained an element of truth. When the War Department implemented a standard architectural form at Andersonville, it had enclosed the cemetery and left the graves of the Confederate guards beyond the pale of its care. Using their "hoarded monument fund," the Americus chapter furnished marble headstones "at the head and foot of each grave" and where possible identified by name the deceased soldier. Following the reinterment, the women of the LMAs joined forces with the United Daughters of the Confederacy to raise money for a monument to honor the Andersonville guards. It took nearly 20 years but the groups erected a monument in 1899 at a cost of $1,800.[25]

As for Southern soldiers who died as prisoners of war or in Union hospitals, exceptions were granted by the federal government so that these particular Confederates could be interred in national cemeteries. For example, the Camp Butler National Cemetery, located some 6 miles northeast of Springfield, Illinois, included a separate Confederate section, which contained the remains of 866 former prisoners of war, primarily from the states of Texas (302), Tennessee (302), and Arkansas (153). The pointed-topped headstones of the Confederate dead were easily distinguishable from the round-topped gravestones of the Union dead. Local legend held that the pointed-shaped Confederate headstones were designed to keep disrespectful Union soldiers from sitting on them, which may have been true to some degree.[26] However, the fundamental purpose of the contrasting shapes of the headstones was to differentiate between Union dead and Confederate dead. Confederate prisoners were also buried in separate Confederate sections of the national cemeteries at Point Lookout, Maryland, and Jefferson Barracks, Missouri.

The cases of Confederate cemeteries at Johnson's Island and Elmira illustrate the inconsistent attitude of the federal government toward the Southern prisoner of war dead and demonstrate a more passionate response from select Northern communities. The condition of the cemetery at Johnson's Island deteriorated quickly after the U.S. Army auctioned off the prison buildings and surplus furnishings and abandoned the island in mid-1866. Leonard Johnson purchased some of the buildings and supplies and planted an orchard of 3,000 fruit trees near the former prison. When visitors from Georgia toured the cemetery in 1889 they discovered rotten wooden grave markers; most of the prison buildings had long since vanished and the prison grounds were overgrown by weeds and brush. A campaign ensued immediately to raise funds in order to purchase marble headstones for the approximately 200 graves. Within a year enough money had been raised and the new headstones were set. Local residents supported the Southern-led effort to honor their fallen, but the federal government offered no assistance even when Leonard Johnson offered to deed the property in return for a paid cemetery superintendent position similar to those at national cemeteries. During the 1890s, the United Confederate Veterans supported financially the care and maintenance of the cemetery, and in 1902 the United Daughters of the

Confederacy, with the help of local citizens, purchased the cemetery land. The federal government assumed responsibility for the cemetery in June 1932.[27]

The Confederate dead at Elmira Prison were buried in Woodlawn Cemetery. Following the war, concerned Southerners paid local resident Sexton Jones $50 annually to maintain the Confederate section of the cemetery; Union soldiers, mainly prison guards, were interred in the cemetery's northwest section. At some point Jones quit after failing to be paid for services rendered. Motivated in part by the accusations raised by Benjamin Hill during the amnesty debate of 1876, Elmira's civic leaders entered negotiations with the War Department about designating Woodlawn as a national cemetery. In December 1877, the city ceded two and one-half acres to the federal government for the sum of $1,500 and Woodlawn became a national cemetery.[28] When ex-Elmira prisoner Marcus B. Toney returned to the city in 1901, he expected to see graves "grown over with briars, weeds, and thistles," but was surprised to find a lush green landscape with "not a weed to be seen!" The "only difference" that Toney detected between the two sections was that marble headstones adorned the Union graves whereas the wooden headboards at the Confederate graves "had all rotted away." The former prisoner thought it would be "futile" for Southerners to attempt to raise funds for marble replacements, feeling "it can only be done by the general government."[29] The U.S. Congress responded just five years later by authorizing the War Department to report on the condition of Confederate graves and "prepare accurate identification of the deceased . . . including grave numbers, name, rank, regiment, and state." During the summer of 1906, each grave site received a new wooden marker. In the spirit of reconciliation, the federal government awarded the Blue Ridge Marble Company of Nelson, Georgia the contract to furnish 2,932 marble headstones at a cost of $8,500 and paid an Elmira firm $733 to set the headstones, work that was completed in October 1907. Every Confederate state was represented in the Woodlawn National Cemetery with North Carolinians occupying almost half (1,233) the burial sites. Less than two years later, the remains of Northern guards and Confederate prisoners, who were killed en route to Elmira in July 1864 and laid to rest near the train crash site at Shohola, Pennsylvania, were exhumed and reinterred at Woodlawn National Cemetery. The federal government even appropriated money for the Shohola Monument as a tribute to the accident victims.[30]

In 1906, the U.S. Congress passed the Foraker Bill, which created the Commission for Marking Graves of Confederate Dead. Ohio Senator Joseph B. Foraker had introduced the legislation. As governor of Ohio, Foraker had supported plans to improve the conditions of the cemeteries at Camp Chase and Johnson's Island. The Foraker Bill established a temporary commission to identify, by headstone or tablet, the graves of Confederate soldiers who died in Union prisons or hospitals. Although not required by legislative mandate, former Confederate officers—William Elliott, William C. Oates, James H. Berry, and Samuel E. Lewis—each served as successive commissioners. They oversaw the location and marking of "at least sixty additional sites that had never been incorporated into any form of federal custody," including the cemeteries of such former prisoner of war camps as Rock Island, Illinois and Point Lookout, Maryland. The commission strictly limited its work to the prisoner and hospital dead. In one instance, it authorized the placement of a tablet on a vault containing the remains of nine Confederate dead. However, the commission only permitted the names of six soldiers to be listed on the tablet because the other three, whose names were known, had not died as prisoners of war or in a Union hospital. Generally speaking, Southerners approved of the federal government's efforts, which led to the identification and marking of 30,000 Confederate prisoner and hospital dead. Nevertheless, the work of the Commission for Marking Graves of Confederate Dead did little to eliminate the sectional tensions over the prisoner of war controversy.[31]

MONUMENTS

As blacks and whites, Northerners and Southerners commemorated the Civil War dead—they assigned different meanings to the war. In attempting to understand what the Civil War meant to the participants of the conflict, historians have identified four primary interpretive or memory traditions. The Union Cause held that the war's primary objective had been to turn back the secessionist threat and to save the world's only democratic republic. The Emancipationist Cause pointed to the destruction of slavery as the most significant consequence of the war. The Lost Cause tradition offered a Southern explanation for the origins of the war and the reasons for Confederate defeat. Its adherents argued that the defense of states rights, not slavery, had necessitated secession and that the Confederacy fell to an industrially superior foe that had unlimited resources. The Reconciliationist Cause downplayed the issues of race and slavery and focused on the heroism exhibited by those individuals who were willing to fight and die for what they believed was right and just. These four memory traditions had been firmly established by the 1880s, a time when veterans groups and commemorative societies erected and dedicated monuments to honor those who fought and died in the Civil War.[32]

Monuments appeared on battlefields, in town squares, in cemeteries, and even at prisoner of war sites. Not surprisingly, Northerners chose Andersonville as the most fitting place to memorialize Union prisoners of war and the national cemetery and the grounds of the prison complex became the scene of the most extensive and sustained commemoration of Northern war captives in the entire nation. In fact, starting with the New Jersey monument dedication in 1899 and ending with the Minnesota monument dedication in 1916, 15 states erected and dedicated monuments to the prisoner dead at Andersonville. Typically, though not always the case, a former prisoner presented a bill to a state legislature requesting an appropriation for the purchase, erection, and dedication of a monument to the soldiers from that state who died at Andersonville. Once the legislature passed the bill and the governor signed it into law he then appointed a commission, which always included a Civil War veteran and usually a former prisoner of war, to oversee and carry out the project. Upon completion of the monument project, the commission submitted a detailed report concerning expenditures, a list of the dead buried at Andersonville, and copies of any speeches or orations delivered at the dedication service. These reports often reveal how the prisoner of war controversy helped to shape and became part of the four Civil War memory traditions.

Figure 5.1 The Connecticut Monument at Andersonville. Photo by Chris Barr, courtesy of Andersonville National Historic Site.

Although a relatively small number, 235, of New Jersey's sons died at Andersonville, the state legislature appropriated $2,000 in 1898 to place a monument in the national cemetery at the former prison site. Badger Brothers of Quincy, Massachusetts won the contract for the construction, transportation, and erection of the monument. The height of the monument exceeded 24 feet, and the front face inscription glistened with state pride:

> Go, stranger, to New Jersey; tell her that we lie here in fulfillment of the mandate and our pledge, to maintain the proud name of our State, unsullied, and place it high on the Scroll of Honor, among the States of this Great Nation.

The monument's long shaft bore a simple inscription: "Death Before Dishonor."[33] The emphasis on duty to country and personal honor carried special meaning for former Union prisoners of war because their integrity had been questioned, on occasion, during the war. A number of Union leaders, both military and civilian, believed that some soldiers allowed themselves to be captured and then paroled in order to avoid the risks of combat. The list of critics included Secretary of War Edwin Stanton. Moreover, when the prisoner exchange program broke down, Union captives had the opportunity to become Galvanized Rebels, men who switched sides and actively participated in the Confederate war effort.[34]

The number of Galvanized Rebels greatly exceeded the totals mentioned by prisoner memoirists such as John L. Ransom, author of the widely popular and influential work, *Andersonville Diary: Escape and List of Dead*. Ransom had also been a prisoner at Camp Lawton in the fall of 1864. In his memoir, he claimed that he only saw "two or three" men take the oath and become Galvanized Rebels. Camp records, however, indicate that 349 Union prisoners took the Confederate oath at Camp Lawton during November 1864, which was roughly 3 percent of the prison's population. Elsewhere the numbers were even higher. By asserting the "Death Before Dishonor" mantra, the New Jersians spoke on behalf of those who perished in captivity, testifying to their patriotism, courage, and their dedication to the preservation of the Union. Rather than betray their cause they had accepted death. Similarly, those who lived to see an honorable release from any Confederate prison had literally imperiled their lives by refusing the Confederate oath of allegiance.[35]

The dedication ceremony occurred on February 3, 1899. The monument was set in the cemetery in a "central and conspicuous" location, "near the greatest number of New Jersey's dead." The commission gathered a number of items and deposited them in a time capsule that was placed under the monument's foundation. The eclectic list of items included newspapers, photos and woodcuts of prominent New Jersians, GAR membership badges, coins, flags, a deck of cards, the register of Andersonville dead, and an assortment of documents from the New Jersey legislature. The commission took great pride in being the first state to place a monument at Andersonville. Other states soon followed New Jersey's lead. Most tellingly, of the fourteen subsequent state monuments erected and dedicated at Andersonville, whether in the national cemetery or on the grounds of the prison stockade, five bore the mantra, "Death Before Dishonor."

Beginning in the late nineteenth century, Southerners, Northerners, and the federal government worked individually and in concert to promote the preservation and care of Confederate prisoner cemeteries. More than 4,500 Confederates died at Camp Douglas, Illinois and many were reburied in unmarked graves in the soldiers section of Chicago's Oakwoods Cemetery. For years, two GAR posts, both under the command of Colonel Charles R.E. Koch, attended to the graves and as early as May 30, 1876 had decorated the Confederate graves as a show of "reconstructive friendship" toward the goal of "national patriotism." The secretary of war granted Chicago's ex-Confederate Association permission to erect a memorial monument in the cemetery and to hold a dedication service. The association raised $25,000 and planned for the dedication to coincide with a Confederate veterans reunion in Chicago. The scheduled date for the dedication, national Decoration Day, prompted the Department of Illinois GAR to voice strong disapproval over the honoring of Southern soldiers on

At Andersonville, during a severe rainstorm in the summer of 1864, an underground spring was uncovered, providing prisoners with much needed drinking water. Some men referred to the event as a miracle and called the well Providence Spring. Following the war, Union veterans often gathered at that exact location. On Decoration Day 1901, the granite Providence Spring monument house was dedicated.

a holiday set aside to pay tribute to those killed while defending the nation from the threat of secession.[36] Despite the protests, the mayor of Chicago, and several former Union officers including John M. Schofield and Medal of Honor recipient John C. Black, participated in the dedication ceremony, spoke at the reunion, or forwarded remarks. A spirit of fraternity also surrounded the dedication of a monument to the Confederate dead at Camp Chase, Ohio. Former Union veteran William Knauss led local efforts to care for the graves beginning in the mid-1890s. By 1902, the Columbus Ohio chapter of the United Daughters of the Confederacy assumed primary responsibility for the care of the graves but Knauss assisted the organization in raising funds for a memorial archway to be placed at the cemetery. On June 7, 1902, Ohio Governor George Nash was among those giving speeches at the dedication. The only inscription on the monument was the word: "Americans."[37]

On June 3, 1908, the state of Maine dedicated a monument at the Salisbury National Cemetery "to perpetuate the memory" of the "patriotic Maine soldiers" who suffered and died in Salisbury Prison. The state, four years earlier, had erected a monument at the Andersonville National Cemetery to honor its men who died at that prison. George B. Haskell, a former prisoner of war and a member of the Maine House of Representatives, introduced the legislation, which was approved with a $5,000 appropriation. The monument commission received five bids for the design and awarded the contract to the Bodwell Granite Company of Vinalhaven, Maine. The completed monument stood 25 feet high. On the second base cut appeared the phrase: "One Country, One Flag." The four faces of the monument's die—essentially the trunk of the monument—included a general tribute and three marital mottoes. The north face read: "Maine's tribute to her soldiers who died while prisoners of war at Salisbury, N.C., 1864–1865." The other three:

East—Neither hunger, thirst nor offered bribes affected their loyalty
South—To live in hearts we leave behind is not to die
West—They fought for peace; for peace they fell; they sleep in peace, and all is well

The east and west die mottoes reflect the commemorative thrust of the Maine Monument Commission.[38] First, the reference to bribes and loyalty refers to the treasonous behavior of the Galvanized Rebels and the sentiment followed in the tradition established by New Jersey at Andersonville nearly a decade earlier. Second, the call for peace was not an unconditional offer of sectional reconciliation. In 1868, Ulysses S. Grant campaigned for the presidency on the slogan, "Let Us Have Peace." As Grant biographer Joan Waugh explains, peace, for men like the former general, was predicated "on southern acceptance of the victor's terms." Their memory of the war honored the sacrifice of those who died, first and foremost, to save the union, and then to destroy slavery. Moreover, Grant "found repugnant, the increasingly popular idea that the Union and Confederate causes were separate but equal," or even worse, "that the two were somehow morally equivalent."[39]

The Maine Monument dedication party, numbering less than 40, left Portland on June 5 and arrived in Salisbury on the morning of June 8. They were met by a welcoming committee from the state of North Carolina, which included Secretary of State J. Bryan Grimes and the town's mayor. The governor of North Carolina ordered state troops to escort the party to the cemetery and 53 Confederate veterans also joined the procession. The displays of cordiality, however, cannot be construed as proof of sectional reconciliation as evidenced by the dedicatorial address of Charles D. Newell. In describing the great war, Newell declared, "History records no other such conflict. It has no equal. Men of the North, brave, and courageous, and determined, against men of the South, impulsive, brave, courageous, but mistaken." Standing near the graves of Salisbury's prisoner of war dead, Newell recalled their "valor and patriotism" and proclaimed them "instrumental in making this one of the greatest nations of the earth." He concluded his remarks by saying their "loyalty and heroism were the best legacy that could be transmitted" to their children and to future generations. Joseph L. Small, a former Salisbury prisoner, spoke with an even harsher tone.[40]

"In yonder stockade 43 years ago," Small began, "thousands of the boys in blue suffered for nearly five months daily martyrdom in body and spirit, rather than dishonor the old flag by swearing allegiance to the Stars and Bars." He did not attempt to paint a picture of the conditions in the prison, but he spoke forcefully about who was responsible for the high death toll:

> at whose door lies the blame that there was a lack of the three primal necessities of life—food, water, shelter. An abundant supply of running water and wood enough for fuel and shelter was within half a mile of the stockade. That these were denied the prisoners could be due only to the negligence, the cold-blooded indifference of the commandant of the prison, Maj. John H. Gee, of the Eleventh Florida Infantry—a man brutal and avaricious, void of all sense of honor, a tool of those higher in authority, who was more anxious to prevent the escape of the prisoners than to preserve their lives.

Small did not blame the people of Salisbury—in fact he cited individual acts of kindness shown to Union prisoners by Southern citizens—but in closing his remarks he reminded the audience that the dead buried in that national cemetery displayed a "steadfast faith in the righteousness of their cause" and gave "to the world new ideals of patriotism which cannot be surpassed."[41]

Captain Henry Wirz was not the only Confederate prison commandant arrested and charged with war crimes. Major John Gee, commandant of Salisbury Prison, was arrested and stood trial for war crimes before a military commission in Raleigh, North Carolina in February 1866. He was acquitted of all charges.

Prior to the bold Unionist statements of Newell and Small, Grimes, the son of a revered Confederate general, delivered an impassioned defense of the Southern cause and the Salisbury Prison. Grimes highlighted the role of North Carolina in the revolutionary struggle with Great Britain and the quest for independence. He reminded his Northern visitors of their tepid response to the War of 1812 and the talk of secession at the Hartford Convention of 1814 where New England Federalists contemplated a separate peace treaty with Great Britain. "It might be said that we learned some of the lessons of secession from you," accused Grimes. The unfortunate suffering and high death toll at Salisbury had been the result of the South's impoverishment, not callous neglect, Grimes bluntly confessed, "We could not feed our soldiers, and we could not feed our prisoners." Furthermore, he blamed the North for harming their own men by refusing to exchange prisoners—quoting the now famous Grant declaration of August 1864—and by rejecting Confederate plans to allow Union surgeons to bring medicines through enemy lines and treat the sick and wounded. Most important, he associated "the glory of the soldier who wore the blue" with "the valor of the soldier who wore the gray" as part of a "common heritage" shared by "all Americans." To Maine's declaration of "One Country, One Flag," Grimes asserted, "This is our flag as much as your flag. It has been laved in the blood of Southern heroes and Carolina heroes, and we of the South have done as much to make it great and glorious as you men of the North have."[42]

THE WIRZ MONUMENT

In his remarks, Grimes echoed what had become a standard Southern response to the prisoner of war controversy and nowhere was the sentiment more fiercely advanced than the state of Georgia. In 1905, the Georgia Chapters of the United Daughters of the Confederacy (UDC) announced a plan to erect in the town of Andersonville a monument "to that brave soldier and humane gentleman, Captain Wirz, whom the north has unjustly reviled." The Wirz monument, the UDC declared, would "stand as the protest of the South against the slanders and false-hoods already in bronze and brass at that place." Clearly, the memorialization of Union soldiers at the Andersonville National Cemetery and the prison site had offended and angered the Daughters of Dixie.[43] Despite the strong desire to vindicate Wirz and the South, the women seemed divided over where exactly to place the monument. During the 1908 Georgia UDC state convention a vote was taken that changed the monument's location to Richmond, Virginia. But then, in 1909, in "one of the most spirited [debates] in the history of the U.D.C of Georgia," the convention reversed the previous decision and selected Andersonville for the site of the monument.[44]

The monument dedication occurred on May 12, 1909 to great fanfare as more than 3,000 spectators flocked to the town of Andersonville. The two principal orators of the day's events, Pleasant A. Stovall of Savannah and Dr. J.C. Olmstead of Atlanta, echoed familiar themes of the Southern version of the prison controversy. For example, both men cast Wirz as a martyr to the Southern cause. They opined that Jefferson Davis was the federal government's real target in the Wirz trial and the prison commandant chose death rather than to falsely implicate the Confederate president. Wirz's selfless act, they proclaimed, defended Southern honor. Olmstead, in particular, declared that the South must not forget its heroic past. "Our cause . . . can only be 'lost,' when patriotism shall cease to be esteemed a virtue, and self-sacrifice for country no longer regarded a duty," he intoned. Olmstead urged the audience to remain vigilant because public schools were vulnerable to the North's "perversions of the truth" that had been printed "unrestrictedly" in the textbooks that filled the classrooms. He defiantly proclaimed, "we have nothing to be ashamed of, nothing to conceal; there is no spot or blemish upon our fair record, which we would seek to erase!"[45] Olmstead equated the defense of Wirz and the record at Andersonville with the entire Confederate cause. Stovall's address focused more on a comparison of Northern and Southern prisons and the causes of prisoner suffering.

Stovall praised Wirz for combating a difficult situation to the best of the commandant's ability. He called special attention to Wirz's handling of the Andersonville Raiders. Wirz revealed his "humanity" in allowing a court martial proceeding to take place, and Stovall highlighted the Raiders as examples of the "desperate men" who committed vicious acts against their comrades in arms. At one point in his speech, Stovall remarked, Wirz "commanded no kindergarten." Ultimately, Stovall believed "that the suffering among the men [at Andersonville] was largely brought about by a spirit of despondency, when they realized that their own government had deserted them, and would not authorize any exchange of prisoners." He repeated the familiar refrain that General Ulysses S. Grant doomed thousands of his own men "to the graveyard of Andersonville" because he feared that a wholesale prisoner exchange would replenish Confederate lines. Regarding the care of Confederate prisoners in Northern camps, Stovall did not want "to engage in a contest of crimination and recrimination." However, he argued that Southern men returned "home with fingers frozen off, suffering from blood poison, emaciated, invalid for life," after their release from such places as Elmira, Fort Delaware, and Rock Island.[46]

Following the conclusion of the speeches and the "singing of Southern anthems," the daughter of Henry Wirz pulled the bunting that unveiled the monument "as guns thundered a salute of honor." The 45-feet-tall monument was shaped in the form of an obelisk. On the base of the monument are four inscribed panels which tell the Wirz story in abbreviated form. The east side panel presents Wirz's biography and credits the Georgia Division of the UDC with the erection of the monument. The south side panel expresses the UDC's belief that Wirz faithfully discharged his duties and was "the victim of a misdirected popular clamor" intended to incriminate Jefferson Davis. The north side panel, a quote from the Confederate president, optimistically asserted that the South would be vindicated "when time shall have softened passion and prejudice, when reason shall have stripped the mask from misrepresentations, then justice, holding evenly her scales, will require much of the past censures and praise to change places." The west side panel bore General Grant's August 1864 justification for refusing to resume the prisoner exchange.[47] The Wirz monument represented a brazen attempt by Lost Cause enthusiasts to perpetuate the Southern version of the prison controversy near the site of one of the war's great tragedies.

Certainly the horrors of Andersonville, as well as other Confederate prisons, had circulated in the Northern press prior to the end of the war. Nevertheless, it was the arrest, trail, and execution of Captain Henry Wirz that defined Andersonville as the dominant narrative of the Union prisoner of war experience. The spirit of acrimony that fueled the politics of captivity animated the hearts and minds of those individuals who joined the effort to commemorate the war dead. The National Cemetery System afforded the North an advantage in honoring their prisoner of war dead and gave them control over the disposition of Confederate prisoner of war dead. Although some historians have written of an attitude of reconciliation that occurred between the sections and among some veterans, the state-led movement to erect monuments to the prisoner dead perpetuated some of the rancor inherent in the prison controversy. The monument movement also became a means for voicing patriotic messages extolling the Union Cause, as did Decoration Day, and African-Americans in particular turned to the novel Emancipation Day holiday as a way to celebrate individual freedom and racial pride, while honoring the war dead. To a large degree, Southerners responded to Northern memorialization by inventing their own holidays, such as Confederate Memorial Day, and by using such displays at the Wirz Monument dedication to advance a Lost Cause interpretation of the war and the prison controversy. These conflicting interpretive perspectives of Civil War prison history are still debated among modern historians and appear in a wide array of popular culture representations.

NOTES

1   Angela M. Zombek, "Libby Prison," and "Castle Thunder Prison," *Encyclopedia Virginia*, http://encyclopediavirginia.org/ (accessed June 10, 2014).

2   Gray, *The Business of Captivity*, 150–152.

3   Marvel, *Andersonville*, 248.

4   Nancy A. Roberts, "The Afterlife of Civil War Prisons and Their Dead," (Ph.D. diss., University of Oregon, 1996), 212–213.

5   John Neff, *Honoring the Civil War Dead: Commemoration and the Problem of Reconciliation* (Lawrence: University Press of Kansas, 2005), 6.

6   Edward Steere, *Shrines of the Honored Dead: A Study of the National Cemetery System*, (Washington D.C.: U.S. Army, Office of the Quartermaster General, 1954 [?]), 7–11.

7   Neff, *Honoring the Civil War Dead*, 134.

8   Stephen B. Oates, *A Woman of Valor: Clara Barton and the Civil War* (New York: The Free Press, 1994), 307–336.

9   Brief histories of national cemeteries can be found at the National Cemetery Administration website: www.cem.va.gov/cem/cems/listcem.asp (accessed June 10, 2014).

10   *New York Tribune*, February 14, 1866.

11   J.T. Trowbridge, *The South: A Tour of Its Battlefields and Ruined Cities, a Journey through the Desolated States, and Talks with the People* (Hartford, CT: L. Stebbins, 1866), 468–474.

12   Sidney Andrews, *The South Since the War: As Shown by Fourteen Weeks of Travel and Observation in Georgia and the Carolinas* (Boston: Ticknor and Fields, 1866), 102–107, 191–200, 301–317.

13   J. Matthew Gallman, Ed., *A Tour of Reconstruction: Travel Letters of 1875* (Lexington: University Press of Kentucky, 2011), 46, 87, 90–91.

14   David Blight, *Race and Reunion: The Civil War in American Memory* (Cambridge, MA: Harvard University Press, 2001), 68–71.

15   Ibid., 71.

16   Frank Moore, *Memorial Ceremonies at the Graves of Our Soldiers* (Washington D.C: Washington City, 1869), 327–333, 627, 678–682.

17   Roberts, "The Afterlife of Civil War Prisons," 178–179.

18   Gallman, *A Tour of Reconstruction*, 82.

19 *New York Tribune*, February 14, 1866.

20 Clara Merritt DeBoer, "Blacks and the American Missionary Association," www.ucc.org/about-us/hidden-histories/blacks-and-the-american.html (accessed February 15, 2011).

21 W. Fitzhugh Brundage, *The Southern Past: A Clash of Race and Memory* (Cambridge, MA: Harvard University Press, 2005), 62.

22 H.W. Pierson, *A Letter to Hon. Charles Sumner: With "Statements" of Outrages upon Freedmen in Georgia, and an Account of My Expulsion from Andersonville, Ga., by the Ku-Klux Klan* (Washington, D.C.: Chronicle Print, 1870), 23–28.

23 Cloyd, *Haunted by Atrocity*, 74–75.

24 Caroline E. Janney, *Burying the Dead but Not the Past: Ladies' Memorial Associations and the Lost Cause* (Chapel Hill: University of North Carolina Press, 2007), 9.

25 Confederated Southern Memorial Association, *History of the Confederated Memorial Associations of the South* (New Orleans, LA: Graham, 1904), 87–88.

26 Camilla A. Corlas Quinn, "Forgotten Soldiers: The Confederate Prisoners at Camp Butler, 1862–1863," *Illinois Historical Journal* 81 (Spring 1988): 35–36.

27 Roberts, "The Afterlife of Civil War Prisons," 117–121, 228, 249.

28 Gray, *The Business of Captivity*, 161–165.

29 Marcus Toney, "Our Dead at Elmira," *Southern Historical Society Papers* 29 (1901): 193–197.

30 Gray, *The Business of Captivity*, 161–165.

31 Neff, *Honoring the Civil War Dead*, 230–235.

32 Matthew J. Grow, "The Shadow of the Civil War: A Historiography of Civil War Memory," *American Nineteenth Century History* 4 (Summer 2003): 77–103.

33 *Report of the New Jersey Andersonville Monument Commissioners* (Somerville, NJ: The Unionist-Gazette Association, State Printers, 1899), 6–8.

34 Glenn Robins, "Race, Repatriation, and Galvanized Rebels: Union Prisoners and the Exchange Question in Deep South Prison Camps," *Civil War History* 53 (June 2007): 117–140.

35 Ibid.; John L. Ransom, *Andersonville Diary: Escape and List of Dead* (1881; reprint New York: P.S. Eriksson, 1963), 164.

36 John Cox Underwood, *Report of Proceedings Incidental to the Erection and Dedication of the Confederate Monument* (Chicago: W.M. Johnson Printing Company, 1896), 6–9; Neff, *Honoring the Civil War Dead*, 3, 201.

37 Cloyd, *Haunted by Atrocity*, 97–98.

38 *Report of the Maine Commissioners on the Monument Erected at Salisbury, N.C., 1908* (Waterville, ME: Sentinel Publishing Company, 1908), 3–6.

39 Waugh, *U.S. Grant*, 3.

40 Ibid., 6–7, 18–21.

41 Ibid., 21–24.

42 *Remarks of J. Bryan Grimes, Responding for the State of North Carolina, Upon the Occasion of the Dedication of the Maine Monument at Salisbury, N.C., May 8, 1908* (Raleigh: J.B. Grimes [?], 1908 [?]), 2–8.

43 *Americus Weekly Times-Recorder*, January 12, 1906, Wirz Monument Folder, Vertical Files, ANHS.

44 *Americus Weekly Times-Recorder*, May 13, 1909, Wirz Monument Folder, Vertical Files, ANHS.

45 Ibid.

46 Ibid.

47 Ibid.

CHAPTER 6

Civil War Prisons in History and Memory

HISTORIOGRAPHY OF THE PRISONS

The single most important, comprehensive, and accessible resource for researchers of the American Civil War is the collection of primary documents compiled, edited, and published by the War Department. This unique series of volumes, entitled *The Official Records of the War of the Rebellion*, is typically simply referred to as the *OR*. It required decades to amass, organize, transcribe, and print, but the result was well worth the trouble. While the *OR* does not include every piece of correspondence created during the war, it does have a remarkable coverage of the conflict, and is a vital source for any researcher examining the war. In 1864, Union Army Chief of Staff Henry W. Halleck began a systematic attempt to maintain as many of the letters, reports, orders, and personal accounts of the events of the war as possible. When Richmond fell to Union troops in early 1865, he extended the project to include as many Confederate documents as possible, beginning with those seized at the Confederate War Department. In 1877, Secretary of War George W. McCrary appointed Captain Robert N. Scott to head the Publications Office of the War Records Division. Scott's primary function was to conduct the final editorial process for publishing the *OR*; as a result, he is listed as the preparer in every volume of the work, even though he was aided by hundreds of clerks, typesetters, and printers. The result of this massive effort is a unique collection of records from both sides of the conflict, consolidated into a single unit.

The *OR* includes 127 serially-numbered books, released in 4 series as the consolidations of specific topics were completed. Series I covers the military operations of the war, grouped into 53 volumes, most containing more than 1 book. It includes the formal reports of field commanders for most battles, plus professional correspondence, orders, and adjutant returns of the Union and Confederate Armies. Each volume covers a geographic region for a set period of time, often on a state-by-state, yearly basis. Thus, all of the records pertaining to the Battle of Gettysburg, which occurred on July 1–3, 1863, can be found in Series I, Volume XXV, "Operations in Northern Virginia, West Virginia, Maryland, and Pennsylvania,

January 26–June 3." This particular volume is printed in two books, one containing all of the military reports, the other containing all of the supporting documentation. Publication of the first series required nearly two decades, with the first volume released in 1880 and the final volume not available until 1898—a testament to the sheer size of the task before the compilation team. Series II of the OR contains all of the correspondence, orders, reports, and returns for both the Union and the Confederacy relating to prisoners of war, including state and political prisoners. It is divided into eight volumes, published between 1894 and 1899. Series III and IV, published in 1899–1900, include documents that were not included in the earlier series, primarily because they were not discovered or forwarded in time to be included, or because they could not be easily classified as relating to a specific topic covered by an earlier volume.

One of the most attractive aspects of the OR is its sheer availability. Because it was produced by the War Department and has been reissued periodically by the Government Printing Office, most research libraries have a full set of the bound volumes. Further, the entire text of all four series is available online, thanks to Cornell University Library's *Making of America* project.[1] The online set can be computer-searched, making it possible to check for even the most obscure terms in moments, eliminating the tedious need to consult the index of every volume of interest. The electronic volumes can also be casually browsed in the same manner as paper copies, and the zoom function can reduce the eyestrain common to researchers used to reading the tiny font of the paper copies.

Survivors' accounts of prison life began to appear before the Civil War had even concluded. Some newspaper accounts served to alert the citizenry of the challenges faced by POWs languishing in captivity, with many allegedly penned by escaped prisoners. Their accounts included graphic descriptions of starving, diseased prisoners being deliberately abused by their captors, in both the North and the South. These accounts sometimes included a plea for rescue attempts, a call for donations of much-needed comfort items, or a demand for speedy exchanges with the enemy. They also occasionally include a call to arms to punish the enemy for their atrocious behavior. Few of these stories can be linked to specific prisoners; their very vagueness makes them suspect as reliable historical sources. In many ways, they tend to reflect the political leanings of the newspapers that printed them, more than a complete description of the camp system.[2]

In 1890, Asa B. Isham, Henry M. Davidson, and Henry B. Furness collaborated on the first substantial attempt to record the overall history of Civil War prisons. The OR volumes related to POWs had not been published, and thus much of their work was derived from POW survivors' accounts, newspaper articles, and the occasional military document. Their work, *Prisoners of War and Military Prisons*, is anything but unbiased, which is unsurprising given that each of the authors served in the Union Army. They castigated Confederate authorities for the terrible conditions in Southern prisons, and reprinted every tale of atrocities that could be found. They massively inflated casualty numbers for Northern POWs, claiming a 39 percent mortality rate for their former comrades. At the same time, they argued that Union camps were well administered and the POWs in them were amply supplied. According to their analysis, only 6 percent of Southern POWs died in Union hands.[3]

Despite its shortcomings, the work has a significant utility as a collection of prisoners' diaries and journals that offers a broad view of prison life in the Confederacy. While the authors' conclusions are suspect, the day-to-day perspectives resonate and offer a wide variety of POW experiences in a single volume.

In 1930, historian William Best Hesseltine published *Civil War Prisons: A Study in War Psychology*. This work systematically draws upon the *OR*, along with a multitude of first-person accounts to flesh out the official narrative. Hesseltine was far enough separated from the events he discussed that he was able to produce a remarkably balanced account that stood as the dominant work in the field for more than six decades, and still holds an important position in the historiography of the prisons. Unlike most of his predecessors, he believed that neither the Union nor the Confederacy deliberately mistreated prisoners. Rather, the horrors of the camps occurred because neither belligerent was prepared to maintain thousands of captives in massive prison compounds when the exchange system broke down. Both governments had their full attention on the propagation of the war—neither wished to spare precious manpower resources on the POW problem. Also, the warring groups each expected the paroles and exchanges to quickly resume, and thus saw no need to create a system that would only be used for a short time. By the time it became clear that the exchanges would not resume, the existing structure had been overwhelmed, and the few officials concerned with the problem scrambled to improvise solutions with mixed success. The Union had greater resources, and a much more robust logistical capability, thus Hesseltine found the Northern prisons to be far better built, while he considered the Southern prisons "the result of a series of accidents."[4]

The next author to tackle the problem of a comprehensive study of Civil War prisons was Lonnie B. Speer, whose *Portals to Hell* appeared in 1997. Speer combined extensive archival research with a close examination of the *OR* to produce a solid historical study, although the work has a decided tendency to portray POWs as victims of deliberately cruel practices. He places special emphasis upon the concept of retaliatory measures, which, while present in the war, did not dominate the experience of most POWs. Speer cross-checked the *OR* with original documents to create the best single-source compilation of POW numbers in each camp. This was done by consulting the returns of every major camp (and most of the minor ones) that have survived in archival collections and finding that the mortality rate in Northern and Southern prisons proved almost equal.[5] In many ways, Speer's book title summarizes his entire picture of the camp systems, and to a certain extent it makes sense, as the worst prisons on both sides accounted for most of the fatalities, and dominated the later discussions of the camps. On the other hand, many of the smaller camps, as well as those run by gifted administrators, demonstrated that not all of the camps included atrocities and deliberate mistreatment, which belies the notion of a nationwide policy of depravity. To Speer, the conditions of captivity that dominated the war were so bad that "to have been killed on the battlefield might have been humane."[6] It is doubtful that those POWs who survived captivity would agree.

Charles W. Sanders, Jr. published another comprehensive study, akin to Speer's, in 2005. His *While in the Hands of the Enemy* argues that the two governments deliberately mistreated their captives through a systematic attempt to render them unfit for further service. According to Sanders, previous historians have been guilty of whitewashing the "darkest chapter of that conflict," rather than rightfully assigning blame.[7] He believes that neglecting one's captives should be equated with deliberately harming them, despite all the evidence that both governments simply became overwhelmed by their wartime responsibilities. In his opinion, both President Abraham Lincoln and President Jefferson Davis were fully aware of the conditions within the camps, but neither was willing to resolve the problem. The supply of troops in the field took precedence over feeding captives, and the same held true for other necessary supplies.

The past two decades have seen a renaissance in scholarship dedicated to Civil War prisons. In particular, historians have turned to studies of individual prison locations. Most are well grounded in primary source materials located at the National Archives in Washington, D.C., the OR, and items specific to the prison being studied, often maintained in state and local archival collections. Interestingly, the old regional rivalries can still be detected, even 150 years after the war. Some partisans still attempt to prove that certain Union prisons rivaled the horrors of Andersonville, despite all evidence to the contrary. Another popular argument is that the mortality rates in Union prisons were due to deliberate policies of neglect and cruelty, while deaths in Southern camps should be blamed upon circumstances beyond the control of Confederate officials. Some authors dedicate their efforts to proving that the story of Andersonville has always been blown out of proportion, others that Andersonville was even worse than has been assumed. Thus, many of the controversies that dominated writings about Civil War prisons in the nineteenth century maintain a substantial influence today. It would be impossible to examine every example of individual prison studies, but there are a number that stand out as worthy of discussion.

In 1999, George Levy's To Die in Chicago made the case for Camp Douglas as the deadliest Union prison.[8] While more Confederates died at Douglas than in any other location, it was also one of the largest and longest-operating prisons in the North, and the percentage of prisoners who died there did not differ markedly from the average for Civil War prisons. Camp Douglas tended to receive massive shipments of POWs after the major surrenders in the Western Theater, and handled them relatively well until communicable diseases began to circulate within the camp. At that point, the camp's medical facilities proved inadequate to the task, and the death toll rapidly rose.[9] In 2000, Benton McAdams took issue with the term "Andersonville of the North" when applied to Rock Island, noting that it was popularized by Margaret Mitchell in Gone With the Wind, regardless of the inaccuracy of the sobriquet.[10] Instead, McAdams considered Rock Island a model prison, regardless of the 16 percent mortality rate, because it had access to fresh food and water, was secure, and had an efficient, stable commander in Colonel Adolphus J. Johnson.[11] Unlike most prisons, the facilities at Rock Island were purpose-built as a prison, giving it a substantial advantage in design over most camps.

The Northern prison that has been most closely compared with Andersonville is Elmira, the subject of an excellent 2001 study by Michael P. Gray. Elmira saw 24 percent of its inhabitants die in a single year of operation. Like Andersonville, it had an inadequate water supply that soon became contaminated, allowing a number of diseases to decimate the population.[12] Inadequate shelter, poor medical care, and an inept commander, Lieutenant Colonel Seth Eastman, exacerbated the problems. Not to be outdone, James R. Hall advanced the idea that Camp Morton, located near Indianapolis, might have been the worst Union prison. Hall tends to accept the claims of a former inhabitant without much scrutiny, particularly regarding allegations of deliberate cruelty on the part of the camp commandant, Colonel Ambrose Stevens.[13] As a result, Hall's work is a cautionary tale for the modern researcher—while the camps were not a pleasant place to spend the war, and their survivors rarely said kind words about the experience, there were certainly different levels of discomfort, even if the individual prisoners had little means of comparison.

In 2007, Roger Pickenpaugh published one of the best and most balanced studies of an individual Union prison. His examination of Camp Chase, Ohio, followed the complex history of the location, beginning with its construction as a training depot and following through its conversion to a prison camp. Unlike most POW camps, Chase had adequate shelter for its inhabitants, which no doubt helped to reduce the mortality rate.[14] Even more surprising, the buildings were replaced in 1864, using prisoner labor; one of the few Civil War examples of POWs being allowed to improve their own lot. Only a late outbreak of disease truly marred the reputation of the camp, although naturally its inhabitants complained about the food supply and rampant boredom, never realizing how lucky they were to have the luxury of such complaints.[15]

The prison camp that has generated far more discussion, and revulsion, than any other is Camp Sumter, more commonly referred to as Andersonville. It had by far the largest Union POW population, and accounted for approximately half of the total Union POW deaths despite being in operation for only a few months. The camp's commandant, Captain Henry Wirz, has been accused of attempting to kill as many of his captives as possible, with a number of survivor's accounts accusing him of openly murdering several POWs who had been recaptured after an escape. None of the sources has much detail to bolster the story: the murdered prisoners are always nameless, and the numbers involved vary. In all likelihood, the story was invented and expanded as it circulated through the POW population, until it became impossible to separate fact from fiction. Some accounts claim that Wirz bragged he was doing more to hurt the Union than any division of the Confederate Army, although little explanation is offered for why Wirz would share such a sentiment with the Union POWs. As the only Confederate official tried for wartime activities and executed for what are now termed "war crimes," Wirz has long been a symbol for the Civil War POW experience. Detractors argue that his depraved indifference and refusal to supply even the most basic necessities led to the death of thousands of prisoners, despite his prison's location in an area full of agricultural produce and readily available timber. Postwar supporters consider Wirz a scapegoat for the failure of Confederate logistics, and suggest he did the best he could for the men under his control, despite his extremely limited resources. The truth is no doubt somewhere in the middle, in that Andersonville's horrors definitely existed, but were probably not due to intentional mistreatment. Although Andersonville continues to dominate much of the scholarship dedicated to Southern prisons, there have also been a number of noteworthy studies of other Confederate prisons recently produced. Some are heavily influenced by a desire to demonstrate that Andersonville did not represent the only important location, and that others were run with more humane results. It is telling that few scholars have attempted to explain the other Confederate camps with extremely high mortality rates, such as Belle Isle or Danville, and have instead focused primarily upon less representative locations in the Western Theater.

In 1990, William O. Bryant published a study of Cahaba Prison, located near Montgomery, Alabama. The prison, an unfinished warehouse, opened in 1863, but sent its entire population to Andersonville less than a year later. When the infamous Georgia prison reached its highest population, and it became clear that a crisis was at hand, Cahaba reopened to handle some of the overflow. It soon held 5,000 officers and enlisted soldiers on less than half an acre. Despite the terrible overcrowding, the prison had a mortality rate below 5 percent.[16] Bryant's study also includes an extensive discussion of the worst river boat disaster in American history. More than 2,000 POWs freed from the prison crowded onto the decks of the *Sultana*, a steamboat rated for no more than 400 passengers. During the trip up the Mississippi River, one of the boilers exploded, destroying the boat and killing more than 1,600 victims.[17] Bryant's study does a remarkable job of recreating a prison that left few records behind, and demonstrating the urgency that most POWs felt to get home, regardless of the risks that such an urgency might create.

Naturally, much scholarship continues to examine Andersonville, especially to discuss why it was such a deadly location. The first modern study of Andersonville was published in 1968 by Ovid L. Futch. He created a solid account of daily life in the prison, without focusing too much attention on the worst tales from the camp. Unlike many Southern apologists, Futch refused to excuse the Confederate leadership of blame for the mortality rate. Although the Union refused to exchange prisoners, Futch believed the Confederates should have unilaterally paroled them rather than allowing them to die by the thousands.[18] In 1994, William Marvel published a broad overview of the prison. He somewhat excused Wirz's failures as the commandant, largely due to his low rank and inability to impress resources.[19] Interestingly, Marvel noted the presence of at least 70 African-American prisoners at Andersonville, whom Wirz refused to turn over to Confederate slavery officials. Marvel argued that these men had a substantially lower mortality rate than their white counterparts, probably because they were utilized on labor details and thus given extra rations, although subsequent historical study has shown the claim to be an error.[20]

In 2008, historian James M. Gillispie addressed the continual debate and accusations regarding Civil War POW camps. His *Andersonvilles of the North* argued that the political sensibilities of the immediate postwar era rendered any description of the camps suspect. Even the passage of decades did little to temper the sectional fervor, which was characterized by accusations, exaggerations, and absolute falsehoods. After demonstrating the extremes of the debate, Gillispie then supplied a micro-analysis of the Northern POW camps, broken into regions. He found that the vast majority of Confederate deaths in captivity, more than 80 percent, were due to communicable, untreatable diseases. Further, Confederate POWs actually had a lower mortality rate in Union prison hospitals than they did in facilities run by their own government. Thus, in Gillispie's view, ignorance of medical treatments, not Union malice, was to blame for the deadly results of the Union camps.[21]

Like Gillispie, Benjamin Cloyd believes that enough time has passed since the Civil War to permit an objective study of the camps. However, his interest is focused upon how the POW system has been retained in the public memory in the intervening decades. His *Haunted By Atrocity* demonstrates that most of the nineteenth-century discussions of Civil War prisons revolved around efforts to demonize the enemy, through accusations and exaggerations. "Waving the bloody shirt" proved a popular and successful ploy to rally political support around a candidate or an idea. This behavior began with the decision to prosecute Wirz for atrocities at Andersonville, an act Cloyd considers inextricably linked with the assassination of Abraham Lincoln.[22] The public's anger, coupled with the terrible accounts from Andersonville survivors, necessitated the prosecution, and sealed Wirz's fate before the first witness could speak. To Cloyd, the nation could not begin to reconcile until the primary actors died. The world wars allowed the United States to rally as a nation, and put the Civil War firmly in the past. By the 1960s, the war was truly American history, a fitting venue for tourism and memorabilia. Over time, Andersonville's meaning changed as well, as it became more than just the worst POW camp. The National POW Museum transformed the site into a center of hope and memorialization, rather than just the location of a terrible tragedy.

A number of studies investigating American POW operations over the course of the nation's history have placed special emphasis upon the American Civil War. Not only was the conflict the only case of Americans holding one another as POWs, it was also a watershed for future U.S. military operations. George G. Lewis and John Mewha's *History of Prisoner of War Utilization by the United States Army, 1776–1945* largely concentrates upon the POW labor camps of World War II. They see the Civil War POW population as an underutilized resource, a labor force that might have been best put to work for its own sustenance. Instead, the captives languished in their camps, contributing nothing and receiving little in return.[23] Richard Garrett's *P.O.W.* differed from most works specializing in Civil War POWs, in that it argued that neither side deliberately mistreated the enemy, although both sides neglected them.[24] Garrett's main focus is upon the POW camps of the Cold War, and thus he may not have looked deeply enough into the Civil War situation to have made an accurate assessment of the camps. Both Howard Levie and A.J. Barker wrote that Civil War POW operations had little influence over later U.S. behavior and that the only important ramification from the war regarding POWs was the development of the Lieber Code.[25] Such an attitude is unsurprising from Levie, a legal historian whose career largely focused upon the development and implementation of the Geneva Conventions. Barker, on the other hand, has no such excuse for dismissing one of the largest (and by far the deadliest) POW efforts in American history.

In a strange coincidence, three new books on POWs in the United States all appeared in 2010, each examining the breadth of American POW policy and practice. Paul J. Springer's *America's Captives* relied the most heavily upon archival research and focused primarily upon the development of American POW policy, with discussions of practices supplied primarily to determine how well the policies were carried into execution. He argued that the lack of forethought and planning in peacetime led to the poorly-improvised wartime solutions to extremely complex problems. The emphasis upon military expediency, coupled with an obsession for economic efficiency, created the conditions for enormous casualties even if the neglect was merely benign. When malicious individuals became involved in certain aspects of POW administration, deliberate atrocities rather than mistreatment due to circumstances became the norm.[26] Robert C. Doyle's *The Enemy in Our Hands* spends most of its time examining the experiences of captivity from the POW perspective. Thus, it is less about why the conditions existed, and more about how the POWs reacted to the situation. In Doyle's view, the Civil War prisons were not as bad as the survivors' accounts claim, with a few exceptions. He notes that Civil War POWs fared better than did individuals admitted to military hospitals. Doyle's Civil War chapter devotes surprisingly little space to military prisoners, as he spends substantial time discussing political prisoners and the imprisonment of Confederate officials after the war. In this regard, he examines important subjects but makes unfortunate decisions to conflate them with POWs.[27] A heavy emphasis upon the legal aspects of POWs, particularly in an international sense, dominates Stephanie Carvin's *Prisoners of America's Wars*. Like Levie and Barker, she considers the creation of the Lieber Code as the most important development from the war. To Carvin, the Lieber Code is more a set of guidelines defining the concept of warfare in terms of natural law than it is a specific set of orders. While she is correct that the Lieber Code's international legal significance was enormous, her tight focus leaves the rest of the POW narrative largely untold, as she devotes only a few pages to a brief summary of POWs in the Civil War. Carvin's primary goal is to examine the modern legal framework of POW operations, particularly in the War on Terror. While she recognizes the importance of history in shaping the modern system, she does not see a lot of influence in current affairs from the Civil War experience.[28]

There are still plenty of topics worthy of study regarding the history of Civil War prisons. One obvious area that is still being expanded is that of individual prison studies. The current literature has a number of first-rate examinations, which demonstrate the utility and feasibility of such studies, but there are dozens more camps that have not been given a full scholarly treatment. In particular, the prisons west of the Mississippi River have been largely ignored, despite being at the extreme end of the logistical lines. Of course, new diaries and journals may appear at any time, or be found in unpublished archival or private collections. While not every prisoner of war kept a diary worthy of modern publication, those offering a unique perspective are certainly worthy of consideration. A series of new interdisciplinary examinations of the archaeological record of various sites also shows tremendous potential, at least for camps that have not become overrun by urban areas. While a number of biographies have been produced about Wirz, few have been very scholarly, and there have been no books published that offer a biography of Hoffman. Finally, examinations looking at specific aspects of prison life, such as the medical treatment of prisoners for example, might enhance our understanding of the Civil War prison system as a whole.

VISUAL IMAGES OF CAPTIVITY

The Civil War prison controversy has not been limited to academic debates. Since the 1860s the issue has been a part of American (and Southern) popular culture and remains so to this day. Most of the photographic and artistic renditions of prisons and prisoners of war have focused on conveying the physical landscape of a prison building or stockade or on illustrating the suffering of captivity. The Andrew Riddle photos exemplify this visual tradition and constitute one of the most reproduced set of images of the Civil War prisoner of war experience. In mid-August 1864, a massive rain storm pummeled the Andersonville Prison and the resulting run-off of water washed away portions of the stockade wall. This same storm uncovered an underground spring that prisoners later christened Providence Spring. Curious about the unusual turn of events, photographer Andrew Riddle boarded a train in Macon, Georgia and headed to nearby Andersonville. Over the course of a sweltering August day, Riddle took portrait photos of General John Winder, the post commander, and Captain Henry Wirz, the commandant of the stockade. In addition, he took nine photos in and around the stockade and two photos in the cemetery.

The Andersonville prisoners certainly noticed Riddle, his assistant, and all of the commotion caused by his enterprise. Sergeant Robert Kellogg, 16th Connecticut Infantry, wrote sarcastically in his diary: "Some artists from Macon have been taking pictures of our misery from posts around the stockade. They will probably adorn the parlor of some chivalrous sons of the South." The prisoners had good reason to be upset. Andersonville was awash in death and suffering. The prison population exceeded 30,000, more than twice its designed capacity, and the average daily death toll for the month of August was 100. By August 1864, 6,000 men had already died at Andersonville since the opening of the prison in February of that same year. Given the deplorable conditions one wonders why the Confederates allowed Riddle to make a record of the dire circumstances in the camp. Most likely the vanity of Winder and Wirz—who were photographed before Riddle proceeded to the stockade—granted the photographer his entrée. From the breach in the stockade wall caused by the rain storm, Riddle shot four photos. He used the vantage point to capture suffering men "hunched over the prison latrine," the rows of dilapidated she-bangs and make-shift shelters, and the ominous deadline. He also climbed up to a guard tower and took a series of photos, several of which focused on Stockade Creek, where men bathed and "squatted promiscuously with their buttocks bared [over the latrine] for the camera." As the afternoon came to a close, Riddle documented the distribution of rations to the sergeants of the messes before moving to the cemetery. He aimed his camera at the graves of the first prison dead. Wooden stakes served as their headboards and only bore a number—no names or dates—which corresponded to a hospital registry that contained their actual identity. The burial detail had just filled Row 1, Section E of the cemetery and Riddle turned his attention to Row 2, an approximately 180 feet long, 7 feet wide, 2.5 feet deep, neatly squared trench. In the midst of the row, the burial detail and several of Riddle's hired hands posed with four corpses.[29] Before Andersonville closed in April 1865, 7,000 more Union soldiers were laid to rest in the cemetery. In many ways Andrew Riddle had harnessed the worst elements of the prisoner of war experience—sickness, measly rations, overcrowding, unsanitary conditions, and death—in a dozen enduring images taken during a hot summer day in southwest Georgia.

Riddle immediately attempted to cash-in on his work. He mounted prints of the photos on four-by-five-inch cards and sold them to the general public. He

Figure 6.1 A prisoner using the latrine at Andersonville. Photo courtesy of Andersonville
    National Historic Site.

ventured to New York after the war, putting the photographs on display with the
hope of selling more prints. Although Riddle never prospered financially from the
photos, his prints became a frequently sought after item by former prisoners.
Interestingly, Kellogg, who rebuked Riddle for his perceived greed and apathy, added
a set of prints to his extensive files on prisoner of war history and Ambrose C. Spencer
used a Riddle photo in his own memoir *A Narrative of Andersonville* (1866).
Reproduced countless times, the War Department obtained copies of the Riddle
photos in 1897 and sets have been donated to or acquired by the U.S. Army Military
History Institute, the State Library of Connecticut, and the University of Georgia.
The Riddle photos are the only surviving photos of Union prisoners held in an
operating Confederate prison.[30]

In contrast to the stark realities depicted in the Riddle photos, Winslow Homer,
one of the war's most original painters, created two pieces, *Prisoners from the Front*
(1866) and *Near Andersonville* (1866) that departed from the prisoner of war visual
norm. Homer was a native of Massachusetts and imbibed the abolitionist atmosphere
of Boston and Cambridge. He honed his artistic skills as an illustrator for news weeklies
and began a successful career as an illustrator for *Harper's Weekly* in 1857. Homer
accompanied General George McClellan's army during the Peninsula Campaign
(March–July 1862) observing the siege at Yorktown and witnessing the Battle of
Seven Pines. He likely spent time near Petersburg during the summer of 1864. In
each of these instances, Homer encountered the carnage and death of war as well as
the large number of war contrabands; the fugitive slaves who sought refuge in the
Union army camps. These personal experiences clearly inspired Homer's artistic

development and his understanding of the war, which can be seen in both *Prisoners from the Front* and *Near Andersonville*.

Homer appears to depict an actual historical scene in *Prisoners from the Front*. The foreground of the painting features three Confederate captives, flanked by a Union guard and officer, while the background conveys a battlefield. Scholars have determined that the Union officer was undoubtedly General Francis Channing Barlow, who enjoyed a public reputation of dignity, gallantry, and patriotism. The painting "celebrates Barlow's heroic capture of several thousand southern troops at Spotsylvania, Virginia" in May 1864. The three Confederates, of various ranks, represent the strata of Southern society and by extension the Confederate army. The central figure among the Rebel prisoners has the dress and physical appearance of a well-to-do Virginian or South Carolinian. An elderly man in haggard attire and resigned expression stands next to the Southern aristocrat, and the third figure, a youthful, "uncouth," "corn-cracker" type looks on defiantly.[31] To many observers, Homer's *Prisoners from the Front* invokes "a pictorial synopsis of the war" by presenting a contrast of character between the victor and the defeated. Barlow's personal virtue typified the American ideal, and the Union's success at Spotsylvania ensured the perpetuity of the nation and the destruction of slavery. Given the way the prisoner of war issue affected the North during the war and continued to divide the sections after the war, Homer's rather benign portrayal of a capture event warrants further reflection. Is Homer implying that the Union soldiers treated Confederate prisoners fairly and respectfully in order to refute allegations of mistreatment? Does he suggest a Southern inferiority that might excuse the harsh conditions in some Northern camps? Or is Homer merely adding to the adoration of General Barlow? Whatever the answers to these questions, Homer's unprecedented use of the contentious prisoner of war issue to celebrate the superiority of the Union cause gives credence to the uniqueness of his Civil War art. Likewise, his painting *Near Andersonville* departs from the conventions of Civil War art.[32]

Scholars have only just begun to study the meaning and symbolism of Homer's *Near Andersonville* because the painting was mistakenly stored in an attic for nearly a century after its original owner, Sarah Kellogg, passed away shortly after she acquired the painting in 1866. In *Near Andersonville*, Homer presented the Civil War as a three-sided conflict between white Southerners, white Northerners, and African-Americans. His placement of an African-American female in the foreground and his relegation of Union prisoners and their Confederate guards to the background makes it a truly remarkable, even revolutionary, reflection on slavery and war in southwest Georgia. Peter Wood, an acclaimed historian of the Colonial South and race relations in America, has long been an admirer of Homer and provides a provocative interpretation of the painting in his book *Near Andersonville: Winslow Homer's Civil War*. Wood notes, in particular, the building in *Near Andersonville*, which is not a slave cabin but could be a small house or plantation outbuilding. The structure's "ambiguity" might suggest the impending end of slavery. The African-American woman emerges from the dark shadows of the building and stands in a doorway to contemplate the fate of the captured liberators, which Wood suggests were the men from Stoneman's failed raid. In July 1864, General George Stoneman, in a prelude to General William Sherman's "March to the Sea," attempted to liberate the Union officer prison camp at Macon, Georgia. Stoneman's noble intentions turned disastrous. His raiding party suffered numerous casualties and 600 of his men became prisoners of war. Most of them were sent to Andersonville. Wood points to specific objects in the painting and produces allegorical interpretations, some of which are of a highly speculative nature. For example, Wood identifies the planks that lay at the doorway, heading in opposite directions, as representative of the respective political planks or platforms of the Republican and Democratic parties during the 1864 presidential election. According to Wood, the Republicans pledged to fight for victory and freedom while the Democrats offered peace and the maintenance of slavery. Similarly, Wood speculates on the meaning of the woman's attire, particularly the red, white, and blue headpiece. Unlike "the black-mammy bandana of popular cartoons," Homer's heroine wears a bandana that "hints at what is known as the Phrygian freedom cap," which manumitted slaves wore in ancient Rome "to imply liberty." Wood also comments on her "Garibaldi blouse," invoking and drawing comparisons to the Italian freedom fighter Giuseppe Garibaldi.[33] Some of Wood's emancipationist allegories, particularly the political planks and Garibaldi blouse reference, have elicited criticisms for distracting observers from the simple force and power of the painting.[34] Homer's black heroine obviously stands on a threshold, "both literally and figuratively," as she faces "a transition between two very different worlds," one slave, one free.[35] This painting combines the Civil War's most infamous prison with the war's emancipationist legacy in a way that few artists ever considered.

LIBBY PRISON MUSEUM

The most unusual popular culture manifestation of the Civil War prisoner of war story transpired at Libby Prison Museum. In 1888, W.H. Gray recruited a group of Chicago investors that included Josiah Cratty, Charles K. Miller, and John A. Crawford for the purpose of purchasing the old tobacco warehouse prison and moving it to Chicago. Gray's group needed $200,000 to purchase the building, demolish it, and transport it to Chicago. Work began in April 1889. The initial plan was "to reconstruct the warehouse in Chicago; enclose it in another, glass-roofed building; surround it with a panoramic view of the James River, and fill it with war relics and images of the Monitor-Merrimac battle." News of the proposed museum sparked an intense backlash. Opponents hoped Richmond, Virginia Mayor W.C. Carrington would block the sale and shipment of the warehouse. One ex-Libby prisoner informed the mayor:

> It might serve to collect dimes and dollars as a ghastly circus exhibition to fill the pockets of sharp, unprincipled speculators—men that have conceived the selfish and despicable idea of violating the sanctity of the soldiers' sufferings and to many the very spot of their deaths.

Northerners and Southerners alike objected to the scheme because they felt the museum would awaken the spirit of animosity over the prisoner of war issue and threaten sectional reconciliation. Throughout the public discussion, the project's sponsors maintained that their intent was simply to make a profit, not inflame regional passions.[36]

Despite the opposition, the museum opened on September 20, 1889. Charles Gunther, the entrepreneurial confectioner and collector, served as president of the Libby Prison War Association, which represented the interests of the museum's stakeholders. Approximately 300 guests attended the grand opening, including members of the Grand Army of the Republic and 10 former Libby prisoners. The investors had settled on a less expensive but still impressive concept for the museum. A stone wall was all that enclosed the converted warehouse, but the museum displayed thousands of relics such as swords, guns, cartridge boxes, flags, photographs of battlefields, life-size oil paintings of Union and Confederate generals, various artillery pieces, and the Appomattox table at which Robert E. Lee accepted Ulysses S. Grant's terms of surrender. In some ways, the museum seemed more of a national Civil War museum than a prisoner of war museum. But, of course, the Libby Prison story was told. An individual exhibit marked the entrance to the tunnel that 109 prisoners had used as an escape route in February 1864. Former prisoners "could purchase a plaque to mark the place where they (or a comrade) slept during their imprisonment." The museum sold 400 plaques. More than simply displaying war relics, the museum also promoted a type of living history. The spacious building hosted veteran reunions and former prisoners frequently appeared at the museum and interacted with patrons. During the first full year of operation, the museum drew an estimated 200,000 visitors; 900 ex-prisoners attended that first year.[37]

The peak year for the museum occurred in 1893 when Chicago hosted the World's Columbian Exposition, which drew approximately 25 million people to the city. As intended, the proprietors earned a substantial profit on their investment. Aside from entrance fees, the museum's souvenir shop hawked such items as Libby Prison brand cigars, military medals, Confederate money, photographs, books, plates, flags, jewelry, flooring from the prison, and gavels made of Libby wood. Despite the profitability of the museum, the investors developed other interests and closed the doors to the public in 1899. The building was demolished and replaced with the new 15,000-seat Chicago Coliseum stadium. Many of the artifacts eventually found their way to the Chicago Historical Society and can still be viewed today. Although the Libby Prison was relatively short-lived, the venture was important for marking a milestone in the intersection of popular culture and the commercialization of the Civil War.[38]

ANDERSONVILLE AND THE PULITZER PRIZE

The eventual passing of the Civil War generation quieted momentarily the prison controversy, but the horrific events of World War II, particularly the Holocaust, compelled historians and novelists to reconsider the Civil War prisons story. Few works garnered more attention than MacKinley Kantor's novel, *Andersonville*, which he published in 1955. Already well-known for *Long Remember*, a novel about the battle of Gettysburg, Kantor spent 25 years researching and writing *Andersonville*. During that time, he visited the Nazi concentration camp at Buchenwald and later spent time at the infamous Confederate prison in 1953. Kantor filled his novel with scores of characters, some fictitious and others actual historical figures such as Henry Wirz, former prisoners and memoirists John Ransom and John McElroy, and William Collins, one of the notorious Raiders. The prison, however, served as Kantor's protagonist. In describing the novel, historian Henry Steele Commanger wrote: "There is neither hero or villain here, nor narrative nor plot in the ordinary sense, but the prison embraces them all, submerges them all in a common humanity or inhumanity."[39] Kantor's *Andersonville* won the Pulitzer Prize.

For historians such as Benjamin Cloyd, the significance of Kantor's novel transcends its popular appeal and its literary success. Cloyd's *Haunted By Atrocity* represents the most sophisticated study of Civil War prisons in American memory to date. He shows how the memory of Andersonville and Confederate prisons intersected with Reconstruction politics, particularly the tactic of "waving the bloody shirt," and how veteran organizations like the Grand Army of the Republic sustained sectional antagonisms for at least a generation after the Civil War concluded. The philosophical impact of World War I and World War II ushered in a new understanding of Civil War prisons, according to Cloyd. His chapter, "Objectivity in the Shadow of Twentieth-Century War," argues that the seemingly senseless and pointless slaughter of World War I, and the brutality of the Nazi concentration camps and Japanese internment camps of World War II led to a realization that "places like Andersonville or Elmira were not isolated examples of unparalleled human cruelty." In Cloyd's estimation, books such as William Hesseltine's *Civil War Prisons: A Subject in War Psychology* and Kantor's *Andersonville* as well as Saul Levitt's play *The Andersonville Trial* promoted:

> Saul Levitt's *The Andersonville Trial* was first presented in New York City on December 29, 1959. Levitt incorporated original trial testimony from former prisoners into the play but the scenes of Henry Wirz testifying on his own behalf were not part of the actual trial.

the belief that modern war inevitably brought a devastation for which no one was really to blame . . . [and] allowed Americans to continue to avoid the daunting task of honestly and more accurately assessing the responsibility for the tragedy of Civil War prisons.[40]

THE NATIONAL PRISONER OF WAR MUSEUM

Kantor's novel intensified interest in Andersonville as well as Civil War prisons much more so than the observance of the Civil War centennial. The resulting increase in visitation to Andersonville coupled with the on-going demands of an active national cemetery motivated the U.S. Army to rid itself of the cemetery and the prison site, which it had administered for more than 100 years and for 60 years respectively. In addition, the burdens of the Vietnam War gave the army the perfect opportunity to make the change. There was precedent too. The first five Civil War military parks, Gettysburg, Antietam, Shiloh, Vicksburg, and Chickamauga, were transferred from the Department of the Army to the National Park Service (NPS) in 1933. When President Lyndon Johnson looked to Senator Richard Russell of Georgia in the late 1960s for help in doing "something"

> The number of Americans held as prisoners of war during the twentieth century breaks down as follows: WWI (4,120), WWII (130,201), Korea (7,140), Vietnam (771), Persian Gulf (23).

that might one day benefit American prisoners of the Vietnam War, and when local and state politicians in Georgia as well as business leaders recognized the potential economic impact that historical tourism could have on the state and individual communities, the transfer became a fait accompli. In 1971, the U.S. Congress passed enabling legislation that created the Andersonville National Historic Site (ANHS) as a component of the National Park Service. The legislation required the NPS to interpret and commemorate the experiences of all American prisoners of war throughout the nation's history, not just those held at Camp Sumter during the Civil War.

Thus, the NPS received an opportunity to influence the public understanding of both Andersonville and the prisoner of war story more generally, but the new mandate occurred within the context of a century-long battle over the site's historical identity, and somewhat predictably generated yet another controversy.[41]

Although Georgia's political and business leaders presented a united front, the United Daughters of the Confederacy called on Georgia's congressional delegation to block federal funding for the measure until there were guarantees that the Southern view of the prison controversy would be part of the NPS' interpretive plan. "We want equal treatment in the allocation of federal funds, the right to place monuments and markers giving the Southern position leading up to the war," announced Evelyn Madry, the treasurer of the Georgia UDC, "and to include in any historical speeches or recordings . . . the South's side of the historical background of the war." Moreover, the UDC suggested that "federal propaganda" had created a false understanding of living conditions and death rates at Andersonville when, in fact, the North's blockade of Southern ports and its refusal to exchange prisoners led to the unfortunate circumstances of the past.[42] To allay the UDC's concerns, U.S. Representative Jack Brinkley, of Georgia's Third Congressional District, publicly assured Southerners that they would be able to place monuments at the national historic site, and promised that he was "personally interested in preserving and protecting our Southern heritage at every opportunity."[43] Ultimately, the proponents of the transfer insisted that the intent was not to blame the South for Union prisoner deaths, but to memorialize all American prisoners of war.

To address its enabling legislation mandate, the ANHS set aside two existing buildings as museums. The Carriage House, the previous residence of the site's caretaker, covered the history of POWs from modern wars and the former cemetery chapel was devoted to Civil War prisoner history. Not until 1984 did the NPS, ANHS, and American Ex-prisoners of War (AXPOW) form a partnership for the purpose of building the National Prisoner of War Museum at Andersonville. The U.S. Congress and the state of Georgia appropriated funding and local governments, and private organizations contributed in numerous ways to the initial efforts. After a decade of minimal progress, former Vietnam POW Pete Peterson introduced a bill in the U.S. House of Representatives that ultimately authorized the Secretary of the Treasury to mint a Prisoner of War Commemorative Coin. The coins sold for thirty dollars each, with ten dollars of the total price going to fund the construction of the POW museum. The Treasury Department sold nearly 300,000 coins. Construction on the museum finally began in the summer of 1996.[44]

"Under a cloudless sky," the National Prisoner of War Museum was formally dedicated on April 9, 1998 before more than 2,000 former prisoners of war, many of whom were accompanied by family and friends. For the Civil War enthusiast, the dedication date of April 9 seemed to have an obvious connotation, Robert E. Lee's surrender to U.S. Grant at Appomattox. However, the official dedication literature highlighted the museum's dedication date as the 56th anniversary of the Bataan Death March. President Bill Clinton, although not in attendance, forwarded prepared remarks for the occasion. The day's keynote speaker, senator and former Vietnam POW John McCain, spoke of the "hallowed ground where 13,000 Americans gave their lives so that they might save a nation." He linked the prisoners of Andersonville to the Bataan Death March survivors at Camp O'Donnell in the Philippines, to the men held in the "desolate" camps in North Korea. These men, McCain remarked, "had been deprived of their liberty" by enemies who "attempted to commit them to the animal caste." They endured "terrible suffering," "may have lost their faith for a time," lived on "meager rations," resisted the "daily regimen of brainwashing," and silently memorized "the ever lengthening roll call of the dead, so that families may one day know the fate of their loved ones." To McCain, the legacy of the American prisoner of war was that throughout their collective ordeals they not only survived the horrors of captivity but they remained loyal to "a cause greater than their self-interest."[45] The dedication of the National Prisoner of War Museum represented a critical juncture in elevating public awareness about the history of America's prisoners of war.

Inside the 10,000 square-foot museum are nine themed exhibit areas covering POW history from the American Revolution to Operation Iraqi Freedom. The themes of the captivity experience are: the formal definition of a POW; capture; journey; living conditions; news and communication; those who wait (POW/MIA families); privation; morale; and freedom. A corridor in the museum, roughly the size of three exhibit areas, holds temporary displays and serves as the de facto exhibit space for Civil War prisons and prisoners. Visitors see in the very first exhibit area—the definition of a POW—examples that illustrate the racial and gender changes in the American military over time and that the American prisoner of war story is not limited to the intrepid deeds of white males.

On September 20, 2013, a Female POW Commemorative Plaque was dedicated at the National Prisoner of War Museum. Among those in attendance was Iraq War POW Shoshana Johnson. U.S. Army Specialist Johnson was the first black woman and Hispanic female to be held as an American prisoner of war.

The museum utilizes a multitude of artifacts such as rations, coffee cubes, Red Cross packages, eating utensils, toiletries, footwear, and clothing, from various conflicts, and an audio-visual interactive orients these items to a specific war. In addition such artifacts as sheet music, smoking paraphernalia, dominoes, and baseball gear demonstrate the ways that prisoners occupied their time. Radios and camp newspapers convey the resilience and ingenuity of many POWs. Video monitors play capture narratives from former prisoners. The dismay in their faces and voices as they tell their individual stories force the viewer to confront the life and death struggle most POWs faced. These soldiers also had to grapple with the sense of failure that often accompanied capture. Spatially, the "those who wait" gallery is the largest exhibit area in the museum. It is also the most inviting with a number of easily accessible benches available for an extended period of observation. Aside from photographs and text displays, a series of video monitors plays interviews with wives and children of former prisoners. They recount the missed birthdays, anniversaries, Christmases, and other holidays as well as one-of-a-kind events such as births, first steps, graduations, and weddings. The release of a loved one produced feelings of relief and joy for POW families; however, new concerns followed as they wondered and worried how the captivity experience changed their husband/wife or father/mother. The privation exhibit contains replicas of the urban prison cells of North Vietnam as well as bamboo "tiger cages," which were used by Asian captors of various wars. Each cell highlights the confined living space and isolation many POWs endured. Hand-cuffs, common to all conflicts, and ball and chain signifying the Civil War era remind visitors of the spartan conditions that characterized prison life. Noticeably absent from the museum as a whole is a discussion of the disease, squalor, and death rates that plagued many prison facilities and led to hundreds of thousands of deaths for American military personnel.[46]

The ANHS attracts an impressive number and variety of visitors. Only once since 1972 has the site's visitation been fewer than 100,000 people. Between 1972 and 2012, the yearly total has exceeded 150,000 visitors 19 times.[47]

During the Civil War sesquicentennial, National Geographic listed Andersonville as a top 10 U.S. Civil War site, and CNN named it one of 12 fascinating Civil War sites in a story on travel and leisure.[48] Andersonville, however, is not simply a Civil War site. Indeed, the Andersonville National Historic Site consists of three distinct but inter-related components: the Camp Sumter prison site, the National Prisoner of War Museum, and the Andersonville National Cemetery. The cemetery remains an active national cemetery open to qualified veterans, their spouses, and their dependents. The Andersonville National Cemetery now averages close to 200 burials per year and by the time it reaches maximum capacity the number of non-Civil War burials will surpass the number of Civil war burials. The museum—whose interpretive theme is the price of freedom—places the story of the American prisoner of war within the broader context of how wars have shaped the nation's history. This reorientation has helped transform the infamous prison site into a patriotic arena that celebrates duty and self-sacrifice.

The Turner Network Television (TNT) miniseries *Andersonville* was released in 1996 and increased interest in the infamous prison. A large portion of the miniseries focuses on the story of the prison gang known as the Raiders.

THE POW LEGACY

The American POW has not always been viewed as a hero. During the Civil War, Northern military and civilian leaders believed that some men voluntarily surrendered in order to avoid combat, and the shameful stigma of betrayal followed the Galvanized Rebels and Galvanized Yankees long after the war ended. For most of the twentieth century, American men and women captured while serving their country during a time of war also battled the perception of failure. No group of American prisoners of war has been more neglected or more maligned than those held during the Korean War. The Department of Defense, concerned that POWs had been brainwashed during indoctrination sessions and alarmed by the roughly 40 percent of servicemen who died in captivity in Korea, appointed an 11-man commission that produced the military Code of Conduct. The Code was first tested during the Vietnam War.

As the Vietnam War came to an end, many Americans, in response to what they considered a tragic military defeat, turned to the prisoner of war as a symbol of bravery and honor. In 1979, the first POW/MIA Recognition Day was observed to celebrate the sacrifices of former POWs and to remember those still missing in action. Beginning in 1986, the third Friday in September has been set aside, by presidential proclamation, as POW/MIA Recognition Day. In addition, the U.S. Congress authorized and President Ronald Reagan signed into law on November 8, 1985 the creation of the Prisoner of War Medal, which could be awarded to anyone held as a prisoner of war after April 5, 1917—the day before America's entrance into WWI. The outpouring of public interest in the stories of Michael Durant and Jessica Lynch testifies to the transformation of the image of the American POW.

THE LEGACY OF THE LIEBER CODE

The importance of the Lieber Code in later international laws regarding the treatment of POWs cannot be overstated. The rise of modern, industrialized warfare promised to create enormous national armies possessing far deadlier weaponry than what had been available only a few years before. What some individuals quickly grasped was that in such wars, the only sure way to eliminate a large enemy force was to compel its complete surrender, as the far longer engagement range of rifled firearms made the complete encirclement and annihilation of it much less likely. Even if such a maneuver could be achieved, the surrounded force would inflict a prohibitively high number of casualties upon the attacker. The aggressor would be forced to fight in the open, while the defender had the advantage of firing from cover, and given only a short time to prepare, from entrenched positions. By the time the Lieber Code had been issued, Civil War troops had mastered the art of quick field fortifications, and could be counted upon to begin entrenchments at almost any opportunity. This made being on the tactical defensive a far stronger position, although it also squandered the initiative to the enemy. Only if a position could be completely cut off would it be guaranteed to fall, and even then, the commander might not be induced to surrender if he was not certain his men would receive acceptable treatment. General Orders No. 100 promised a minimum standard for the maintenance of prisoners, and thus in its own way, not only did it protect POWs, it made their capture far more likely. It injected a certain degree of humane behavior into the brutal undertaking of war.

Other agreements, pronouncements, and organizations of the era also tried to mitigate the worst aspects of conflict. Agents of the U.S. Sanitary Commission ranged through the Civil War battlefields, offering medical care to wounded troops and captives. In 1864, representatives from 16 nations met at Geneva to discuss ways to ameliorate the suffering of soldiers on modern battlefields. Representatives of 10 states signed the Geneva Convention of 1864, a document that directly led to the creation of the International Committee of the Red Cross (ICRC). National subsidiaries were quickly formed in nearly every European nation, and the idea spread throughout the world. In 1881, the American Red Cross was founded, primarily through the efforts of Clara Barton, who had witnessed the horrors of Civil War battlefields first-hand. The ICRC leadership was aware of the Lieber Code, but believed that it did not do enough to protect the wounded on the battlefield, despite the provisions that enemy medical personnel should not be regarded as POWs and that wounded enemies should be medically treated.

The obvious utility of the Lieber Code was not lost upon the ICRC and other international negotiators, but it still required decades before a multilateral convention declaring the rules of civilized warfare could be completed. In 1874, delegates from 15 nations met at Brussels, Belgium, with the intention of crafting an international treaty codifying the laws of war. The assembled diplomats used the Lieber Code as the basis for the Brussels Declaration. Unfortunately, most nations either did not sign the convention or did not ratify it, and thus it is considered a failure. However, it served as the point of departure for later attempts, including the creation of the *Oxford Manual of the Laws and Customs of War* in 1880, the Hague Conventions of 1899 and 1907, and the Geneva Conventions of 1929 and 1949. Ironically, despite supplying the underlying document, the American negotiators argued that the Brussels Declaration would potentially violate U.S. neutrality and sovereignty, and refused to sign the finished product. This position reflected a renewed isolationism in the American government, which refused to even sign the Geneva Convention of 1864 until 1882. The work of Barton and other humanitarian activists, coupled with a new push to provide pensions to disabled veterans, including former POWs, finally pushed President Chester A. Arthur to authorize its signature.

American isolationism did not completely abate until well into the twentieth century, although it began to relax with the expansionist moves of the 1890s. When the United States declared war upon Spain in 1898, General Orders No. 100 remained in force, and provided a domestic guide for American behavior regardless of international standards. American commanders cited the decades-old orders when determining the proper treatment of captured Spanish troops, who by all accounts were well maintained and quickly repatriated to Spain. In the peace treaty to end the war, the United States purchased the Philippines, where an insurrection against the Spanish colonial government soon turned against the newly-arrived Americans. Once again, General Orders No. 100 was relied upon to determine the acceptable limits of American military activities, and also to justify harsh, punitive acts against native rebels who employed unconventional tactics. General Jacob H. Smith, brought up on war crimes charges for his brutal policies on the Island of Samar, cited aspects of General Orders No. 100 regarding illegal combatants and retaliatory measures. He argued that the Lieber Code only applied to civilized populations who followed its provisions, and hence the participation of partisans, guerrillas, and assassins in the Philippines, especially in areas under military occupation, justified the nastiest retaliatory responses. His defense was only partially successful—while he was not convicted of war crimes, he was still found guilty of conduct prejudicial to good order and military discipline and forced to retire.

While the United States fought to quell the Filipino guerrilla movement, Tsar Nicholas II of Russia called for a new international conference to meet at The Hague in 1899. Diplomats met at The Hague in 1899 and 1907 to craft what they expected to be a global understanding of the laws of war. The Hague Conference had three primary objectives. First, its representatives hoped to codify the laws of war between civilized nations, once again relying upon the Lieber Code as a starting position. Second, the Conference sought to create a global judicial oversight system through the formation of a World Court. This neutral body would exist to consider international disputes, in the hope of preventing their escalation into wars. Third, the signatories hoped to provoke a major arms reduction movement, on the assumption that smaller and less well-equipped military forces would reduce the probability of future wars. The United States sent a delegation to The Hague under Andrew D. White.

The provisions of their finished documents included a substantial portion of the Lieber Code, either copied directly or in paraphrased form. Unfortunately, these agreements contained a fatal flaw, in that they required all parties of a conflict to be signatories before their provisions could be considered in effect. The negotiators had not envisioned an all-encompassing conflict such as World War I, and thus they hoped to ensure that no party of a war would be held to a higher standard than its opponents. When World War I erupted, all of the major belligerents had signed and ratified the Hague Conventions, but the relatively minor participants Serbia and Montenegro had not. As a result of their reticence, the Conventions were not legally binding, and nations were free to mistreat their prisoners if they wished to do so. Thankfully, relatively good treatment of POWs was the norm for the war, and to prevent unnecessary retaliatory blunders, the enemies agreed to allow camp inspections by a neutral "Protecting Power." For the first three years of fighting, both the United States and Switzerland provided oversight, until the United States joined the war, at which time the Swiss assumed full responsibility. Switzerland, which houses the headquarters of the ICRC, continues to offer neutral inspections of POW camps, as does the ICRC itself.

Although most of the participants in World War I essentially followed the Hague Convention of 1907's provisions regarding POWs, the technicalities used by some powers to officially ignore it illustrated one of its fundamental flaws. Other weaknesses included an insufficient explanation of the types of labor that prisoners might be expected to perform, and how their labor should be compensated, if at all. The differences between officers, noncommissioned officers, and enlisted personnel required further discussion. Also, an unclear explanation of how much food and other supplies had to be provided, and which classes of personnel should be immune from capture, caused their share of difficulties in interpretation. In 1924, the ICRC began a call for another meeting to iron out the remaining problems, eventually prompting a meeting at Geneva in the summer of 1929. The Geneva Conventions sought to build upon the Hague agreements, retaining their core but expanding upon them. Once more, Lieber's 1863 document served as the foundation with surprisingly few modifications in substance, despite the passage of more than six decades. The new conventions did not achieve full agreement of all the nations that joined World War II, but specified that their provisions applied to signatory nations at war regardless of the participation by other belligerents. Thus, even though Japan refused to sign, and the Soviet Union did so only with specific reservations that effectively nullified the agreement, virtually all of the major powers joined the system.

The vast majority of nations might have signed the Geneva Conventions, but that does not mean they were followed in World War II. On the European Eastern Front, the conflict was considered one of national survival. Millions of prisoners fell into the German and Soviet hands, and few returned home at the end of the war. The bulk of POWs on each side were sent to industrial slave camps and worked to death, with no sanction against summary executions. In contrast, American, British, and French troops captured by the Germans were treated relatively well, and for all intents within the provisions of the Geneva Conventions. The primary exceptions were troops captured by the much-feared Waffen-SS, fanatical troops who executed groups of prisoners on a number of occasions. They, in turn, received little quarter from advancing allied forces, who soon learned to spot them by their uniforms and, when necessary, by checking them for a tattoo of their blood type, found in their armpits.

Naturally, World War II exposed some problems with the existing system, and the Geneva Conventions were revisited in 1949. Further protocols have been subsequently attached, in 1977 and 2005. In each iteration, though, the Lieber Code remains starkly evident, with most of the changes related not to the theoretical conception of warfare that Lieber espoused, but rather to the practices of handling POWs on a day-to-day basis. The adjustments have tended to focus upon maintenance and an expansion of the specificity of the conventions. In the United States, General Orders No. 100 still have substantial reverberations in the nation's doctrine and field manuals, particularly where the treatment of enemy prisoners are concerned. The continuing influence of the Lieber Code is a testament to how well the original document served as a tool to guide commanders in the field.

NOTES

1   The online version is machine-searchable and allows printing. It can be found at http://ebooks.library.cornell.edu/m/moawar/waro.html (accessed June 10, 2014).

2   An excellent example is John J. Geer, *Beyond the Lines; Or, A Yankee Prisoner Loose in Dixie* (Philadelphia: J.W. Daughaday, 1864), with prominent accusations of mistreatment on pages 64–65, 81–84, 210–211, and 250–251. Interesting but not always factually accurate accounts of this type include John McElroy, *This Was Andersonville* (Washington, D.C.: National Tribune, 1879); Alonzo Cooper, *In and Out of Rebel Prisons* (Oswego, NY: R.J. Oliphant,

1888); and Charles Hopkins, *The Andersonville Diary of Charles Hopkins* (Kearny, NJ: Belle Grove Publishing Company, 1988, first published 1890).

3   Asa B. Isham, Henry M. Davidson, and Henry B. Furness, *Prisoners of War and Military Prisons* (Cincinnati, OH: Lyman & Cushing, 1890), 475–476.

4   William B. Hesseltine, *Civil War Prisons: A Study in War Psychology* (Columbus: Ohio State University Press, 1930), ix.

5   Lonnie B. Speer, *Portals to Hell: Military Prisons of the Civil War* (Mechanicsburg, PA: Stackpole Books, 1997), xviii–xix.

6   Ibid., xix.

7   Charles W. Sanders, Jr., *While in the Hands of the Enemy* (Baton Rouge: Louisiana State University Press, 2005), 5.

8   George Levy, *To Die in Chicago: Confederate Prisoners at Camp Douglas, 1862–1865* (Evanston, IL: Evanston Publishers, 1999), 272–274.

9   Ibid., 97.

10   Benton McAdams, *Rebels at Rock Island: The Story of a Civil War Prison* (DeKalb: Northern Illinois University Press, 2000), ix.

11   Ibid., xii, 3.

12   Michael P. Gray, *The Business of Captivity: Elmira and its Civil War Prison* (Kent, OH: Kent State University Press, 2001), 27, 153.

13   James R. Hall, *Den of Misery: Indiana's Civil War Prison* (Gretna, LA: Pelican Publishing, 2006), 35–40.

14   Roger Pickenpaugh, *Camp Chase and the Evolution of Union Prison Policy* (Tuscaloosa: University of Alabama Press, 2007), 34.

15   Ibid., 107, 131.

16   William O. Bryant, *Cahaba Prison and the Sultana Disaster* (Tuscaloosa: University of Alabama Press, 1990), 1–3.

17   Ibid., 118, 137.

18   Ovid L. Futch, *History of Andersonville Prison*, revised ed. (Gainesville: University Press of Florida, 2011), 118–119.

19   William Marvel, *Andersonville: The Last Depot* (Chapel Hill: University of North Carolina Press, 1994), 107.

20   Ibid., 154–155.

21   James M. Gillispie, *Andersonvilles of the North: The Myths and Realities of Northern Treatment of Civil War Confederate Prisoners* (Denton: University of North Texas Press, 2008), 238–246.

22   Benjamin G. Cloyd, *Haunted by Atrocity: Civil War Prisons in American Memory* (Baton Rouge: Louisiana State University Press, 2010), 31–35.

23   George G. Lewis and John Mewha, *History of Prisoner of War Utilization by the United States Army, 1776–1945* (Washington, D.C.: Department of the Army, 1982), 27–42.

24   Richard Garrett, *P.O.W.* (Newton Abbot, UK: David & Charles, 1981), 81–97.

25   Howard Levie, *Prisoners of War in International Armed Conflict*, volume 59 of *International Law Studies* (Newport, RI: Naval War College Press, 1978), 7–8; A.J. Barker, *Prisoners of War* (New York: Universe Books, 1975), 12–15.

26   Paul J. Springer, *America's Captives: Treatment of POWs from the Revolutionary War to the War on Terror* (Lawrence: University Press of Kansas, 2010), 80–102.

27   Robert C. Doyle, *The Enemy in Our Hands: America's Treatment of Enemy Prisoners of War, From the Revolution to the War on Terror* (Lexington: University Press of Kentucky, 2010), 89–96.

28   Stephanie Carvin, *Prisoners of America's Wars: From the Early Republic to Guantanamo* (New York: Columbia University Press, 2010), 63–66.

29   William Marvel, "The Andersonville Artist: The A.J. Riddle Photographs of August 1864," *Blue & Gray Magazine* 10 (August 1993): 18–23.

30   Bob Zeller, *The Blue and Gray in Black and White: A History of Civil War Photography* (Westport, CT: Praeger, 2005), 151; Robert Scott Davis, *Ghosts and Shadows of Andersonville: Essays on the Secret Social Histories of America's Deadliest Prison* (Macon, GA: Mercer University Press, 2006), 135–139.

31   Charles Colbert, "Winslow Homer's Prisoners from the Front," *American Art* 12 (Summer 1998): 66–69.

32   Nicolai Cikovsky, Jr., "Winslow Homer's Prisoners from the Front," *Metropolitan Museum Journal* 12 (1977): 155–172.

33   Peter Wood, *Near Andersonville: Winslow Homer's Civil War* (Cambridge, MA: Harvard University Press, 2011), 60–75.

34   Christopher Benfey, "Winslow Homer: The Stern Facts," *The New York Review of Books* (March 24, 2011): 8–9; Benjamin Cloyd, Review of Peter H. Wood, *Near Andersonville: Winslow Homer's Civil War*. H-CivWar, H-Net Reviews. March, 2011. www.h-net.org/reviews/showrev.php?id=32768 (accessed June 10, 2014).

35   Wood, *Near Andersonville*, 61–62.

36   Jennifer Bridge, "A Shrine of Patriotic Memories," *Chicago History* 32 (Summer 2003): 3–12.

37   Ibid., 12–19.

38   Ibid., 19–23.

39   Henry Steele Commager, "A Novel of an Infamous Prison in the Civil War," *The New York Times Book Review* (October 30, 1955): 1.

40   Cloyd, *Haunted By Atrocity*, 111, 143.

41   Fred Boyles interview with author, May 13, 2009. For more on the first five military parks see Timothy B. Smith, *The Golden Age of Battlefield Preservation: The Decade of the 1890s and the Establishment of America's First Five Military Parks* (Knoxville: University of Tennessee Press, 2008).

42   *Americus Times-Recorder*, November 2, 1972, Park Passes From Army to National Park Service Folder, Vertical Files, ANHS.

43   *Americus Times-Recorder*, November 3, 1972, Park Passes From Army to National Park Service Folder, Vertical Files, ANHS.

44   From the official dedication day program, National Prisoner of War Museum, Andersonville Georgia, Dedication, April 9, 1998 (n.p., 1998), 7–17.

45   John S. McCain, "Remarks at the National POW Museum," www.mccain.senate.gov/public/index.cfm?FuseAction=PressOffice.Speeches&ContentRecord_id=90cca1f7-6c1c-4428-980d-2be918bb2d37&Region_id=&Issue_id=bc036142-6f29-470a-9be9-37d306822ccf (accessed January 1, 2013).

46   Glenn Robins, "The National Prisoner of War Museum," *The Journal of American History* 99 (Summer 2012): 275–279.

47   For visitation statistics see National Park Service "Visitation Statistics," https://irma.nps.gov/Stats/SSRSReports/Park%20Specific%20Reports/Annual%20Park%20Recreation%20Visitation%20%281904%20-%20Last%20Calendar%20Year%29?Park=ANDE (accessed July 2, 2014).

48   "Top 10 U.S. Civil War Sites," http://travel.nationalgeographic.com/travel/top-10/civil-war-sites/ and "12 Fascinating Civil War Sites," http://cnn.com/2012/09/04/travel/civil-war-sites-travel-leisure/ (both accessed June 10, 2014).

Documents

Selections from General Orders No. 100, April 24, 1863 (The Lieber Code)

*T*he Lieber Code included 157 articles, and was designed to cover virtually every aspect
of military behavior for the United States Army while it was in the field. The selections
in this section are the portions of the Code that relate to prisoners of war.

SECTION I

Martial Law—Military jurisdiction—Military necessity— Retaliation

Art. 11.

The law of war does not only disclaim all cruelty and bad faith concerning
engagements concluded with the enemy during the war, but also the breaking of
stipulations solemnly contracted by the belligerents in time of peace, and avowedly
intended to remain in force in case of war between the contracting powers.

It disclaims all extortions and other transactions for individual gain; all acts of
private revenge, or connivance at such acts.

Offenses to the contrary shall be severely punished, and especially so if committed
by officers.

Art. 15.

Military necessity admits of all direct destruction of life or limb of armed enemies,
and of other persons whose destruction is incidentally unavoidable in the armed
contests of the war; it allows of the capturing of every armed enemy, and every
enemy of importance to the hostile government, or of peculiar danger to the captor;
it allows of all destruction of property, and obstruction of the ways and channels of
traffic, travel, or communication, and of all withholding of sustenance or means of
life from the enemy; of the appropriation of whatever an enemy's country affords
necessary for the subsistence and safety of the army, and of such deception as does
not involve the breaking of good faith either positively pledged, regarding agreements
entered into during the war, or supposed by the modern law of war to exist. Men
who take up arms against one another in public war do not cease on this account
to be moral beings, responsible to one another and to God.

Art. 16.

Military necessity does not admit of cruelty—that is, the infliction of suffering for
the sake of suffering or for revenge, nor of maiming or wounding except in fight,
nor of torture to extort confessions. It does not admit of the use of poison in any

way, nor of the wanton devastation of a district. It admits of deception, but disclaims acts of perfidy; and, in general, military necessity does not include any act of hostility which makes the return to peace unnecessarily difficult.

Art. 21.

The citizen or native of a hostile country is thus an enemy, as one of the constituents of the hostile state or nation, and as such is subjected to the hardships of the war.

Art. 22.

Nevertheless, as civilization has advanced during the last centuries, so has likewise steadily advanced, especially in war on land, the distinction between the private individual belonging to a hostile country and the hostile country itself, with its men in arms. The principle has been more and more acknowledged that the unarmed citizen is to be spared in person, property, and honor as much as the exigencies of war will admit.

Art. 27.

The law of war can no more wholly dispense with retaliation than can the law of nations, of which it is a branch. Yet civilized nations acknowledge retaliation as the sternest feature of war. A reckless enemy often leaves to his opponent no other means of securing himself against the repetition of barbarous outrage.

Art. 28.

Retaliation will, therefore, never be resorted to as a measure of mere revenge, but only as a means of protective retribution, and moreover, cautiously and unavoidably; that is to say, retaliation shall only be resorted to after careful inquiry into the real occurrence, and the character of the misdeeds that may demand retribution.

Unjust or inconsiderate retaliation removes the belligerents farther and farther from the mitigating rules of regular war, and by rapid steps leads them nearer to the internecine wars of savages.

SECTION II

Public and private property of the enemy—Protection of persons, and especially of women, of religion, the arts and sciences—Punishment of crimes against the inhabitants of hostile countries.

Art. 42.

Slavery, complicating and confounding the ideas of property, (that is of a thing,) and of personality, (that is of humanity,) exists according to municipal or local law only.

The law of nature and nations has never acknowledged it. The digest of the Roman law enacts the early dictum of the pagan jurist, that "so far as the law of nature is concerned, all men are equal." Fugitives escaping from a country in which they were slaves, villains, or serfs, into another country, have, for centuries past, been held free and acknowledged free by judicial decisions of European countries, even though the municipal law of the country in which the slave had taken refuge acknowledged slavery within its own dominions.

Art. 43.

Therefore, in a war between the United States and a belligerent which admits of slavery, if a person held in bondage by that belligerent be captured by or come as a fugitive under the protection of the military forces of the United States, such person is immediately entitled to the rights and privileges of a freeman. To return such person into slavery would amount to enslaving a free person, and neither the United States nor any officer under their authority can enslave any human being. Moreover, a person so made free by the law of war is under the shield of the law of nations, and the former owner or State can have, by the law of postliminy, no belligerent lien or claim of service.

SECTION III

Deserters—Prisoners of war—Hostages—Booty on the battle-field.

Art. 48.

Deserters from the American Army, having entered the service of the enemy, suffer death if they fall again into the hands of the United States, whether by capture, or being delivered up to the American Army; and if a deserter from the enemy, having taken service in the Army of the United States, is captured by the enemy, and punished by them with death or otherwise, it is not a breach against the law and usages of war, requiring redress or retaliation.

Art. 49.

A prisoner of war is a public enemy armed or attached to the hostile army for active aid, who has fallen into the hands of the captor, either fighting or wounded, on the field or in the hospital, by individual surrender or by capitulation.

All soldiers, of whatever species of arms; all men who belong to the rising en masse of the hostile country; all those who are attached to the army for its efficiency and promote directly the object of the war, except such as are hereinafter provided for; all disabled men or officers on the field or elsewhere, if captured; all enemies who have thrown away their arms and ask for quarter, are prisoners of war, and as such exposed to the inconveniences as well as entitled to the privileges of a prisoner of war.

Art. 50.

Moreover, citizens who accompany an army for whatever purpose, such as sutlers, editors, or reporters of journals, or contractors, if captured, may be made prisoners of war, and be detained as such.

The monarch and members of the hostile reigning family, male or female, the chief, and chief officers of the hostile government, its diplomatic agents, and all persons who are of particular and singular use and benefit to the hostile army or its government, are, if captured on belligerent ground, and if unprovided with a safe conduct granted by the captor's government, prisoners of war.

Art. 51.

If the people of that portion of an invaded country which is not yet occupied by the enemy, or of the whole country, at the approach of a hostile army, rise, under a duly authorized levy en masse to resist the invader, they are now treated as public enemies, and, if captured, are prisoners of war.

Art. 52.

No belligerent has the right to declare that he will treat every captured man in arms of a levy en masse as a brigand or bandit. If, however, the people of a country, or any portion of the same, already occupied by an army, rise against it, they are violators of the laws of war, and are not entitled to their protection.

Art. 53.

The enemy's chaplains, officers of the medical staff, apothecaries, hospital nurses and servants, if they fall into the hands of the American Army, are not prisoners of war, unless the commander has reasons to retain them. In this latter case; or if, at their own desire, they are allowed to remain with their captured companions, they are treated as prisoners of war, and may be exchanged if the commander sees fit.

Art. 54

A hostage is a person accepted as a pledge for the fulfillment of an agreement concluded between belligerents during the war, or in consequence of a war. Hostages are rare in the present age.

Art. 55.

If a hostage is accepted, he is treated like a prisoner of war, according to rank and condition, as circumstances may admit.

Art. 56.

A prisoner of war is subject to no punishment for being a public enemy, nor is any revenge wreaked upon him by the intentional infliction of any suffering, or disgrace, by cruel imprisonment, want of food, by mutilation, death, or any other barbarity.

Art. 57.

So soon as a man is armed by a sovereign government and takes the soldier's oath of fidelity, he is a belligerent; his killing, wounding, or other warlike acts are not individual crimes or offenses. No belligerent has a right to declare that enemies of a certain class, color, or condition, when properly organized as soldiers, will not be treated by him as public enemies.

Art. 58.

The law of nations knows of no distinction of color, and if an enemy of the United States should enslave and sell any captured persons of their army, it would be a case for the severest retaliation, if not redressed upon complaint.

The United States cannot retaliate by enslavement; therefore death must be the retaliation for this crime against the law of nations.

Art. 59.

A prisoner of war remains answerable for his crimes committed against the captor's army or people, committed before he was captured, and for which he has not been punished by his own authorities.

All prisoners of war are liable to the infliction of retaliatory measures.

Art. 60.

It is against the usage of modern war to resolve, in hatred and revenge, to give no quarter. No body of troops has the right to declare that it will not give, and therefore will not expect, quarter; but a commander is permitted to direct his troops to give no quarter, in great straits, when his own salvation makes it impossible to cumber himself with prisoners.

Art. 61.

Troops that give no quarter have no right to kill enemies already disabled on the ground, or prisoners captured by other troops.

Art. 62.

All troops of the enemy known or discovered to give no quarter in general, or to any portion of the army, receive none.

Art. 66.

Quarter having been given to an enemy by American troops, under a misapprehension of his true character, he may, nevertheless, be ordered to suffer death if, within three days after the battle, it be discovered that he belongs to a corps which gives no quarter.

Art. 67.

The law of nations allows every sovereign government to make war upon another sovereign state, and, therefore, admits of no rules or laws different from those of regular warfare, regarding the treatment of prisoners of war, although they may belong to the army of a government which the captor may consider as a wanton and unjust assailant.

Art. 68.

Modern wars are not internecine wars, in which the killing of the enemy is the object. The destruction of the enemy in modern war, and, indeed, modern war itself, are means to obtain that object of the belligerent which lies beyond the war.

Unnecessary or revengeful destruction of life is not lawful.

Art. 72.

Money and other valuables on the person of a prisoner, such as watches or jewelry, as well as extra clothing, are regarded by the American Army as the private property of the prisoner, and the appropriation of such valuables or money is considered dishonorable, and is prohibited. Nevertheless, if large sums are found upon the persons of prisoners, or in their possession, they shall be taken from them, and the surplus, after providing for their own support, appropriated for the use of the army, under the direction of the commander, unless otherwise ordered by the government. Nor can prisoners claim, as private property, large sums found and captured in their train, although they have been placed in the private luggage of the prisoners.

Art. 73.

All officers, when captured, must surrender their side arms to the captor. They may be restored to the prisoner in marked cases, by the commander, to signalize admiration of his distinguished bravery or approbation of his humane treatment of prisoners before his capture. The captured officer to whom they may be restored can not wear them during captivity.

Art. 74.

A prisoner of war, being a public enemy, is the prisoner of the government, and not of the captor. No ransom can be paid by a prisoner of war to his individual captor or to any officer in command. The government alone releases captives, according to rules prescribed by itself.

Art. 75.

Prisoners of war are subject to confinement or imprisonment such as may be deemed necessary on account of safety, but they are to be subjected to no other intentional suffering or indignity. The confinement and mode of treating a prisoner may be varied during his captivity according to the demands of safety.

Art. 76.

Prisoners of war shall be fed upon plain and wholesome food, whenever practicable, and treated with humanity.

They may be required to work for the benefit of the captor's government, according to their rank and condition.

Art. 77.

A prisoner of war who escapes may be shot or otherwise killed in his flight; but neither death nor any other punishment shall be inflicted upon him simply for his attempt to escape, which the law of war does not consider a crime. Stricter means of security shall be used after an unsuccessful attempt at escape.

If, however, a conspiracy is discovered, the purpose of which is a united or general escape, the conspirators may be rigorously punished, even with death; and capital punishment may also be inflicted upon prisoners of war discovered to have plotted rebellion against the authorities of the captors, whether in union with fellow prisoners or other persons.

Art. 78.

If prisoners of war, having given no pledge nor made any promise on their honor, forcibly or otherwise escape, and are captured again in battle after having rejoined their own army, they shall not be punished for their escape, but shall be treated as simple prisoners of war, although they will be subjected to stricter confinement.

Art. 79.

Every captured wounded enemy shall be medically treated, according to the ability of the medical staff.

Art. 80.

Honorable men, when captured, will abstain from giving to the enemy information concerning their own army, and the modern law of war permits no longer the use of any violence against prisoners in order to extort the desired information or to punish them for having given false information.

SECTION VI

Exchange of prisoners—Flags of truce—Flags of protection

Art. 105.

Exchanges of prisoners take place—number for number—rank for rank wounded for wounded—with added condition for added condition—such, for instance, as not to serve for a certain period.

Art. 106.

In exchanging prisoners of war, such numbers of persons of inferior rank may be substituted as an equivalent for one of superior rank as may be agreed upon by cartel, which requires the sanction of the government, or of the commander of the army in the field.

Art. 107.

A prisoner of war is in honor bound truly to state to the captor his rank; and he is not to assume a lower rank than belongs to him, in order to cause a more advantageous exchange, nor a higher rank, for the purpose of obtaining better treatment.

Offenses to the contrary have been justly punished by the commanders of released prisoners, and may be good cause for refusing to release such prisoners.

Art. 108.

The surplus number of prisoners of war remaining after an exchange has taken place is sometimes released either for the payment of a stipulated sum of money, or, in urgent cases, of provision, clothing, or other necessaries.

Such arrangement, however, requires the sanction of the highest authority.

Art. 109.

The exchange of prisoners of war is an act of convenience to both belligerents. If no general cartel has been concluded, it cannot be demanded by either of them. No belligerent is obliged to exchange prisoners of war.

A cartel is voidable as soon as either party has violated it.

Art. 110.

No exchange of prisoners shall be made except after complete capture, and after an accurate account of them, and a list of the captured officers, has been taken.

SECTION VII

Parole

Art. 119.

Prisoners of war may be released from captivity by exchange, and, under certain circumstances, also by parole.

Art. 120.

The term Parole designates the pledge of individual good faith and honor to do, or to omit doing, certain acts after he who gives his parole shall have been dismissed, wholly or partially, from the power of the captor.

Art. 123.

Release of prisoners of war by exchange is the general rule; release by parole is the exception.

Art. 124.

Breaking the parole is punished with death when the person breaking the parole is captured again.

Accurate lists, therefore, of the paroled persons must be kept by the belligerents.

Art. 126.

Commissioned officers only are allowed to give their parole, and they can give it only with the permission of their superior, as long as a superior in rank is within reach.

Art. 127.

No noncommissioned officer or private can give his parole except through an officer. Individual paroles not given through an officer are not only void, but subject the individuals giving them to the punishment of death as deserters. The only admissible exception is where individuals, properly separated from their commands, have suffered long confinement without the possibility of being paroled through an officer.

Art. 128.

No paroling on the battlefield; no paroling of entire bodies of troops after a battle; and no dismissal of large numbers of prisoners, with a general declaration that they are paroled, is permitted, or of any value.

Art. 129.

In capitulations for the surrender of strong places or fortified camps the commanding officer, in cases of urgent necessity, may agree that the troops under his command shall not fight again during the war, unless exchanged.

Art. 130.

The usual pledge given in the parole is not to serve during the existing war, unless exchanged.

This pledge refers only to the active service in the field, against the paroling belligerent or his allies actively engaged in the same war. These cases of breaking the parole are patent acts, and can be visited with the punishment of death; but the pledge does not refer to internal service, such as recruiting or drilling the recruits, fortifying places not besieged, quelling civil commotions, fighting against belligerents unconnected with the paroling belligerents, or to civil or diplomatic service for which the paroled officer may be employed.

Art. 133.

No prisoner of war can be forced by the hostile government to parole himself, and no government is obliged to parole prisoners of war, or to parole all captured officers, if it paroles any. As the pledging of the parole is an individual act, so is paroling, on the other hand, an act of choice on the part of the belligerent.

SECTION X

Insurrection—Civil War—Rebellion

Art. 153.

Treating captured rebels as prisoners of war, exchanging them, concluding of cartels, capitulations, or other warlike agreements with them; addressing officers of a rebel army by the rank they may have in the same; accepting flags of truce; or, on the other hand, proclaiming Martial Law in their territory, or levying war-taxes or forced loans, or doing any other act sanctioned or demanded by the law and usages of public war between sovereign belligerents, neither proves nor establishes an acknowledgment of the rebellious people, or of the government which they may have erected, as a public or sovereign power. Nor does the adoption of the rules of war toward rebels imply an engagement with them extending beyond the limits of these rules. It is victory in the field that ends the strife and settles the future relations between the contending parties.

Art. 154.

Treating, in the field, the rebellious enemy according to the law and usages of war has never prevented the legitimate government from trying the leaders of the rebellion or chief rebels for high treason, and from treating them accordingly, unless they are included in a general amnesty.

Source: *OR*, II:5:671–682.

DOCUMENT 2

Rates of Exchange

*D*uring the American Civil War, many of the legal precedents and practical solutions to *thorny issues were provided by earlier conflicts. The War of 1812, fought with Great Britain, included a formal exchange agreement for prisoners of war that supplied the exchange rates used in the Civil War as well.*

RATE OF EXCHANGE ADOPTED IN THE CARTEL BETWEEN GREAT BRITAIN AND THE UNITED STATES, SIGNED MAY 12, 1813

General commanding in chief or admiral, 60 men; lieutenant-general or vice-admiral, 40 men; major-general or rear-admiral, 30 men; brigadier-general or commodore, with a broad pennant and a captain under him, 20 men; colonel or captain of a line-of-battle ship, 15 men; lieutenant-colonel or captain of a frigate, 10 men; major or commander of a sloop-of-war, bomb-ketch, fire-ship, or packet, 8 men; captain or lieutenant or master, 6 men; lieutenant or master's mate, 4 men; sub-lieutenant or ensign, or midshipman, warrant officers, masters of merchant vessels and captains of private armed vessels, 3 men; non-commissioned officers or lieutenants and mates of private armed vessels, mates of merchant vessels and all petty officers of ships of war, 2 men; private soldiers or seamen, 1 man.

Source: *OR*, II:1:166–167.

DOCUMENT 3

Rules for Camp Morton

*T*he U.S. War Department established Camp Morton as a POW facility in February of *1862, under the command of Colonel Richard D. Owen. These rules governed the conduct of the prisoners during their confinement.*

RULES FOR CAMP MORTON

1. The entire camp prisoners will be divided into thirty divisions, each under charge of a chief selected by the companies composing the division from among the first sergeants of companies. At the bugle call for first sergeants they will report themselves at headquarters.
2. These chiefs of divisions will draw up the provisions returns for their divisions, care for and be responsible for the general appearance, police and welfare of their divisions. The first fifteen will constitute a board of appeal for the hearing of grievances, settlement and punishment of misdemeanors, subject to the approval of the commander of the post in their fifteen divisions. The other fifteen will form a like court for the remaining fifteen divisions.
3. Among the crimes and misdemeanors which first sergeants are expected to guard and which they will punish on detection are counterfeiting the commandant's, doctor's, adjutant's, or chaplain's hands for requisitions, making improper use of premises, refusing to take a reasonable share in the details according to the roster, selling to the sutler any articles issued to them as clothing, appropriating things belonging to others or insulting sentinels.
4. The prisoners' returns will be handed in for approval at 10 a.m. each alternate day previous to the one on which the issue is made. The issues of tobacco and stationery will be made on Wednesdays and Saturdays at 2 p.m. by the chaplain, as well as the distribution of reading matter. Letters will be given out between 2 and 3 p.m. and mailed between 3 and 4 p.m.
5. Daily inspections will be made by the commandant or officer of the day to see that the policing so essential to health has been thoroughly performed, and facilities will be afforded for sports and athletic exercise also conducive to health, as well as bathing by companies, if permission can be obtained from the proper authority.
6. The first sergeants of companies will look after the general wants of their companies and maintain the necessary order, discipline and police essential to health and comfort, and will make requisitions, first on chiefs of divisions, and they afterwards at headquarters, for clothing, camp and garrison equipage absolutely necessary; also for tobacco wanted, and the like.
7. The inside chain of soldiers, except a small patrol with side-arms, will be removed, and the quiet and good order of the camp as well as the policing for health and comfort, the construction of new sinks when necessary and the daily throwing in of lime and mold to prevent bad odors will be entirely under the supervision of the sergeants of prisoners.
8. Vessels for the washing of clothing and ropes for clotheslines will be furnished, and no bed or other clothing will be put on roof tops or on fences.
9. Prisoners will carefully avoid interrupting sentinels in the discharge of their duty, and especially will not curse them, use abusive language or climb onto fences or trees, as the sentinels are ordered to fire if such an offense occurs after three positive and distinct orders to desist, even in daytime. At night, only one warning will be given to any one climbing on the fence tops.

10. A prisoners' fund will be created by the deduction as heretofore of small amounts from the rations of beef, bread, beans, &c., a schedule of which will be placed at the commissary department. This fund will be used for the purchase of tobacco, stationery, stamps and such other articles as the chiefs of divisions may report, and which should be drawn on requisitions handed in by first sergeants between 9 and 10 a.m. each day.
11. Every endeavor will be made by the commandant to give each and every prisoner as much liberty and comfort as is consistent with orders received and with an equal distribution of the means at disposal, provided such indulgence never leads to any abuse of the privileges.

Source: *OR*, II:3:518–519.

DOCUMENT 4

Hoffman's Inspection Tour

In late 1863, Commissary General of Prisons William Hoffman undertook an inspection tour of the major Union POW camps. He was shocked to find how squalid the living conditions were at many of the camps, but had few solutions to offer in his report.

WASHINGTON, D.C., DECEMBER 3, 1863, HON. E.M. STANTON, SECRETARY OF WAR, WASHINGTON, D.C.

Sir: I have the honor to submit the following report of my inspection of the condition of Camp Douglas and other prison camps, made pursuant to your instructions of the 13th ultimo.

I left this city on the evening of the 13th and proceeded at once to Camp Douglas, it being the chief object of the service upon which I was ordered, to inquire into the cause and extent of the fire which had occurred at that camp, by which the barracks for six companies and considerable extent of fencing had been destroyed. I arrived at Chicago on Sunday morning and immediately after breakfast repaired to Camp Douglas, which is on the outer limits of the city.

On inspection of the ground I was gratified to find that the destruction of the fence was much less than had been reported, being only about 400 feet instead of 1,000, as was first estimated. The destruction of the barracks was more serious, involving, as had been reported, the quarters for six companies, with mess and cook rooms, a commissary store, and other outbuildings. In addition to the buildings destroyed there was also consumed a considerable quantity of public property, arms, and accouterments and quartermaster stores and private property, consisting of clothing and other articles belonging to officers and soldiers.

The fire occurred about mid-day and originated in a room occupied by officers during the absence of the inmates at dinner. It appears that there was a large fire in the stove and either through the over-heating of the pipe or some defects in it near the roof the ceiling took fire, and when it was discovered it had made such progress it was impossible to check it. A high wind was blowing at the time, and when the door of the room in which it began was opened the flames were given such power that it was not possible to check it.

Prompt means were immediately taken by the commanding officer, Col. C.V. De Land, Michigan sharpshooters, to check the fire and at the same time to restrain the prisoners of war from any attempt to take advantage of the opportunity it gave them to make their escape. To confine the fire to as small a limit as possible a portion of the line of barracks was torn down, and as the wind was across the line this plan accomplished the object and checked the fire in that direction, but the wind carried the flames directly over the cook-houses and other buildings and fencing in the rear and they were all consumed in a few moments. The engines of the city were promptly on the ground, but the fire had done its work before they could get there.

The fire was accidental, but there was probably some carelessness with it. A large fire was probably left in the stove without any precaution to guard against its being communicated to the buildings, and by the over-heating of the pipe, or in some other way, the ceiling and tarred roofing were set on fire and in a few minutes it was beyond control.

There was some excitement among the prisoners at the time, and some cheering, but as a part of the command was placed under arms as soon as the alarm was given the demonstrations of the prisoners were soon put a stop to.

As soon as the fire was extinguished the acting quartermaster at the camp, Captain Goodwin, with commendable energy, took immediate steps to have the fence which had been destroyed rebuilt, and before night of the same day it was accomplished.

I inclose herewith a report, made to me by Colonel De Land, of the public and private property destroyed. There have been similar occasions when officers and men have lost clothing and other personal property that it has been made good to them by the Government, and I respectfully suggest that at the least the clothing lost by the enlisted men be replaced by an extra issue.

By direction of the General-in-Chief, I ordered Captain Potter, assistant quartermaster at Chicago, to rebuild the barracks which had been destroyed with as little delay as possible; until this is done the troops who form the guards must be very much crowded, as all have to be accommodated in the barracks, which are sufficient for only a part.

The guard at Camp Douglas consists of the Michigan sharpshooters, under Col. C.V. De Land, and six companies of the Invalid Corps, under Colonel Sweet, giving an aggregate of 1,196, but of these only 859 enlisted men are for duty, and as the invalids cannot count on more than two-thirds of their strength for guard duty in all weather the actual force for service is small. Just previous to my visit the sharpshooters had been ordered to join General Grant's army, but on my representations of the necessity of their presence at the camp till relieved by an equivalent force the order has been suspended by the General-in-Chief.

Colonel Sweet thinks that with one regiment of the First Battalion of the invalids and two companies of the Second Battalion he will be able to take charge of the prisoners of war at Camp Douglas, but considering the unavoidable inefficiency of that organization I doubt if less than fifteen companies will be competent for the service. The guard and the prisoners are within the same inclosure, which makes a larger proportion of guard necessary.

There are between 6,000 and 7,000 prisoners at Camp Douglas, and in consequence of the burning of a part of the barracks by paroled troops last winter they are very much crowded, having now to occupy buildings which were formerly used as cook-houses and which are very indifferently fitted up with sleeping arrangements. To relieve them somewhat from unwholesome crowding I propose to order about a thousand to the depot at Rock Island, unless there is a prospect that large numbers of prisoners will be sent there from General Grant's Army.

The sick in hospital are very comfortable, but they are too crowded, and there are many in the quarters who should be in the hospital. Two additional buildings, with enlarged accommodations for dispensary, store-rooms, laundry, &c., are being erected, which will greatly improve the condition of the sick.

An abundant supply of water has just been introduced into the camp, and an extensive system of sewerage has been constructed, which will be of great benefit to the camp by the greater facilities it will afford for preserving a good state of police and by carrying off the surface water, freeing the camp from the mud which has heretofore been a source of much annoyance.

One square formerly occupied by prisoners of war is now vacant, the buildings having been destroyed by fire last winter. Barracks for 2,000 prisoners could be erected on this ground for $10,000 to $12,000, and since it is inclosed and the rent of the ground has to be paid it would seem to be economy in the end to rebuild the barracks. A large part of the expense could be paid from the prison fund.

I found at Camp Douglas five officers who had passed themselves off as enlisted men until this deception had been detected. Two of them were among some who had made their escape and were sent back from Louisville, where they were recaptured. One of them had been the ringleader in all the disturbances in the camp, and for their greater security, and on account of the offense which they had committed in misrepresenting their rank, I ordered them to be sent to Fort Warren to be held in close confinement.

On Monday evening I left Chicago for Rock Island, which I reached the next morning. The inclosure and the barracks for prisoners are completed and are ready for occupation, though there is yet some unfinished work. In consequence of the extent to the inclosure and the less efficient character of the Invalid Corps than other troops the accommodations for the guard will have to be more extensive than was anticipated, and some little time will elapse before the additions which are in progress will be completed. This, however, will not delay the reception of prisoners. I found but four companies present, two of which had just arrived, and as no medical officer had been appointed I applied to assistant surgeon-general in Louisville for one to be ordered there, with a supply of medicines and stores. My request was immediately complied with, and I have since asked that other medical officers may be ordered there. Since my return to this city the guard has been increased to a regiment and the depot is placed under the command of Col. R.H. Rush, of the Invalid Corps, who, I feel confident, will soon have it so organized and administered as to give the most satisfactory results.

With the exception of a small part of it Rock Island belongs to the United States, and it is very desirable that it should be placed under martial law, in order that the commanding officer may have it in his power to prevent the intrusion of persons who will take advantage of every opportunity to enter into an illicit traffic with the guard or the prisoners. The Chicago and Rock Island Railroad crosses the island and should not be allowed, without the permission of the commanding officer, to land passengers on the island.

On Tuesday evening I left Rock Island for Sandusky, where I arrived on Thursday morning and proceeded at once to the depot on Johnson's Island, where I met General Cox, who had a considerable force with him, drawn there by the threatened attempt from Canada to rescue the prisoners. I met there also Captain Carter, of the Navy, the commander of the U.S. steamer Michigan, which was lying off the island.

As the Michigan had been lying in Sandusky Bay at the request of the War Department some ten days when the report of the threatened invasion was made there was not possible chance of its being attended with any success, even if the rebels could have been sufficiently secret in their preparations to have left a Canada port without detection, but that, as the results show, was not possible.

Some threats, it is reported, have been made by the prisoners on the island to take advantage of some opportune moment to overcome the guard and make their escape to Canada, but their situation must be much more desperate than it is now before they will attempt, with naked hands, to attack a vigilant guard armed with muskets and revolvers, when success, which is only within the reach of possibility after great sacrifices, would only place them on an island from which they could not escape.

General Cox will withdraw all his troops except five companies of cavalry recruits, who will remain on the island until relieved by some of the companies ordered to be added to the battalion to make it up to a regiment. I doubt if quarters for more than two companies can be built this season, and with this increase of the strength of the guard I think the prisoners will be perfectly secure for the winter.

In consequence of the dangers which it has been represented would attend her wintering in Sandusky Bay the Michigan has been ordered to return to Erie before the navigation of the lake closes.

While General Orme, who accompanied me to the island, was inspecting the prisoners in pursuance of your instructions I examined the ground with a view to decide on the best location for the barracks about to be erected, and having attended to this I gave all necessary instructions in relation to the restrictions which should be put upon the prisoners in the receipt of clothing and other particulars. The sutler's store had been closed pursuant to your orders and remained closed.

The affairs of this depot under Lieutenant-Colonel Pierson have been very creditably managed; but one prisoner is known to have escaped, and it is believed he was enabled to do so by taking the place of an enlisted man who was of a party ordered from the island. There are now at the island 2,350 officers, 33 citizens, and 10 enlisted convicts.

After completing my duties at the depot, I left Sandusky that evening in company with General Orme, for Columbus, Ohio, where we arrived the following morning. After breakfast we proceeded together to Camp Chase, where I inquired into the management of the affairs of the camp, the condition of the prisons, &c., and gave such instructions as seemed to be necessary.

The camp is commanded by Col. William Wallace, Fifteenth Ohio, and the guard is composed of eleven companies of the Invalid Corps, giving an aggregate [of] 771 men, and for duty 562 enlisted men. There are three different prisons, all requiring guards, which make the guard duty more arduous than it would be for the same command if all the prisoners were within the same inclosure, but the duty can probably be performed by a small increase of the present guard without too much oppressing the men.

There are now in this prison upward of 2,500 men, when 1,800 is calculated as its full capacity. To relieve it from this excess, and the Alton military prison from a like excess, I have applied for a guard to be sent to Camp Butler, near Springfield, Ill., where General Ammen, who commands the district, informs me 3,000 prisoners can be accommodated.

I did not visit the prisoners in the Ohio penitentiary, because I had recently received a very detailed report from General Mason showing that they were well and securely quartered and provided for, and the duties in my office requiring my return at the earliest day possible I was unwilling to make a delay which would cause my return to this city delayed beyond Sunday. I was anxious to have seen His Excellency Governor Tod, to have consulted with him in relation to the organization of the six companies which are to be added to the battalion at Johnson's Island, making it up to a regiment, but the Governor was absent from the city and I was unable to accomplish this part of the object of my visit to Columbus.

On that evening I left for Pittsburg, where, on the following day, I had an interview with Major-General Brooks relative to the prisoners of war in the Allegheny Penitentiary. They are held there at an expense of 48 cents a day per man, and they are much better provided for and more comfortable, from the nature of the prison, than they deserve to be. I am informed that the political sentiments of the officials who have the management of the affairs of the prison, with one exception, incline them to have sympathy for the prisoners, and I would recommend that they be sent elsewhere for safe-keeping and to lessen the expense, but I can find no suitable place to which they can be ordered; none of our forts have sufficient room which can be made available for this purpose.

I returned to this city on Sunday, the 22d.

I have the honor to be, very respectfully, your obedient servant,

W. Hoffman
Colonel Third Infantry and Commissary-General of Prisoners

Source: *OR*, II:6:632–636.

DOCUMENT 5

Isaiah White's Andersonville Report

Isaiah H. White served as the chief surgeon of the Andersonville Prison hospital. His observations demonstrate the rapidly devolving situation within the compound walls, including the expanding medical crisis.

SANITARY REPORT OF C.S. MILITARY PRISON HOSPITAL, ANDERSONVILLE, GA., FOR THE QUARTER ENDING JUNE 30, 1864

There is nothing in the topography of the country that can be said to have influenced the health of the command, except, perhaps, in the immediate camp, through which passes a stream of water, the margins of which are low and swampy, and have recently been drained with a view of reclaiming it sufficiently for camping purposes, the result of which has been to expose to the rays of the summer sun a large surface covered with decomposing vegetable matter, a condition favorable to the production of malarial diseases. (This surface is now being covered with dry sand.) With this exception the land is high and well drained, the soil light and sandy. The prisoners, being from the United States, have been influenced perhaps as much by the climate as any other agency. The prison was built to accommodate 10,000 prisoners, in which have unavoidably been placed over 26,000, causing them to become so crowded as to prevent a proper circulation and due allowance of atmospheric air. With this crowded condition there is an absence of barracks or tents, the only protection from the weather being little huts made of boughs, blankets, and small picket-tents used in the U.S. Army, which being irregularly arranged obstruct the free circulation of air. Within the last few days the stockade has been increased ten acres, relieving the crowded condition heretofore existing. Barracks are also being constructed. It, however, is an immense task and will not soon be completed. The diet of the prisoners is the same as that issued to Confederate soldiers in the field, viz, one pound beef or one-third pound bacon, one and one-fourth pound meal, with an occasional issue of beans and rice. There is a great lack of cleanliness on the part of the prisoners. The chief cause of disease and mortality is long confinement in prison, which, in connection with the diet (having produced scurvy among them), has so lowered their vitality as to render them unable to resist disease. The hospital, in the early part of the quarter, being situated within the stockade, it was impossible to supply the sick with the necessary comforts; hospital bedding, diet, &c., being stolen from the hospital by the prisoners. In the latter part of the month of May authority was granted to move the hospital without the stockade. The condition of the sick has been much improved by the change. They are now treated in a hospital camp well supplied with shade and water. The tents are for the most part small and illy adapted to hospital purposes, insufficient in number to accommodate the large number of sick to be treated. The tents are all filled to excess, and many men are refused admission to hospital for want of room. During the quarter the prison has been on several occasions without any medicines whatever. Requisitions are made for one month's supply, which are filled in such diminished quantities as to create the necessity for other requisitions during the month. These have to go to Atlanta for approval. In consequence of the irregularity of the mail they do not return frequently under eight or ten days. They have then to be sent to the medical purveyor at Macon, where they are usually filled with promptness. But before they are received one-half of the period drawn for has elapsed and the former supply entirely exhausted. The number of medical officers on duty at the prison is inadequate to perform the required duties. There are over 26,000 prisoners with only thirteen medical officers; of this number, five attend the hospital, where there are 1,134 sick.

Respectfully submitted.

Isaiah H. White
Chief Surgeon of Post

Source: *OR*, II:7:426–427.

DOCUMENT 6

Voices of Captivity

*T*hese are the diary entries of William Tritt. Private Tritt, 21st Wisconsin Infantry, was captured on September 20, 1863 and was exchanged on February 27, 1865. The January entries cover a portion of his time at Danville Prison and the October entries cover a portion of his time at the Confederate prison in Florence, South Carolina.*

January 1, 1864 [Friday]

Cool and wet. Also freezing smart. One hundred of No. 5 were moved into No. 3 stockade. Over 100 men to No. 4 after delay. Full of sleeping men.

2nd

Cool and windy. 90 cases of Measles reported this morning in building.

3rd

Cool, but clear and pleasant. The Presbyterians sent in a number of their tracts and papers. The messenger wanted us to send to the North for some to supply us with Bibles.

4th

The tracts and papers give us a very hard name indeed. Outlawed, unprincipled, disobedient, anything but good. I cannot see how they know. It must be here-say.

5th

Since we came to Danville, 115 cases of death from various diseases. Out of 4,000 men sent here, some cases of Small Pox and lung disease yet. In hopes this unholy war will soon play out.

6th

Ground bare yet, but chilly. The winters seem to be harder to get used to than Wisconsin.

7th

We miss the warm rooms very much, indeed, the food warm meals our gallant mothers used to get for us. The Negroes are used by the Rebs for all labor save the Manual of Arms. I find by close observation there is a sprinkling of the Negro blood in the ranks. Cold with wind. Trading off shoes for rice, salt and bread. Some cases of Pox yet.

8th

An addition of 50 crackers today to our rations seems good. Froze so as to carry a wagon, a little sheet of snow 1 inch deep.

9th

All quiet. News of being exchanged gives much joy. Very pleasant. Many seem to be sick or getting sick. A bringing in of the Negroes a little closer to assist in carrying on the war.

10th

News that we are exchanged. Rebs call Butler "Beast Butler."

11th

Very pleasant. Many seem to think that Charleston is surrendered. Did some washing. Everything growing seems to be used by the Rebs to carry on the war.

12th

Very pleasant. Good weather to get out the flag. No snow on the ground. The first time since I came to this prison.

13th

Warm and raining. News of no exchange. Some little smartness by the Rebs on the Rappahannock. Winters are rainy and muddy. No business going on touching improvement of farms.

14th

A pain in my back long on account of being shut up in prison. Teaming is done on wagons. Negroes do the teaming. Seems rather poor.

15th

Things all quiet. Guard mountains [?] every morning by the Rebs. Clubs and paddles are used to walk with. Some boxes have come to hand.

16th

Rumors of exchange, but nothing certain.

17th

Cabbage, tripe, cornbread and beef. Pleasant and the sun shone. I think much about home and desire very much to see you all.

18th

Warm and raining, mixed bread, corn and flour, beef and cabbage soup as rations. No frost on the ground at this date. Winter seems like Murfreesboro, Tennessee. Health of this house improving some.

19th

Chilly and windy. Was very unwell of cold feet and limbs and pain in the head, which made me feel very bad.

20th

Four months today a prisoner. I am some better this morning. A very pleasant day. Rumors of being sent home.

21st

Pleasant like a summer day, the singing of birds and many other gay things. The sweet melody of birds is much gayer in the North than in the South on account of spraying & breeding in the South.

22nd

Some letters came in. North Carolina press recommended a convention to consider our return to the old Union. Pleasant indeed is the weather and not cold. Seems to look better. Two more boxes have come to hand.

23rd

Small Pox have not made their appearance for several days in Nov. 4. It has not been very fatal, though some have died. Pleasant days. Health of this building is good at this date. One fight on the first floor.

24th

Health seems to improve generally. A good feeling among the ranks. Rations playing out. Very small raw cabbage sent in to soldiers.

25th

Weather very pleasant. Rice 50 c per pound; sugar $2.50 per pound; shoes $10.00 per pair, pants $10.00 per pair. Things are very high.

26th

Hospital returning our members back fast. Another fight. Raw cabbage sent in. not as good quality as ours.

27th

Coming in fast out of the hospital's care. Running away. Our building full. Rations getting short. No snow, most pleasant, most like summer. I feel well.

28th

A guard made a business of fooling with a Negro wench, taking her on the streets, stopping her by charging on with bayonet. Got a gun loaded and finally the gun went off and the ballast through the left breast of the wench. One of the boys fell down in the well about 40 feet, came out alright in water 10 feet deep.

29th

John Jorday Collier Berir is dead. Died in hospital. Residence is Oshkosh, Co. B, 21st Regiment. Still pleasant, 100 reported making their escape out of No. 5 last night and were shot by the guard.

30th

Some preparation to leave or run away, but adjourned the men. About 50 engaged.

31st

Boys tried to go through the board fence of the yard. Guard fired on them, passing through the board that they were cutting off and entering the window, passing through the house and out again. Nobody hurt.

October 1, 1864 [Saturday]

Sun arises very nice. Cool and pleasant. On some trees the leaves are beginning to fall off.

2nd

Cloudy and cool. Hospital stewards leaving, know not where. The most that is going on is the wasting of the number of men in camp. Some fighting the traders, or full bellies do it. Sometimes they slap or shove a hungry man for taking something that is not his. Ordered this morning to move into a new stockade about 1 mile off. It was quite a sight to see 500 men on the move, loaded with their traps, tents and kettles.

October 3rd

Cloudy, cool and refreshing. Got meal, molasses, a very little flour and salt at a late hour last night, which made our empty bellies feel warm and which made into mush and ate with molasses. Got a reasonable place for a tent, 2 of us. William Horn of Co. E-86, Indiana and myself. A dead man was robbed of shirt, blouse and boots before being carried out.

4th

The most unprincipled, the traders, and those who have a little to trade, generally Irish or half breed. Most of the Oath men are Eastern.

5th

1500 of the old prisoners from Charleston arrived. One man shot at the watering place on account of a blunder. It wants fixing all blame to the managers of the place, for some guards have no judgment.

6th

Very pleasant and mild. Some acquainted with the new prison. We are fixing for a long stay, building shanties of all kinds and fashions. I feel well, but not content. Taking the Oath seems to be adjourned and played out.

7th

Rained last night. Wet us some. At 3 o'clock yesterday we were ordered to move into detachments, leaving streets to pass about on and made quite a stir and bustle. Smoke settles around mornings, especially lowry [?] mornings, and is disagreeable to the eyes. The balance of the Charleston prisoners came on some.

8th

Very cool and raw wind. Many shivering of cold. All kinds of complaints. Sounds like the bad Faith of the Children of Israel in the Wilderness.

9th

Very chilly and windy. Much yelling and noise.

10th

Chilly, clear and fair. Brass band working outside the stockade. The first heard since I have been a prisoner.

11th

Very chilly nights and hot by day. News of Yanks breaking up officers and all, and taking the town of Columbus.

12th

Cool nights and hot, sunny days.
[October 13, 14, and 15 missing]

16th

Clear and pleasant. Feels and looks like fall. Some men have sold the clothes off their bodies and can't put them into doing anything, so they look bad and are perishing.

17th

Cool and airy. Some cloudy. A majority have caves and tents to live in. Some are lying out yet. I visited the gate to see the things that are in line to march. 250 to take the Oath.

18th

No rations yesterday. Then this morning on Main Street were stands to sell onions, potatoes and beans, but they were ordered off with their trade. Some did not and lost their stuff. This street was so crowded that it was unsafe for a civil man to get through, also all trade save potatoes, salt and tobacco.

19th

Cool and pleasant, Fair Fall weather. The dishonesty going on between the Quartermaster and some trade in here stopped. Quartermaster tried and condemned Yankees. Stands turned upside down, rations increased soon after.

20th

Sun rises very beautiful. Fair and warm. Issuing blankets 5 to 100 or to be divided amongst the destitute. Rations reasonable. 13 months a prisoner this evening. After sundown I wrote a letter.

21st

Cool nights and pleasant daytime. News of Sherman cleaning out Hood and Beauregard. Also a good report from Grant.

22nd

Cool windy and sprinkling. Clothes not adequate to the necessity of the case. Not one article more than we should have. Some will do, but many are destitute in a manner.

23rd

Clear and cool. Sun arose very pleasant. Hospital was moved inside in the Northwest corner on the ground that was occupied by the first thousand, moved to another place.

24th

Fair, fine and beautiful. Hood seems to be still in Sherman's rear. I am waiting with all patience for the result to be sent. May they be sent headlong to the wall Army for causing so much misery.

25th

Used up all the lumber and are chopping and digging out the stumps and roots for wood or fuel. Fair and pleasant. Crows are coming south in their own way, promiscuously, not organized like pigeons. In lines of battle, so are the Robin Redbreasts.

26th

Pleasant and cool. Better supply of shirts, drawers, hats and socks. Quite a sprinkling of gray and red shirts. A few more prisoners arrive to make 11 thousand full. Much talk of exchange, to be *ready* to exchange.

27th

The hospital receives all the sick, but poorly managed. The strong eat the provisions and sell them to the soldiers or prisoners while the weak are suffered to die. 32 dead lay before the gate yesterday forenoon. Our men run the concern.

28th

Much talk of dissatisfaction against the police and traders in camp on account of high prices and whippings. They are called Galvanized Rebs. Some mean Oath men by this phrase. I was taken with the 100 to get clothes, but was turned away empty.

29th

Clear and pleasant. Much distress on account of shoes and socks, or the want of them. Some shoes were sold to the Rebs, others left as a snake leaves its skin. Things seem in a running condition with the Armies.

30th

Clear and pleasant. Many vegetables in camp for sale. Potatoes retailed at $5.00 per bushel. The poles over which men rest to do their business gave way and let them into the sewer, making awful work.

31st

Smoky and cool. Health of camp good.

Source: William Tritt Diary, Andersonville National Historic Site.

DOCUMENT 7

Reflections on Captivity 1

" *A Toast"* was offered by Charles A. Rubright during a gathering of Civil War veterans. *Corporal Rubright, 106th Pennsylvania Infantry, was captured on June 22, 1864 and was held briefly at Libby Prison and Belle Isle before moving to Andersonville in late July. He was exchanged on April 1, 1865.*

"A TOAST"

There was confined at this prison, about 31,000 prisoners, out of that number there were about 21,000 buried at that place, that accounts for some of our absent comrades. I am not able to give you a picture of Andersonville, nor am I able to find language to convey the horrors of that place. The very thought of what passed before my eyes during my confinement there, even at this late date, fills me with horror and baffles all descriptions. We were all huddled in a stockade without any cover, exposed to the scorching rays of the sun, and the drenching storms of that climate. There was never a time when sufficient food was provided, and what was provided, and what was doled out to us, was not fit for brutes to eat. We were not brutes, and yet, it would be difficult for us to pass ourselves off for human beings. We could not recognize each other. We were simply moving skeletons. In August 1864, the average daily deaths at that prison was 91, and many of them died from starvation. There was no medical attendance on the sick . . . thousands of our absent comrades are there today, their graves are marked with the word "unknown."

With all their suffering they made no murmur, they all loved the old flag, and longed to see it triumph. They went out from good homes to fight the battles of liberty, they mostly gave their lives for their country. They do not respond to our roll call tonight they are numbered among our absent comrades.

It was through the sacrifice and suffering of our absent comrades, and brave soldiers who have survived the war, with all its havoc of disease, and starvation in prison pens, and the shot of shell of the battlefield, that our country was restored, and those absent ones will never be forgotten while a single soldier of the republic survives.

Source: Charles Rubright Papers, Special Collections, Auburn University Libraries.

DOCUMENT 8

Reflections on Captivity 2

The poem, "They Have Left Us Here to Die," was very familiar to Union prisoners of war and was often copied in diaries or recited at reunions. The author was most likely Private James W. Hyatt, 116th Pennsylvania Infantry.

"THEY HAVE LEFT US HERE TO DIE"

1st

When our country called for me we came from forge and store and mill.
From workshop, farm and factory the broken ranks to fill;
We left our quite happy homes, and ones we loved so well;
To vanquish all the Union foes, or fall where others fell;
Now in a prison drear we languish and it is our constant cry;
Oh! Ye who yet can save us, will you leave us here to die?

2nd

The voices of slander tells you that our hearts are weak with fear.
That all or nearly all of us were captured in the rear;
The scars upon our bodies from musket ball and shell;
The missing legs and shattered arms a true tale will tell;
We have tried to do our duty in the sight of God on high;
Oh! Ye who yet can save us, will you leave us here to die?

3rd

Then are hearts with hopes still beating in our pleasant Northern homes
Waiting; waiting; for the footstep that may never more return;
In Southern prisons pining; meager; tattered; pale and gaunt;
Growing weaker; weaker; daily from pinching cold and want;
Their brothers; sons; and husbands; poor and helpless captured be;
Oh! Ye who yet can save us, will you leave us here to die?

4th

Just out our prison gate there is a grave yard near at hand;
Where lie twelve thousand Union men beneath the Georgia sand;
Scores and scores we lay beside them as day succeeds each day;
And this it will be ever until they all shall pass away;
And the last can say when dying with upturned and glazing eye;
Both love and faith are dead at home, they have left us here to die.

Source: Lyle Adair Diary, February 28, 1865, Andersonville National Historic Site.

Bibliography

MANUSCRIPT COLLECTIONS

Andersonville National Historic Site

Lyle G. Adair Diary
John Duff Diary
John Ely Diary
William Seeley Diary
William J. Tritt Diary
M.J. Umsted Diary
James Vance Diary

Auburn University

Madison P. Jones Letters
Charles Rubright Papers

National Archives and Records Administration, Washington, D.C.

Record Group 45: Naval Records Collection of the Office of Naval Records and Library
Record Group 94: Records of the Adjutant General's Office, 1780s-1917
Record Group 249: Records of the Commissary General of Prisoners

Published Primary Source Collections

U.S. House of Representatives. *Trial of Henry Wirz*. 40th Congress, 2nd Session, 1866, Serial 1331.

U.S. War Department. *The War of the Rebellion: A Compilation of the Official Records of the Union and Confederate Armies*. 127 vols. Washington, D.C.: Government Printing Office, 1880–1901.

Washington, George. *The Writings of George Washington from the Original Manuscript Sources, 1745–1799*. 39 vols. Edited by John C. Fitzpatrick. Washington, D.C.: Government Printing Office, 1931–1944.

CIVIL WAR PRISONER ACCOUNTS

Abbott, A.O. *Prison Life in the South: At Richmond, Macon, Savannah, Charleston, Columbia, Charlotte, Raleigh, Goldsborough, and Andersonville During the Years 1864 and 1865.* New York: Harper & Brothers, 1865.

Adair, Lyle. *They Have Left Us Here to Die: The Civil War Diary of Sgt. Lyle Adair, 111th U.S. Colored Infantry.* Edited by Glenn Robins. Kent, OH: Kent State University Press, 2011.

Barbiere, Joe. *Scraps from the Prison Table at Camp Chase and Johnson's Island.* Doylestown: W.W.H. Davis Printer, 1868.

Carpenter, Horace. "Plain Living at Johnson's Island," *Century Magazine* (March 1891): 705–717.

Chesnut, Mary Boykin Miller. *Mary Chesnut's Civil War.* Edited by C. Vann Woodward. New Haven, CT: Yale University Press, 1981.

Cooper, Alonzo. *In and Out of Rebel Prisons.* Oswego, NY: R.J. Oliphant, 1888.

Corcoran, Michael. *The Captivity of General Corcoran, The Only Authentic and Reliable Narrative of the Trials and Sufferings Endured During his Twelve Month's Imprisonment in Richmond and Other Southern Cities.* Philadelphia, PA: Barclay & Co., 1862.

Domschcke, Bernhard. *Twenty Months in Captivity: Memoirs of a Union Officer in Confederate Prisons.* Translated by Frederic Trautmann. Rutherford, NJ: Fairleigh Dickinson University Press, 1987.

Geer, John James. *Beyond the Lines; Or, a Yankee Prisoner Loose in Dixie.* Philadelphia: J.W. Daughaday, 1864.

Hawes, Jesse. *Cahaba: A Story of Captive Boys in Blue.* New York: Burr, 1888.

Hopkins, Charles. *The Andersonville Diary & Memoirs of Charles Hopkins, 1st New Jersey Infantry.* Edited by William B. Styple and John J. Fitzpatrick. Kearny, NJ: Belle Grove Pub. Co., 1988.

Isham, Asa B., Henry M. Davidson, and Henry B. Furness. *Prisoners of War and Military Prisons.* Cincinnati, OH: Lyman & Cushing, 1890.

Keiley, Anthony. *In Viculus or the Prisoner of War.* New York: Blelock & Co., 1866.

Kellogg, Robert. *Life and Death in Rebel Prisons.* Hartford, CT: L. Stebbins, 1865.

Kiner, F.F. *One Year's Soldiering: Embracing the Battles of Fort Donelson and Shiloh, and the Capture of Two Hundred Officers and Men of the Fourteenth Iowa Infantry, and Their Confinement Six Months and a Half in Rebel Prisons.* Lancaster, PA: E.H. Thomas Printer, 1863.

McElroy, John. *Andersonville: A Story of Rebel Military Prisons.* Toledo, OH: D.R. Locke, 1879.

Makely, Wesley. *I Fear I Shall Never Leave This Island: Life in a Civil War Prison.* Edited by David R. Bush. Gainesville: University Press of Florida.

Merrell, W.H. *Five Months in Rebeldom, or Notes from the Diary of a Bull Run Prisoner at Richmond.* Rochester, NY: Adams & Dabney, 1862.

Ransom, John L. *John Ransom's Andersonville Diary.* Philadelphia: Douglass Brothers, 1883.

Ransom, John L. *Andersonville Diary: Escape and List of Dead.* 1881; reprint New York: P.S. Eriksson, 1963.

Smith, W.B. *On Wheels and How I Came There: Giving the Personal Experiences and Observations of a Fifteen-Year-Old Yankee Boy as a Soldier and Prisoner in the American Civil War.* New York: Hunt & Eaton, 1893.

Toney, Marcus. "Our Dead at Elmira," *Southern Historical Society Papers* 29 (1901): 193–197.

Witherspoon, T.D. "Prison Life at Fort McHenry," *Southern Historical Society Papers* 8 (February 1880): 77–82; (March 1880): 111–119; (April 1880): 163–168.

Ziegler, W.T. *Half Hour with an Andersonville Prisoner: Delivered at the Reunion of Post 9, G.A.R., at Gettysburg, Pennsylvania, January 8, 1879.* N.p.: J.W. Tate, 1879.

GENERAL BIBLIOGRAPHY

Andrews, Charles. *The Prisoners' Memoirs or Dartmoor Prison.* New York: Self published, 1815.

Andrews, Sidney. *The South Since the War: As Shown by Fourteen Weeks of Travel and Observation in Georgia and the Carolinas.* Boston: Ticknor and Fields, 1866.

Bangert, Elizabeth C. "The Press and the Prisons: Union and Confederate Newspaper Coverage of Civil War Prisons," M.A. Thesis, College of William and Mary, 2001.

Barker, A.J. *Prisoners of War.* New York: Universe Books, 1975.

Bauer, K. Jack. *The Mexican War, 1846–1848.* New York: Macmillan, 1974.

Benfey, Christopher. "Winslow Homer: The Stern Facts," *The New York Review of Books* (March 24, 2011): 8–9.

Berlin, Ira, Ed. *Freedom: A Documentary History of Emancipation, 1861–1867.* New York: Cambridge University Press, 1982.

Berry, Stephen. *House of Abraham: Lincoln & The Todds, A Family Divided By War.* New York, Houghton Mifflin, 2007.

Bird, Vivian. *The Dartmoor Massacre: A British Atrocity against American POWs at Princetown Jail during the War of 1812.* Washington, D.C.: Barnes Review, 2002.

Blakey, Arch Fredric. *General John H. Winder, C.S.A.* Gainesville: University of Florida Press, 1990.

Blight, David. *Race and Reunion: The Civil War in American Memory.* Cambridge, MA: Harvard University Press, 2001.

Bollett, Alfred Jay. *Civil War Medicine: Challenges and Triumphs.* Tucson, AZ: Galen Press, 2002.

Bridge, Jennifer. "A Shrine of Patriotic Memories," *Chicago History* 32 (Summer 2003): 4–23.

Brown, D. Alexander. *The Galvanized Yankees.* Urbana: University of Illinois Press, 1963.

Brundage, W. Fitzhugh. *The Southern Past: A Clash of Race and Memory.* Cambridge, MA: Harvard University Press, 2005.

Bryant, William O. *Cahaba Prison and the Sultana Disaster.* Tuscaloosa: University of Alabama Press, 1990.

Bush, David R. *I Fear I Shall Never Leave This Island: Life in a Civil War Prison.* Gainesville: University Press of Florida, 2011.

Carvin, Stephanie. *Prisoners of America's Wars: From the Early Republic to Guantanamo.* New York: Columbia University Press, 2010.

Chipman, Norton P. *The Horrors of Andersonville Rebel Prison.* San Francisco: Bancroft, 1891.

Cikovsky, Nicolai, Jr. "Winslow Homer's Prisoners from the Front," *Metropolitan Museum Journal* 12 (1977): 155–172.

Cimprich, John. *Fort Pillow, a Civil War Massacre, and Public Memory.* Baton Rouge: Louisiana State University Press, 2011.

Cloyd, Benjamin G. *Haunted by Atrocity: Civil War Prisons in American Memory.* Baton Rouge: Louisiana State University Press, 2010.

——. Review of Wood, Peter H. *Near Andersonville: Winslow Homer's Civil War.* H-CivWar, H-Net Reviews. March, 2011. www.h-net.org/reviews/showrev.php?id=32768 (accessed July 2, 2014).

Colbert, Charles. "Winslow Homer's Prisoners from the Front," *American Art* 12 (Summer 1998): 66–69.

Commanger, Henry Steele. "A Novel of an Infamous Prison in the Civil War," *The New York Times Book Review* (October 30, 1955): 1, 32.

Confederated Southern Memorial Association. *History of the Confederate Memorial Associations of the South.* New Orleans, LA: Graham, 1904.

Coulter, E. Merton. " 'Amnesty for all Except Jefferson Davis': The Hill-Blaine Debate of 1876," *Georgia Historical Quarterly* 57 (Summer 1973): 453–494.

Crabtree, Beth G. and James W. Patton, Eds. *"Journal of a Secesh Lady:" The Diary of Catherine Ann Devereux Edmondston, 1860–1866*. Raleigh, NC: Division of Archives and History, 1979.

Davis, Robert Scott. "Escape from Andersonville: A Study in Isolation and Imprisonment," *Journal of Military History* 67 (October 2003): 1065–1082.

——. *Ghosts and Shadows of Andersonville: Essays on the Secret Social Histories of America's Deadliest Prison*. Macon, GA: Mercer University Press, 2006.

Dean, Eric T. *Shook Over Hell: Post-Traumatic Stress, Vietnam, and the Civil War*. Cambridge, MA: Harvard University Press, 1999.

DeBoer, Clara Merritt. "Blacks and the American Missionary Association," www.ucc.org/about-us/hidden-histories/blacks-and-the-american.html (accessed July 2, 2014).

Derden, John K. *The World's Largest Prison: The Story of Camp Lawton*. Macon, GA: Mercer University Press, 2012.

Doyle, Robert C. *The Enemy in Our Hands: America's Treatment of Enemy Prisoners of War, from the Revolution to the War on Terror*. Lexington: University Press of Kentucky, 2010.

——. *Voices From Captivity: Interpreting the American POW Narrative*. Lawrence: University Press of Kansas, 1994.

Emberton, Carole. "The Minister of Death," http://opinionator.blogs.nytimes.com/2012/08/17/the-minister-of-death/?_r=0 (accessed July 2, 2014).

Fetzer, Dale and Bruce Mowday. *Unlikely Allies: Fort Delaware's Prison Community in the Civil War*. Mechanicsburg, PA: Stackpole Books, 2000.

Futch, Ovid L. *History of Andersonville Prison*. Revised edition. Gainesville: University Press of Florida, 2011.

Gallman, J. Matthew, Eds. *A Tour of Reconstruction: Travel Letters of 1875*. Lexington: University Press of Kentucky, 2011.

Garrett, Richard. *P.O.W.* Newton Abbot, UK: David & Charles, 1981.

Gillispie, James M. *Andersonvilles of the North: The Myths and Realities of Northern Treatment of Civil War Confederate Prisoners*. Denton: University of North Texas Press, 2008.

Glasson, William Henry. *History of Military Pension Legislation in the United States*. 1900, reprint; New York: AMS Press, 1990.

Glatthaar, Joseph T. *Forged in Battle: The Civil War Alliance of Black Soldiers and White Officers*. New York: The Free Press, 1990.

Grand Army of the Republic, *Proceedings of Enlistment & Muster of the Grand Army of the Republic*. Springfield, IL: B. Richards, 1866.

Gray, Michael P. *The Business of Captivity: Elmira and Its Civil War Prison*. Kent, OH: Kent State University Press, 2001.

Grow, Matthew J. "The Shadow of the Civil War: A Historiography of Civil War Memory," *American Nineteenth Century History* 4 (Summer 2003): 77–103.

Hall, James R. *Den of Misery: Indiana's Civil War Prison*. Gretna, LA: Pelican Publishing, 2006.

Halloran, Fiona Deans. *Thomas Nast: The Father of Modern Political Cartoons*. Chapel Hill: University of North Carolina Press, 2012.

Harris, William C. "Conservative Unionists and the Presidential Election of 1864," *Civil War History* 38 (December 1992): 298–318.

Heidler, David S. and Jeanne T. Heidler. *Encyclopedia of the American Civil War: A Political, Social, and Military History*. 5 vols. Santa Barbara, CA: ABC-CLIO, 2000.

Hesseltine, William B. *Civil War Prisons: A Study in War Psychology*. Columbus: Ohio State University Press, 1930.

Hill, Benjamin Harvey. *Senator Benjamin H. Hill of Georgia: His Life, Speeches, and Writings*. Atlanta, GA: T.H.P. Bloodworth & Co., 1891.

Horrid Massacre at Dartmoor Prison. Boston: Nathaniel Conerly, 1815.

Horseman, Reginald. "The Paradox of Dartmoor Prison," *American Heritage* 26 (February 1975): 13–17.

Huffman, Alan. *Sultana: Surviving the Civil War, Prison, and the Worst Maritime Disaster in American History*. Washington, D.C.: Smithsonian, 2009.

Ingersoll, Robert. *Political Speeches of Robert G. Ingersoll*. New York: C.P. Farrell, 1914.

Janney, Caroline E. *Burying the Dead but Not the Past: Ladies' Memorial Associations and the Lost Cause*. Chapel Hill, University of North Carolina Press: 2007.

Johnson, Donald Bruce (compiler). *National Party Platforms, Volume 1 1840–1956*. Urbana: University of Illinois Press, 1956.

Jones, Terry L. "Brother Against Microbe," http://opinionator.blogs.nytimes.com/2012/10/26/brother-against-microbe/ (accessed June 10, 2014).

Koerting, Gayla M. "The Trial of Henry Wirz and Nineteenth Century Military Law," Ph.D. diss. Kent, OH: Kent State University, 1995.

Levie, Howard. *Prisoners of War in International Armed Conflict*. Naval War College International Law Studies 59. Newport, RI: Naval War College Press, 1978.

Levin, Kevin M. *Remembering the Battle of the Crater: War as Murder*. Lexington: University Press of Kentucky, 2012.

Levy, George. *To Die in Chicago: Confederate Prisoners at Camp Douglas 1862–65*. Evanston, IL: Evanston Publishers, 1999.

Lewis, George G. and John Mewha. *History of Prisoner of War Utilization by the United States Army, 1776–1945*. Washington, D.C.: Department of the Army, 1982.

Lindsay, Arnett G. "Diplomatic Relations between the United States and Great Britain Bearing on the Return of Negro Slaves, 1783–1828," *Journal of Negro History* 5 (October 1920): 391–419.

McAdams, Benton. *Rebels at Rock Island: The Story of a Civil War Prison*. DeKalb: Northern Illinois University Press, 2000.

McCain, John S. "Remarks at the National POW Museum," www.mccain.senate.gov/public/index.cfm?FuseAction=PressOffice.Speeches&ContentRecord_id=90cca1f7-6c1c-4428-980d-2be918bb2d37&Region_id=&Issue_id=bc036142-6f29-470a-9be9-37d306822ccf (accessed July 2, 2014)

McConnell, Stuart. *Glorious Contentment: The Grand Army of the Republic, 1865–1900*. Chapel Hill: University of North Carolina Press, 1992.

McGee, Charles M., Jr. and Ernest M. Lander, Jr., Eds. *A Rebel Came Home: The Diary and Letters of Floride Clemson, 1863–1866*. Columbia: University of South Carolina Press, 1989.

McInvale, Morton R. "'That Thing of Infamy,' Macon's Camp Oglethorpe During the Civil War," *Georgia Historical Quarterly* 63 (Summer 1979): 279–291.

McKee, Christopher. "Foreign Seamen in the United States Navy: A Census of 1808," *William and Mary Quarterly* 42 (July 1985): 383–393.

McPherson, James. *Ordeal By Fire: The Civil War and Reconstruction*. New York: Alfred A. Knopf, 1982.

———. *For Cause and Comrades: Why Men Fought in the Civil War*. New York: Oxford University Press, 1998.

Marten, James. *Sing Not War: The Lives of Union and Confederate Veterans in Gilded Age America*. Chapel Hill: University of North Carolina Press, 2011.

Marvel, William. "The Andersonville Artist: The A.J. Riddle Photographs of August 1864," *Blue & Gray Magazine* 10 (August 1993): 18–23.

——. *Andersonville: The Last Depot.* Chapel Hill: University of North Carolina Press, 1994.

——. "Johnny Ransom's Imagination," *Civil War History* 41 (September 1995): 181–189.

Meserve-Kunhardt, Dorothy and Kunhardt, Philip B. *Twenty Days: A Narrative in Text and Pictures of the Assassination of Abraham Lincoln and the Twenty Days and Nights that Followed.* New York: Harper and Row, 1965.

Miller, Robert Ryal. *Shamrock and Sword: The Saint Patrick's Battalion in the U.S.-Mexican War.* Norman: University of Oklahoma Press, 1989.

Moore, Frank. *Memorial Ceremonies at the Graves of Our Soldiers.* Washington D.C.: Washington City, 1869.

——. *Rebellion Record: A Diary of American Events.* 8 vols. Reprint. New York: Arno Press, 1977.

Morrow, Rising Lake. "The Early American Attitude toward Naturalized Americans Abroad," *American Journal of International Law* 30 (October 1936): 647–663.

National Prisoner of War Museum, Andersonville Georgia, Dedication, April 9, 1998. n.p., 1998.

Neff, John. *Honoring the Civil War Dead: Commemoration and the Problem of Reconciliation.* Lawrence: University Press of Kansas, 2005.

Oates, Stephen B. *A Woman of Valor: Clara Barton and the Civil War.* New York: The Free Press, 1994.

Pickenpaugh, Roger. *Camp Chase and the Evolution of Union Prison Policy.* Tuscaloosa: University of Alabama Press, 2007.

——. *Captives in Gray: The Civil War Prisons of the Union.* Tuscaloosa: University of Alabama Press, 2009.

——. *Captives in Blue: The Civil War Prisons of the Confederacy.* Tuscaloosa: University of Alabama Press, 2013.

Pierson, H.W. *A Letter to Hon. Charles Sumner: With "Statements" of Outrages upon Freedmen in Georgia, and an Account of My Expulsion from Andersonville, Ga., by the Ku-Klux Klan.* Washington, D.C.: Chronicle Print, 1870.

Quaife, Milo M. "The Fort Dearborn Massacre," *Missouri Valley Historical Review* 1 (March 1915): 531–573.

Quimby, Robert S. *The U.S. Army in the War of 1812: An Operational and Command Study.* 2 vols. East Lansing: Michigan State University Press, 1997.

Quinn, Camilla A. Corlas. "Forgotten Soldiers: The Confederate Prisoners at Camp Butler, 1862–1863," *Illinois Historical Journal* 81 (Spring 1988): 35–44.

Remarks of J. Bryan Grimes, Responding for the State of North Carolina, Upon the Occasion of the Dedication of the Maine Monument at Salisbury, N.C., May 8, 1908. Raleigh: J.B. Grimes [?], 1908.

Report of the Maine Commissioners on the Monument Erected at Salisbury, N.C., 1908. Waterville, ME: Sentinel Publishing Company, 1908.

Report of the New Jersey Andersonville Monument Commissioners. Somerville, NJ: The Unionist-Gazette Association, State Printers, 1899.

Roberts, Nancy A. "The Afterlife of Civil War Prisons and Their Dead," Ph.D. diss., University of Oregon, 1996.

Robins, Glenn. "The National Prisoner of War Museum," *The Journal of American History* 99 (Summer 2012): 275–279.

——. "Race, Repatriation, and Galvanized Rebels: Union Prisoners and the Exchange Question in Deep South Prison Camps," *Civil War History* 53 (June 2007): 117–140.

Robinson, Ralph. "Retaliation for the Treatment of Prisoners in the War of 1812," *American Historical Review* 49 (October 1943): 65–70.

Rutherford, Mildred Lewis. *Facts and Figures vs. Myths and Misrepresentations: Henry Wirz and Andersonville Prison*. Athens, GA: United Daughters of the Confederacy, 1921.

Sampson, Richard. *Escape in America: The British Convention Prisoners, 1777–1783*. Chippenham, UK: Picton Publishing, 1995.

Sanders, Charles W., Jr. *While in the Hands of the Enemy*. Baton Rouge: Louisiana State University Press, 2005.

Sears, Stephen W. "McClellan and the Peace Plank of 1864: A Reappraisal," *Civil War History* 36 (March 1990): 57–64

Smith, John David, Ed. *Black Soldiers in Blue: African American Troops in the Civil War Era*. Chapel Hill: University of North Carolina Press, 2002.

Smith, Timothy B. *The Golden Age of Battlefield Preservation: The Decade of the 1890s and the Establishment of America's First Five Military Parks*. Knoxville: University of Tennessee Press, 2008.

Speer, Lonnie R. *Portals to Hell: Military Prisons of the Civil War*. Mechanicsburg, PA: Stackpole Books, 1997.

Springer, Paul J. *America's Captives: Treatment of POWs from the Revolutionary War to the War on Terror*. Lawrence: University Press of Kansas, 2010.

Starbuck, Mary Eliza. *My House and I: A Chronicle of Nantucket*. Boston: Houghton Mifflin, 1929.

Steere, Edward. *Shrines of the Honored Dead: A Study of the National Cemetery System*. Washington D.C.: U.S. Army, Office of the Quartermaster General, 1954 [?].

Sterling, David L. "American Prisoners of War in New York: A Report by Elias Boudinot," *William and Mary Quarterly* 13 (July 1956): 376–393.

Stevens, Peter F. *The Rogue's March: John Riley and the St. Patrick's Battalion*. Washington, D.C.: Brassey's, 1999.

"Summing Up," *Southern Historical Society Papers* 1 (April 1876): 325–327.

Tap, Bruce. *Over Lincoln's Shoulder: The Committee on the Conduct of the War*. Lawrence: University Press of Kansas, 1998.

Trowbridge, J.T. *The South: A Tour of Its Battlefields and Ruined Cities, A Journey through the Desolated States, and Talks with the People*. Hartford, CT: L. Stebbins, 1866.

Underwood, John Cox. *Report of Proceedings Incidental to the Erection and Dedication of the Confederate Monument*. Chicago: W.M. Johnson Printing Company, 1896.

United States Sanitary Commission. *Narrative of Privations and Sufferings of United States Officers and Soldiers while Prisoners of War in the Hands of the Rebel Authorities*. Philadelphia: King & Baird, 1864.

U.S. Congress, House. *Report on the Treatment of Prisoners of War by the Rebel Authorities*, 40th Congress, 3rd Session, 1869, Report No. 45.

Urwin, Gregory J.W. *Black Flag Over Dixie: Racial Atrocities and Reprisals in the Civil War*. Carbondale: Southern Illinois University Press, 2005.

Ward, Thomas J., Jr. "Enemy Combatants: Black Soldiers in Civil War Prisons," *Army History* (Winter 2011): 33–41.

Waugh, Joan. *U.S. Grant: American Hero, American Myth*. Chapel Hill: University of North Carolina Press, 2009.

Weiner, Marli F. Ed. *A Heritage of Woe: The Civil War Diary of Grace Brown Elmore, 1861–1868*. Athens: University of Georgia Press, 1997.

Wheelan, Joseph. *Libby Prison Breakout: The Daring Escape from the Notorious Civil War Prison*. New York: Public Affairs, 2010.

White, William W. *The Confederate Veteran*. Tuscaloosa, AL: Confederate Publishing Company, 1962.

Williams, Walter L. "Again in Chains: Black Soldiers Suffering in Captivity," *Civil War Times Illustrated* 20 (May 1981): 36–45.

Wilson, Charles Reagan. *Baptized in Blood: The Religion of the Lost Cause.* Athens: University of Georgia Press, 1980.

Winslow, Hattie Lou and Joseph R.H. Moore. *Camp Morton 1861–1865: Indianapolis Prison Camp.* Indianapolis: Indiana Historical Society, 1995.

Wood, Peter. *Near Andersonville: Winslow Homer's Civil War.* Cambridge, MA: Harvard University Press, 2011.

Young, James R. "Confederate Pensions in Georgia, 1886–1929," *Georgia Historical Quarterly* 66 (Spring 1982): 47–52.

Younger, Edward. *Inside the Confederate Government: The Diary of Robert Garlick Hill Kean.* New York: Oxford University Press, 1957.

Zeller, Bob. *The Blue and Gray in Black and White: A History of Civil War Photography.* Westport, CT: Praeger, 2005.

Zombek, Angela. "Libby Prison," and "Castle Thunder Prison," *Encyclopedia Virginia*, http://encyclopediavirginia.org/ (accessed July 2, 2014).

INTERNET SOURCES

National Cemetery Administration website: www.cem.va.gov/cem/cems/listcem.asp (accessed June 10, 2014).

National Park Service. "Myth: The Mystery of Felix de la Baume." www.nps.gov/ande/history culture/felixdelabaume.htm (accessed June 10, 2014).

National Park Service "Visitation statistics." https://irma.nps.gov/Stats/Reports/ReportList?id=ANDE (accessed June 10, 2014).

"Top 10 U.S. Civil War Sites." http://travel.nationalgeographic.com/travel/top-10/civil-war-sites/ (accessed June 10, 2014).

"12 Fascinating Civil War Sites." http://travel.nationalgeographic.com/travel/top-10/civil-war-sites/ (accessed June 10, 2014).

OTHER SOURCES

Fred Boyles interview with Glenn Robins, May 13, 2009.

Americus Times-Recorder

Mobile Advertiser and Register

New York Tribune

Richmond Examiner

Index